WOMEN
Experiencing
FAITH

Edited By
Janel Apps Ramsey & Thomas Jay Oord

SacraSage

SacraSage Press
Grasmere, ID 86753-09
© 2018 Janel Apps Ramsey and Thomas Jay Oord

SacraSage Press provides resources that promote wisdom aligned with sacred perspectives.

ISBN: 978-1-948609-09-8 (Print)
ISBN: 978-1-948609-10-4 (Electronic)

Printed in the United States of America

Library of Congress Cataloguing-in-Publication Data
Janel Apps Ramsey and Thomas Jay Oord. Editors
Women Experiencing Faith / Apps Ramsey and Oord

The Women Experiencing Faith Project
womenxfaith.com

Janel's Dedication

To **Jane Apps**, **Julie Hardison**, and **Nena Kuhr**
Three of the many women who have shaped my life so deeply.

To **Baird Ramsey**, the love of my life,
who works so hard for our family,
and is my number one advocate and ally.
For believing in the work of equality in everything you do:
at home, at work, and in the church.

Thomas's Dedication

To **Cheryl Oord, Andee Oord, Alexa Oord,** and
Sydnee Freiburghaus
The women who have shaped my life so much
these past 30 years.

To **Louise Oord-Kelley**
The woman who brought me into this world
and has nurtured and supported me ever since.

CONTENTS

INTRODUCTION

Let Their Voices Speak

The Women Experiencing Faith project came out of a discussion with a friend about the lack of female voices talking about faith. In particular, we were discussing how podcasts predominantly featured men's voices.

Fortunately, things are changing. Since having that conversation, many women have entered the podcasting arena to share their stories. This is so encouraging. So many women have said they felt alone in the midst of faith transition, discrimination, ministry, family life, or friendship struggles.

This volume (and the corresponding podcast) was created to help us hear the voices of religious (or once religious) women. The women represented here come from Judeo-Christian backgrounds, many of which were quite conservative. This was the original invitation we as editors sent potential contributors:

We want to hear how being a woman interacts with, intersects with, and informs your faith practice, experience, or journey. We hope that this book will let people see how women experience the faith journey. All perspectives are welcome including successes, wounds, growth, hardship, rejection, or embrace. Here are a few examples of what your essay might address:

- *How has being a woman informed your faith over the course of your life?*

- *How has being single/married/a mother/disabled/a person of color/a survivor/queer/widowed informed your faith as a woman?*

- *How has the objectification of women, especially the purity or modesty of our bodies, driven church culture and influenced faith?*

- *How does the way the church deals with women (positive and negative) affect our faith experience?*

- *What leadership perspectives and roles, positive or negative, shape your view of faith?*

- *What are the practices that fill up your soul? Do you have a particularly interesting experience or insight about being female you could share?*

- *What ways has the church silenced or expanded your voice?*

These may be sensitive topics. If to speak clearly you would like to use a pseudonym, you are welcome to do so.

Out of this invitation, we received 50 submissions. They fall into seven categories: Women in Ministry, Biography, Faith Transition, Bodies, Reflection, Being Female, and Equality. Some wrote happy stories and some hard stories. There are stories of triumph and confusion. Some wrote stories filled with anger. Many speak of pain and even abuse. Readers will find much Heart, Perseverance, Strength, Power, and Life. Some women didn't think anyone would want to hear their stories.

We're happy to have provided a space for them to be heard!

Janel's life was changed and challenged when preparing this volume. She felt less alone and so much sympathy and empathy for her sisters and friends. She also felt anger over how the church has so often failed the majority of its population.

May we learn by listening to the voices here and around us how to do better in making space for the women in our lives.

EDITING PRIORITIES

As Janel started working on this volume, it became clear how important it was to maintain the voices of the women who shared. So often in our world, we remake things to be 'correct' or 'right' or 'polite'. We change words to make things less offensive, less harsh, or less particular. We censor women's voices to be appealing to men, just as we expect their bodies and image to be attractive to them.

What we need to do is listen.

Janel did her best to edit the content without losing the voice. Readers may find things they would have edited differently. But Janel encourages readers set aside the differences in grammar or voice and just listen.

If we want to change the way our culture and our churches treat women, we need to hear women as they are. Women face hundreds if not thousands of images each day telling them *who* they should be, *what* they should be, *how* they should look, and *how* they should sound. Let's allow this collection to live independently, expressing who the authors are.

BUT THEY'RE SO ANGRY

Many writers in this book have had tough experiences. They're angry, and they have every right to be. We sometimes are conditioned to see angry women in a negative light — that they're not good women, not Christ-like, unforgiving, selfish, or proud. Those terms are buzzwords used to police tone. Tone policing occurs when we dismiss someone because we don't like the way they communicate. This may be unconscious bias or the way many of us have been trained.

There is nothing wrong with women expressing strong emotions. When men express them, we describe them as tough, strong, and powerful. Why don't we attribute those things to women?

If you find yourself feeling disturbed by the tone of one of these essays, we encourage you to step back, take deep breaths, and engage the piece again. Put yourself in the position of the writer and try to experience what she has experienced. If you are still feeling defensive, read the material out loud.

When Janel shared some of these essays at the Wild Goose Festival in 2018, she read them aloud. They were powerful when read this way, because they expressed images straight from the hearts of the authors. To hear the words helps us empathize with their experiences. We look forward to recording these women in their literal voices on the Women Experiencing Faith podcast.

TRIGGERING CONTENT

This book contains intimate stories. Some material may trigger a negative reaction. Out of respect for the readers, we included trigger warnings under the essay title/author. There is no graphic material in this volume. However, some descriptions of the emotions and ways women were treated can be intense.

We thank you so much for joining us in the Women Experiencing Faith journey. We hope you encounter the lives of these women and be changed by their stories. We also encourage you to ask the women in your life to tell their stories. You might be surprised by what you hear!

Janel and Tom

WOMEN IN MINISTRY

"When I began to lean into my gifts with complete abandon, opportunities and relationships flourished. I found myself preaching more boldly, reading more voraciously, and creating deep and lasting friendships. I discovered that my ability to understand scripture, to preach confidently, and to think theologically are not things to be hidden but to be enhanced, encouraged, and used boldly."

ROBBIE

DECONSTRUCTING EXPECTATIONS

L Michaels

BRING IT ON

I haven't always been a raging feminist. Realistically, I'm probably still not *exactly* a raging feminist, although I do talk pretty big. After growing up an only child with a devout, Baptist mom who did not work outside the home and a non-practicing, Catholic dad who worked tirelessly to provide for our family; theology was confusing to me, but gender roles were not.

Women tended to domestic responsibilities, and from either side there was no question that women could *not* be pastors. This was not up for debate. It was a deeply ingrained 'truth.' I spent a large part of my early adulthood proclaiming that I would be completely happy if I was barefoot and pregnant for the rest of my life, and then I actually brought five people into the world to prove it. I stayed home with them. I homeschooled them. I bake awesome desserts, make 21-cheese mac & cheese, homemade pizza, and fried chicken from scratch. Shame me if you have to, but you might want to read the rest of this first.

When God called me to the traditionally male dominated vocational field of theology, I was blown away. In addition to my earlier tendency to fit neatly into conventionally female roles, this is probably the part where I should admit that I had to drop out of my high school speech class, because it *literally* made me sick. I took my general education speech requirement for my undergraduate degree online.

Processing my call went something like this: So let me get this straight, God — you want me to preach, and speak, and teach? You want me to spend the rest of my life standing up in front of groups of people and making words come out of my mouth? OK, whatever. Who am I to say no? Bring it on.

Never say that — the whole, "bring it on," thing. It sounds so cool and tough and strong, but it's overrated. You have no idea what you're getting yourself into! I promise.

GLASS CEILINGS ARE REAL

I never want to jump on a soapbox and shout, "Being a female theologian sucks, because everybody hates us!"

This is simply not true. However, there are some unique challenges. Several years ago, I wrote a piece about them, and then I continued to learn how very difficult these things are, as I simultaneously leaned into becoming who I was created to be.[1]

Glass ceilings are real, and I will keep throwing stones against them and using my own weight, my own reputation, and the very core of my being to push against the splintering shards in order to prevent the ceiling from being repaired. If that sounds dramatic, it is. And it used to be a preoccupation of mine. But these days, I find myself less concerned with pushing and clawing my way to the top of some invisible ladder and, instead, engaging in deep, meaningful relationship with colleagues and friends. A quote that has become important to me reads as follows: "I'm not interested in competing with anyone. I hope we all make it."[2]

Even though I believe this, there are frustrations that accompany the quest to live legitimately into it. To be a 'successful' woman in a male dominated field, I often find myself either desperately trying to fit into the mold as "one of the guys" or eluding whispers of scandal. Both are equally ridiculous!

One of the most freeing things anyone has ever said to me went something like this: "You don't have to pretend to be someone you are not in order to fulfill the call on *your* life!"

---

1. http://www.flipflopsglitterandtheology.com/2015/06/unique-i-think-challenges-for-female.html

2. This quote accredited to Erica Cook can be found in the realm of social media but does not appear to have any official origin for a citation that I could find.

Those words might make more sense than most words I have ever heard or spoken. God calls women for precisely the same reasons God calls men. A recent examination of John 4:27 brought me some clarity on this topic: "Just then his disciples came. They were astonished that he was speaking with a woman, but no one said, 'What do you want?' or, 'Why are you speaking with her?'"[3]

Granted, this is a weird interaction! Jesus, a Jewish teacher, is conversing with an adulterous Samaritan woman as she draws water from a well. It's justifiable that the disciples are surprised, but just because something is surprising doesn't mean it's wrong (or even questionable). There is no need for Jesus to defend his communion with this woman in much the same way there is no need for me to defend my call to preach and teach. Disciples know this, and they don't even ask!

I am called, because God spoke these words into my heart. It is completely reasonable for me to continue to be me (lover of glitter, coffee, Disney, and flip flops in the snow), because women called to pastoral ministry are people called by God, apart from gender considerations. We are not statistics, but human beings.

With that in mind, I think women called to ministry often possess some gifts that are overlooked or even dismissed as less than valuable. Qualities such as emotion and nurture should be celebrated. Clearly, not all women exhibit these characteristics and, certainly, many men do; but I think everyone in ministry who is perceived as sensitive or emotional runs the risk of being considered weak or fragile. Instead, we should honor this ability to care deeply and empathetically, because this is often what people need most in a broken world that has fewer and fewer listeners and advocates as time goes on.

STOP BRINGING IT ON!

I'm glad I've been called to ministry. I cannot imagine doing anything else with my life, but I would be lying if I said it wasn't hard. By hard, I mean heartrending, life changing, breaking me down to the core hard. And at times: blood, sweat, too many tears, and scar-inducing hard. And so, for this reason, I admit that I have sometimes prayed, "Oh, Dear God, please don't call my kids to this."

---

3. John 4:27, NIV

I thought we were doing OK. I have kids who want to be video game programmers, composers, and architects. I have one who wants to be a theological paleontologist and discover the back-story of the creation of the world. I don't really know if that's a thing, but it sounds pretty safe, right? And then I have a seven year old who declared pretty early on that she was going to be an OBGYN, which I thought was a lofty (if somewhat specific) goal for second grade . . . until she approached me one afternoon and proclaimed that she needed to preach. Well, crap.

Like any good pastor mom who wishes her kid would choose something less risky, like logging, fishing, piloting airplanes, collecting garbage, or construction (five deadliest jobs in the United States); I put her off. But she was relentless. Finally, I told her that she could preach *if* she prepared a manuscript. I mean, what seven year old is going to put in *that* kind of work? The answer — mine. I came home from the office the next day and found her with a stack of papers that included not only her sermon but an entire order of worship (call to worship, music, children's moment with 'Pastor M,' (that's what I get for using only one initial), Scripture, and prayer.

We listened to Pastor M^2 (that's what I decided to call her) as she preached. Her siblings laughed too much. I made them sit up front for the 'children's moment.' I don't care that they're teenagers. Of course, I joined her, kneeling on the floor for prayer. She was missing one of her papers, so she rustled through them with a confused look on her face before throwing her hands up in the air. I turned to my husband and said, "Oh my gosh, she's just like me."

When we sang "Jesus Loves Me," as the closing hymn; she marched her little self right out the door and waited to shake each of our hands and thank us for coming to church. There were fist bumps, as well.

I confess; I'm still holding out hope that this is a phase . . . Mommy's a pastor, I love Mommy, and I should be a pastor, too . . . It's the kind of thing that could fade with time and age. If I'm honest, which I try to be, I'm proud. I'm proud of her, and I will be regardless of what she decides to 'do' when she grows up, and I'm proud of myself (which is probably something you shouldn't admit in a piece that is published if you ever hope to be humble). I'm proud because I am raising this girl in a world where it can still be difficult to be female. And as much as it's up to me, she will never believe there is *anything* she cannot do, and she will certainly never believe there is anything to which God cannot call.

WHERE DOES THIS LEAVE US

One chapter in a book, an article here or there, and a growing volume of blog posts do not the patriarchy smash. I've learned that this life is mostly about relationships and community, so stereotypes tend to dissolve slowly, person by person. I have great hope that one day the systemic changes we desperately need will take place, and I realize I must choose every day to be a part of the solution, however long and grueling the process may be. In the meantime, as I teach my children well, as I communicate professionally and relationally with my colleagues of each gender, and as I simply do my job in the world, fulfilling the calling on my life; I hope I will exude the kind of love, grace, and strength that causes people to take pause, because they see what God can do through willing, responsive people as we wait actively and expectantly for redemptive transformation.

MEET THE AUTHOR

L Michaels is a follower of Jesus, theology student, author, blogger, editor, educator, local director of compassionate ministries and family ministries, wife, mom, and aspiring peacemaker. She has a B.S.M. (business management) from Indiana Wesleyan University and an M.A. and M.Div. (both in theology/spiritual formation) from Northwest Nazarene University. L writes and podcasts about theology, the sacraments, political hot button topics, and ministry to the least of these at Flip Flops, Glitter, and Theology (.com). In her spare time, L sings and dances with babies (AKA teaches early childhood music), plans outlandish vacations, drinks voluminous amounts of Peppermint Bark Mocha (preferably at local coffee shops), and masquerades as Catholic, so she can participate in the Eucharist more often. www.flipflopsglitterandtheology.com.

CAR PREACHING

Rev. Abigail A. Henrich

Iwas twenty when I started preaching. I had no congregation, had never studied Greek or Hebrew, and had never heard of the phrase 'biblical exegesis.' I began preaching on the long solitary car rides home after visiting my college boyfriend. He was attending law school, I was an undergraduate, and I was in love with the limitless possibility of the future. My preaching was impassioned. My sermons were manifestos. I believe, even now as I look back twenty years later, the Holy Spirit was very much present.

I have no idea why I started preaching this way, nor do I remember the first time I "car preached." Even more amusing: I don't ever remember thinking it was odd. In fact (I am embarrassed to admit this), I thought about placing a tape recorder in my car so I could preserve my sermons. With a bit of bemusement, I wonder, all these years later, "Why did I car preach?"

I know the story that surrounds those car sermons. At twenty, I had discerned my intention to pursue a Masters in Divinity as well as ordination. Neither my decision to enter the ministry nor my early desire to preach was connected to a powerful moment of call. Instead, I had an intimation of the transformative power of preaching.

My boyfriend and I broke up; I found someone much more suited to my idea of a lifelong partnership. I never, however, stopped preaching. What began during those car rides has become a love affair. With the exception of three brief maternity leaves and a four-month hiatus from ministry as I searched for a new call, I have preached almost every Sunday since I was 25. I think I was born to preach the way my artist mother was born to paint.

My preaching has evolved dramatically since my early impassioned car sermons. As a twenty-two-year-old seminarian, I was often dismissed by my peers, and even by faculty, as a real candidate for preaching. It was suggested that I consider associate ministry, youth ministry, or children and family ministry. I was too cute, too young, and, of course, I was born with a vagina.

After preaching my first ever sermon to a congregation, one woman commented as she shook my hand in the receiving line, "You are so beautiful I couldn't pay attention to anything you said." She meant it as a compliment, but I was bewildered. Perhaps if I quit wearing mascara, I could preach the gospel? The next time I preached, I got more serious. I wore a plain blue suit, tucked my hair back, and preached (and I mean preached) the knock you in the gut Gospel. Ironically, the only African-American couple in the congregation found me at the end of service to tell me that they had never heard such powerful preaching in that particular church. They recommended a preacher in the city they thought I should hear. The next day at the church's staff meeting, I was given just one comment from the senior pastor: "Your voice is too high," he said. I went home and wept.

I worked harder. I followed the rules. I mastered researching the social and historical context of any given text and became an expert at using the computer program BibleWorks. I analyzed the original Greek and Hebrew in my sermons. I graduated from seminary and received a call as the solo pastor of a church poised to grow. I worked diligently at my sermons and crafted each word. Every Saturday night I went to the church, laid my notes before me on the pulpit, and preached to the empty pews. For an hour, I would mark out phrases, add pauses, and change words.

I wish I could say I worked so hard solely for the Gospel. If I am to be authentic, I think I worked so hard so that someone would take me seriously. I worked so hard to gain authority. My preaching was nothing like my first impassioned, genuine proclamations. They were for others, for the wrong reasons. The Holy Spirit was not palpable.

Mary had no "authority" to bear Jesus. She was a young, poor, uneducated woman (who maybe even had a high voice). Mary didn't own a blue suit or a computer with Bible Works. Yet she became the Mother of the Word. Her authority rested solely in the Holy Spirit and her willingness to answer the call.

Currently, I am the pastor of two churches: Grace Community Boston, an emergent Christian community, and Stratford Street United Church, a traditional Boston neighborhood church that is trying to reinvent itself. I have no experience with startup churches, no specialized training; my authority rests solely in the call from each community. Similarly, neither community has strong, if any, denominational affiliation. Our collective "authority" as those who call themselves a church rests solely in the Holy Spirit's calling us to begin a new pilgrimage.

What has happened to my preaching in these past five years is profound. I no longer look to BibleWorks. I rarely read commentaries. I do not write down my sermons or even approach Sunday with any notes in hand. My robe and my blue suit are collecting dust in my closet. Instead, I stand up before my community, clad in leggings (and occasionally something dressier) and my hair in a ponytail. In a woman's voice, I unabashedly proclaim the Gospel I received from the Holy Spirit. I have never preached better in my life. At last, my sermons pour from the very core of my being in the same way my early car sermons did.

I am well aware that I am the product of excellent formal education and have been blessed by years of biblical scholarship. I have not yet thrown out files upon files of my written sermons. And I am uncertain if, in ten years, my preaching style will be the same. Perhaps I will return to notes. Also, there are dangers in the way I preach: If my prayer life is pushed aside, my preaching can become more about me, than the gospel. I risk incredible vulnerability.

Yet I continue. I am now acutely aware that my authority does not rest in my education, carefully chosen clothes, voice pitch, personal journey, or theological precision. No — my authority rests in the Holy Spirit, who inexplicably called a twenty-year-old girl-woman to preach.

I am no Mary. If the Holy Spirit called me to bear Jesus, I would have turned the angel Gabriel down. But, like Mary, I was called to bear the word, and, like Mary, my authority rests in the Holy Spirit. Finally, at age 40, I have embraced my call with the same Spirit I did when I was 20.

MEET THE AUTHOR

Rev. Abigail A Henrich is an ordained minister who earned her stripes at Princeton Theological Seminary and Colgate University. She is married to a theologian, Jon Paul Sydnor, and has three magnificent and exhausting children. Abby is a mother-pastor-spouse who lives in a kinetic state of chaos as she moves between her many vocations: folding laundry, preaching, returning phone calls, sorting lunch boxes, answering emails, and occasionally thinking deep thoughts in the shower. She is unabashedly a progressive Christian who believes some shaking up has got to happen in the church. When she's not driving children around, she enjoys collecting stories, baking, and knitting.

One of Those

Teanna Sunberg

We belly laugh as we wind through the cobbled streets of Budapest and settle into a little Cajun spot called 'Soul Food'. My colleague from the Wesleyan church, also an ordained woman, has just come from a Christian meeting where she introduced herself as an ordained minister. A man from the group responded with an uncomfortable grimace and an, "Oh, you're one of those."

In other words, one of those women who has gone and gotten herself ordained.

Ordained women. Within the evangelical community, we birth those awkward silences for some and become the point of John Piper-like posts for others.

Ordained women. Perhaps we are a bit or a lot like Mary — pregnant with a story to bear that begins like this, 'God asked'. God has asked us to do something beautiful, something hard, something that may bring scorn, it may cause men to question our worth, and it may cause other women to question our character. 'Pregnant Mary' — the wording sounds vulgar sitting on this side of her story where we have prettied up her narrative and made it familiar and soft with fireside lights and decorative manger scenes. That burgeoning belly, the dilating cervix, the virgin breasts, the moans, the blood, and the groans of birth, shame, and dirt; the quaking of a teenage girl having been shushed for the love of everything appropriate. We have erased the clicking tongues, the awkward silences, the emboldened stares boring into that ever-swelling belly of shame. "She says God asked her to do this."

Mary, what kind of strength of character did it take to wake up and face the world every day? What kind of mettle were you made of that you stood tall and courageous and visibly obedient while the community mocked, scorned, and questioned your sanity, your morals, and your worth?

Oh, Mary. Pregnant and visible. Asked by God, for the love of God, to do something beyond yourself: bare your soul and bear the Word. It's a messed up, messy proclamation that at its genesis feels nothing like good news.

It feels nothing like good news today, under the power of words that have stripped and scripted a woman's role down into the pretty, proper, and feminine borders of a manger scene. It is hard to hear you. It is hard to see you. But Mary, your story is vital for us here because you bear witness to the movement of God upon you, to the presence of his Spirit within you, to his call, and your submission to that call. It is a call to bear the Word into the world. And that call came to you, a woman; *because* you were a woman and not in spite of the fact that you were a woman. And that same holy call and the submission to that call search and find us today.

Mary. Woman. Mother of God. Woman of God. We are one of you. You are one of us. We are #OneOfThose — ordained to bear the Holy Word into the brokenness of our world.

This God-call, this ordination, it pulls me from the warm cocoon of my covers, past the kitchen with the often lingering reminders of last night's meal and to the table while the breaths of children and husband lie heavy and peaceful on the before-the-dawn air. Mother, like Mary. Woman, like Mary. Full with the presence of God, like Mary. Called to serve, like Mary. Visibly obedient — and here the tap-tap of fingers on keyboard skips a heartbeat — pauses, falters. This long and visible obedience is more than hard. My body, it remembers the turmoil, the tearing, the sweat of the gritty pushing from the core of my being to move life's newest squeal through the threshold and into this world.

This bearing of the Word into our day and into our time for this generation, it asks of us that Mary-like, long, visible obedience. This is an obedience to be present and pregnant with the promises of God — in the pulpit, in the classroom, in the halls of academia, and in the pages of the published medium. This is a call to dig past the resources that daily sustain and to call upon some deeply embedded strength to push. Push against this glass threshold and feel it shatter.

#OneOfThose, you are called. Called to be visible for the hope of this generation and the one that comes after because our visible obedience is grace — grace for those who tread this cobblestoned way after us. We mark this way for them, we open our arms and bring them along, we walk strong and tall and Mary-like.

At the age of 14, my pigtails would have nodded in the negative over God-ordained, God-spoken womanly tones in the pulpit. I found Jesus in a community church nestled into the heart of Kansas where the topic of women as pastors never touched lips. Women were never visible in leadership. The pastor was a man, worship was led by men, and the youth pastor was a man. There were a plethora of women heaving and bearing that church of believers to glory, but their praying and their ministering and their mentoring were just what good Christian women did.

I stumbled into a Nazarene college and studied education because I wanted to minister and women can be teachers, or so we thought in the days before Mr. Piper. In a random conversation, someone asked me if I thought women should be pastors. "No," I piped. There were no women in visible pastoral roles in the churches I attended. The chaplain of the university was a man. The professors in the religion department were all men. It was a period in our denominational history where only a few women were in ministerial roles, and I knew none of them personally. The North American church was heavily influenced by a fundamentalism that taught that women were meant to submit to the authority of the man. "A woman's place was in the home and not in the pulpit", they said.

I was 14 when God called me to be a missionary, but it never occurred to me that he would want me to study religion.

By 18, I was training to teach because it was a ministry opportunity, but it never occurred to me that I should consider preaching.

By 22, I was married to a seminary student, and I imagined my ministry role would be as a support system for his ministry.

All of my female role models lived out their Christian ministry in traditional women's roles: wives of pastors and youth pastors, secretaries in a religion department, secular careers in the helping professions, and hospitality out of the home. I had never attended a church where a woman was pastoring or preaching from the pulpit.

The only Mary I knew was perched in a manger scene — one quiet, peaceful, prettily poised woman in the midst of a manger of men: Joseph, the three kings, and the shepherd boy doing God's work.

Nobody said that I could be 'one of those'.

Nobody said that I could not be 'one of those'.

Nobody said much at all about women pastoring, preaching, and being ordained. But the pulpit was always filled by the presence of a man and God is referenced as the Father and rarely, if ever, are the mothering qualities of God mentioned. Jesus was a man, and the Holy Spirit has no body. And the manger scene is mostly men in a dollhouse.

Meanwhile, the broader Christian community taught that a woman in the pulpit was outside of God's will.

But then, God sent us to Russia.

With the lingering scent of communism still in the air, I found myself in the hotspot of mission. Here, women were being called into and trained for pastoral ministry and church leadership. The women were from Russia, Bulgaria, Ukraine, Romania, and Albania. Here, I found myself elbow to elbow in ministry with a handful of missionary women who had seminary degrees. Here, I heard, saw, and experienced denominational leaders considering women's names for ministerial preparation, just as they considered the names of men. Here, I watched my own husband support, resource, encourage, and appoint women, in equal measure to men, for ministry positions. Here, I began to imagine, and then to believe, that God could and was calling me to be 'one of those'.

Looking back to the 14-year-old, pig-tailed version of myself — that sweet girl thumping Kansas dirt with her bare and dusty toes — that girl before womanhood, and babies, and pulpits, and messages from Mr. Piper. To that girl, I would say, "Grab your belly, woman-child. Grab your belly deep and preach from your soul. Preach for the joy of being called. Preach through the pain of being called. Preach your Mary-message. Preach as you stand tall and strong and visibly obedient. Deliver this good news as #OneOfThose. Preach like Mary, "I am the Lord's servant. Let it be unto me as you have said."

You are. We are. Like Mary. #OneOfThose

MEET THE AUTHOR

Teanna is passionate about the message of God on mission. She writes and speaks about justice with a focus on refugees and anti-trafficking, missiology, and cultures. Teanna has an M.A. in Missional Leadership and is an ordained elder in the Nazarene Church. She currently lives with her husband Jay and their 4 daughters in Budapest, Hungary. She is a contributor to The Junia Project and writes for her blog at www.teannasunberg.com.

Stages of Faith

Donnamie K. Ali

*"Trust in the Lord with all thine heart; and lean not unto thine own
understanding. In all thy ways acknowledge him, and he shall direct
thy paths."* (Prov. 3:5-6, KJV)

The above quotation from the classic King James Version of the *Bible* is
the first verse I committed to memory after surrendering my life to the
Lordship of Christ in November 1977. Memory fails in describing the number
of times those words came to my rescue when confusion invaded my mind following some life event. They have informed my faith in ways that mere words
can't describe.

Knowing that women are different in many ways from their male counterparts, I believe that our experience of faith indeed differs from that of men.
Our approach to life is different. Our sensitivities and intuition influence how
we experience the events that occur in our lives.

My faith journey began in childhood. Growing up in the Roman Catholic
faith, I had a strong sense of the presence of God around me. I was very religious, and even when I was not taken or sent to church, I was influenced by the
belief that God was right next to me. I reached out in childlike faith to this yet
unknown God and always wanted to know and experience more. This was the
beginning of my Christian faith.

MUSTARD SEED FAITH

I find myself asking God for more faith regularly since I do not possess the gift of faith. In spite of that, I continue to praise God because the Bible says, "Truly I tell you, if you have faith as small as a mustard seed, you can say to this mountain, 'Move from here to there,' and it will move. Nothing will be impossible for you." (Matt. 17:20, NIV) This commitment to faith has defined my Christian journey for the past 41 years. I confess that the words "Be anxious for nothing" (Phil. 4:6) reverberate in my mind many times when I grow anxious about some life situation.

How can I, having accepted Jesus' finished work on the cross, still find myself anxious? Is it personality? I confess that my melancholy/choleric personality combination does not help. I thank God for His unending grace that has always helped me keep moving, and keep trusting even when feeling faint. Without that grace, I would have turned to the world and its philosophies. I would not have been in ministry these many years.

CHRISTIAN WOUNDS

One can't be in ministry for any length of time without being wounded from hardships or rejection. What characterizes those who complete the journey is a doggedness which is fueled by their belief that there is a Creator whose plans and purposes are more important than human sensibilities.

I recall a missionary book about Dr. Nina Gunter, General Superintendent Emeritus. Dr. Gunter had served for many years as the Director of the Nazarene World Missionary Society (NWMS/NMI). She was well known among Nazarene circles as a powerful preacher of God's word. The book, *Preacher with a Mission: The Story of Nina Griggs Gunter,* touches on some of the opposition Dr. Gunter faced because she exercised her call to preach. Though many denominations have accepted women's role as preachers/pastors, there is still skepticism, in some instances, to female preachers.

I have experienced mean-spiritedness in various forms during my years of ministry, and while not always tied to my gender, at times was influenced by it. Daring to further my ministerial education, I was met with veiled hostility at times and I felt that being a woman, rather than a man, in ministry, was the root cause. While this bothered me a bit, I did not let it hinder me from moving forward. There were some difficulties in this pursuit, but I trusted God to work out the details.

My role as assistant pastor was not one that I sought. However, in the depths of my soul, I believed that God would have me play the supportive role to my husband in pastoral ministry and I have done just that over the years. There were times when I felt that the difficulties were too much for me to bear, but it was at these times that I ran to my God for reassurance and gained the strength to go on.

LEADERSHIP PERSPECTIVES

By knowing myself and my abilities, I know when to resist accepting roles just because they are offered. I have leadership characteristics, but they shine only when placed in secondary leadership roles. I learned this from numerous personality type tests over the years and from experience.

Not having the gift of faith in abundance, I have had to learn to "walk by faith and not by sight" many times in doing what I knew God required of me. Perhaps it is because I am a woman in ministry, that I have always placed my family before outside commitments. Over the years, I have turned down several ministry opportunities because I knew they would adversely affect my family life. It is not that I didn't have the faith that God would make a way. Rather it is that God gave me enough wisdom to set priorities.

REGULAR PRACTICES

Before even reading Brother Lawrence's book, *The Practice of the Presence of God*, I was doing just as he did. Prayer, for me, does not only happen during concentrated times in the morning or evening, or on specially called days or times. I have an ongoing conversation with my Lord because I genuinely believe that God is with me every step of the way. Thus, I am hardly ever lonely even while being alone. My contemplative personality thrives in solitude.

I subscribe to a few devotions that come to my inbox daily: *Reflecting God, Soul Care, My Utmost for His Highest*, and *Our Daily Bread*. These scripture-centered thoughts speak into my life; sometimes speaking into my life just what I need to hear. They are an essential aspect of my ongoing spiritual formation.

Part of being female is being intuitive. Without any hard evidence, I know when others are hurting. My faith in the God who answers prayer drives me to pray for those whose countenance reflects inner pain. I believe that these prayers, the calls/messages that are made serve as the hands and feet of God in giving hope and encouragement.

Reading is not only an enjoyable pastime, but it also provides life-changing information. I read widely. Missionary books, biographies of people such as Billy Graham and contemporary authors such as Max Lucado, add fuel to the measure of faith that I have.

THE INFLUENCE OF THE CHURCH

I am so thankful to God for allowing me the privilege of ministry in the Church of the Nazarene. Being asked to let my name to be on a ballot for local missions' president, a mere three months after committing my life to Jesus Christ tested my faith. I told my pastor's wife that I knew nothing about NWMS. She encouraged me, and the rest is history. Forty years later, I am still involved in Nazarene missions today. Each stage of leadership was a faith journey: local president, district president, global representative, and field coordinator (at present). I accepted each ministry with trembling, trusting not in myself but in the One who has called me.

The call to the pastoral ministry, alongside my husband, produced perhaps the greatest inner quaking of my soul. Being fully aware that I was not primarily gifted for a pastoral role, I committed to helping my husband fulfill his calling. This opportunity afforded me the chance to preach and teach, giving voice to the deep thoughts that I have had about biblical and spiritual subjects. These two areas of ministry, along with the few years I spent as a lecturer with Caribbean Nazarene College, expanded a voice that would by choice remain in the background silently.

INFLUENCE OF OTHERS

As I reflect on the journey of faith that has brought me to this point in my life, I realize that God used a number of people along the way to help me on my journey. I will admit to not admiring people easily. I seek integrity, genuine love, and compassion in others, and I seek God for these virtues to be lived out in my own life. Those who have demonstrated these through their actions unknowingly influenced me. I am a woman of faith whose life has mostly been influenced by her husband. His integrity and love have been evident throughout our life together.

THE JOURNEY CONTINUES

Many years ago during a Christian Education course, I learned about James Fowler's stages of faith development. My understanding of these stages of faith widened by reading a gem of a book called, *The Critical Journey*. I am not where I was as a newly committed Christian in 1977. Life experiences, spiritual growth, and a deeper knowledge of the Word of God have helped me grow in my faith.

My Christian life has been a journey towards a place of genuine love towards God and human beings; the latter being all embracing and outside the narrow confines of ethnicity and nationalism. Each stage of this journey has had some interesting twists and turns.

Compassion for others comes more easily when I remember how far God has moved me in this journey. During that journey inward, I became legalistic and narrow-minded. I cringe at the thought. What an unattractive place to be! Nevertheless, God can still bring beauty from the ashes of legalism, since He is not finished with me. I once heard somewhere that one of the main pitfalls of the Holiness Movement is legalism. That tendency has been relegated to the background with the passing years. Glimpses of it still seek to emerge, but I usually am quick to recognize it and treat others the way I would want to be treated.

Total surrender of my will to God took some years. I made many trips to the altar because I wanted to please God even though part of me wanted to keep some areas privately sacred. Thank God for the grace that was given to me. I realize that I am an unfinished work still on the anvil. It is faith that keeps me moving forward even when I falter.

MEET THE AUTHOR

Donnamie K. Ali has been walking in faith since 1977. Donnamie is an ordained elder in the Church of the Nazarene, lives in Trinidad, part of the twin island Republic of Trinidad & Tobago W.I. She and her husband David, also an ordained elder, have been pastors for the past ten years. They have three adult children and four grandchildren. Donnamie earned her M.Div. (Spiritual Formation) from NNU in 2017.

FAITHFUL WOMEN

Robbie Cansler

Every morning as children, my sisters and I would sit down at our breakfast table. My mom was insistent that we ate a hot breakfast every morning. So, while many of our peers were rushing off with a handful of pop-tarts, we were lovingly forced to sit in front of eggs and toast.

But it wasn't just for the eggs and toast that our mom gathered us around the breakfast table. Within minutes of sitting down, she would grab a brown book and open it up to the current page. She had the entire Bible in a set, broken into sections with pictures, and complete with questions at the end. We worked our way through that series more than once, and when we didn't know the answers to the questions at the end of a section, she would often look at us reproachfully.

Following our scripture reading, she or my dad would pray. They would pray for each family member by name, and would always add that God would give us the strength to be the salt and light in our school.

My mom led these morning devotional times. It was my mom who bought us age appropriate Bibles and devotionals throughout the years, and who continues to purchase Bibles and books about faith for the grandchildren. She was the spiritual leader in our home and is the spiritual matriarch in our family.

This reality never seemed odd to me. My mom was gifted and loved Jesus more than anyone I knew. Where my dad's faith is quiet and still, my mom's faith is loud, warm, and encouraging. Where my dad's faith was a steady constant in the background, my mom's faith was brightly colored in the foreground of my life. It fit like a glove for her to take the lead in encouraging us to follow Jesus.

Questioning my mom's spiritual leadership in our home never entered into my mind, until I began to be immersed into the purity culture of the 1990's and early 2000's. Reading books like *When God Writes Your Love Story* and *Passion And Purity*, began to make me second guess the leadership in our home. These stories, and the prevailing narrative of the purity culture, were that men took the lead in relationships and in a woman's spiritual life. That I was supposed to wait for a man, a man that God specifically chose just for me, to enter into my life. The right man would then lead and guide me into a deeper intimacy with Christ.

The idea that giftings weren't as important as gender, when it came to leadership in relationships, was only strengthened when I began attending an evangelical university. When I was a freshman, I began dating a guy who was much more passive than I was. I remember finally telling him, "If you aren't going to take the lead, then this isn't going to work out." I passionately told him that he needed to lead, and if he couldn't deal with it, we couldn't be together. He was flabbergasted by that revelation, and while he tried to make a defense for egalitarian relationships, and living into our individual gifts, he got shot down by nearly all of my friends who parroted back the same ideas found in the myriad of books produced by evangelical purity culture.

I even began to tell people that the fact my mom took the lead in our spirituality growing up, made me uncomfortable. It's strange to think about now, but the narrative of the culture was so pervasive that I began to insert feelings of discomfort and unease towards my family, where I had been comfortable and happy. These feelings of discomfort were only increased when I immersed myself in books like Stacey Eldridge's *Captivating* which told me that I must have a father wound and that until that father wound is healed I will feel incomplete. I would discuss this particular text with other women on campus, and I began to believe that I must have a father wound too and that something must be wrong with the way my family of origin was organized.

While I still believed adamantly that women could lead churches, be pastors, and preach and teach, I felt that the standard was different for home life and relationships. I was supposed to follow the lead of the man I was in a relationship with.

So, when I began dating a guy seriously in college who said my ability to understand and talk about scripture and church history better than him made him feel intimidated, I stopped talking about scripture and church history. If he was supposed to take the lead, then making him feel intimidated about spiritual matters was not his issue or his problem, but rather was mine, for overstepping my role in the relationship.

When the same man told me that, when we got married someday, I couldn't be a pastor and a mother, I took it deeply to heart. I considered breaking up with him, but friends of mine told me that people can change and that maybe there was something to this idea. So I stayed in a relationship that urged me to be a silent partner; discouraging me from living into the call of God on my life.

Going through the inevitable break up that happened months later felt like the worst thing in the world at the time, but I now view it with gratefulness. The shattering of that relationship, which was more silencing than complementary, gave me time to reevaluate what relationships should look like. I took the time to evaluate who I was and decided that I could not be in a relationship until I felt complete and whole with myself.

Gratefully, I was able to intern with a female youth pastor, who not only pastored as an equal partner with her spouse, but who was also raising children at the time. She did both; and she did it with grace, love, intelligence, and boldness. Her creative leadership allowed me to see myself in a different way.

We had long conversations about this God who calls women and men to the ministry. A God who gifts us in specific ways, not to be silenced, but to share our gifts with the world. These lies that had weaved their way into my heart were being undone by the grace of someone who lived into her life as a daughter of God.

That summer was transformative for me. I entered my senior year of college with a different lens. My life was no longer consumed with waiting for the right man who would lead me to happiness, but discovering that I was a whole and complete person on my own. That my relationship with God did not need to be confined to a romantic relationship, and that I needed to live into my gifts and talents with boldness.

When I began to lean into my gifts with complete abandon, opportunities and relationships flourished. I found myself preaching more boldly, reading more voraciously, and creating deep and lasting friendships. I discovered that my ability to understand scripture, to preach confidently, and to think theologically, are not things to be hidden but to be enhanced, encouraged, and used boldly.

Romantic relationships were then not about hiding my gifts, but about life lived with people who enhanced my gifts and challenged me to be better. When I married my husband, I walked down the aisle with confidence that I was marrying a partner. There has never been a question that I will continue to preach, teach, lead, and pastor, *with* children. As we have navigated what that looks like, my husband continues to champion me in those gifts. There was never a question that we would lead together in our home, in the ways we are best gifted.

In a way, I had to relearn what I was taught as a child. God gifts all of us in unique ways, and we are to lean into those gifts with confidence. We need quiet, steady, people of faith; even if that's not me, and certainly not my mom. We are loud, bold, and passionate people. Just because we are women, does not mean we should be relegated to the background, we were meant to lead. God gifted us in a unique way, and both of us are being used mightily for the kingdom of God by being exactly who we were created to be.

After years of theological education, I now have more language and knowledge to support the idea of egalitarian leadership. I have more of a biblical foundation as to why it is important for us to lean into our giftings. But nothing has been more powerful in teaching me about my purpose, gifts, and leadership than the example of the women in my life. I've served with women pastors who have shown me what it looks like to pastor boldly. I've listened to women preachers, who fearlessly share the word. I've learned from female professors who have helped me see scripture in new ways. I've read works written by female theologians who have helped me view myself as being created in the image of God in new ways. I've witnessed mothers, including my own mother and now my sisters, who are gifted to share the life of faith with their children in beautiful and bold ways.

These women have taught me that I can change the world. So now, I seek to do the same. It has been my prayer that my faithfulness to God might encourage others to be faithful too. That somewhere someone has found her voice, has leaned into her gifts, has been able to think of herself with the lens of the Holy Spirit, and is now serving faithfully, because of my example.

There is a saying, "Here's to strong women. May we know them. May we be them. May we raise them." I hope that in the church we can say in addition:

"Here's to faithful women. May we know them. May we be them. May we raise them." I pray that it is so.

MEET THE AUTHOR

Robbie Cansler is the pastor of The Mission Church of the Nazarene in Hammond, Indiana. She is married to her husband Mac, and their infant son Michael. They seek to live hospitably towards everyone and enjoy cooking for friends and family. Robbie writes regularly for The Foundry, at thefoundrycommunity.com, as well as writing pastors resources for Advent and Lent. She also co-hosts In All Things Charity, a Wesleyan Feminist Theology podcast. You can find her on Twitter, Instagram, Facebook, and her blog hammondmissionchurch. blogspot.com.

Shaped in Faith

Rev. Sarah K. Riley

Many people have shaped my life. There are the more obvious ones like my parents, brother, and friends. Then there are those you come across who choose to pick you up where you are, listen to you, and enable you to move forward through their words, actions, and encouragement, into a new future. These people brought strength and beauty into my life. A third group of people shaped me as well. They were the people whose words or actions left gaping wounds. My favorites, of course, are those who helped me grow and change in the midst of a world where I sometimes felt stuck.

As a woman called to ministry, these stories are varied and sometimes way more colorful than they really need to be. Things that seem simple for young men — seeing your path modeled for you, being mentored, encouraged to participate in conversations with male leaders — were a bit more complicated as a woman. I did not, at first, recognize these things. They were normal in the world in which I had been raised and I did not recognize how these things shaped me or that anything was missing from my experience. But the fact that somehow my way forward was different, slowly dawned on me as I begin to look for space and a way to live out my call.

I grew up in a conservative, blue-collar church. They were good people, and I have mostly good memories. My years in youth ministry were particularly formative. One youth leader, a woman, took the time to get to know me. She identified in me the ability to lead and entrusted me with responsibilities. She told me I was an iron fist in a velvet glove. I held on to that image because it was the first time I felt someone identify in me a strength and a grace that allowed me to be confident in who I was and yet gentle in my love for others. She encouraged me and lovingly pushed me forward to face a world where I was uncertain of my place.

A few years later, as a sophomore in college, I began to feel a call to ministry. My now husband as well as professors at the university encouraged me to change my major and pursue an internship. I was already helping with the youth at my home church, so that became my internship. As I changed classes and learned about what it meant to be called, I was told that to pursue ordination I would need to be granted a Local License from my church, as this is how the church affirms one's call to ministry. I was a little hesitant since I didn't want to preach at the time, but the path to ordination as an Elder (the ordination of those called to preach) and a Deacon (the ordination of those called to ministry, but not a preaching ministry) began the same way, with the Local License.

I boldly approached my pastor to ask about a license. I told him I didn't want to preach but felt called to ministry. He quietly shook his head and said I didn't need one. A few weeks later, he publicly granted a license to another woman in the congregation who had openly stated she wasn't called to ministry. I was hurt, confused, and discouraged. I had served the youth and children, played in the orchestra, participated in every drama, VBS, and potluck, and yet he did not recognize my call. I didn't know what this meant for my future. That moment created a small wound that soon grew into a gaping hole as some difficult events unfolded at the church. My heart was broken, left raw by the church that had raised me, and by the leaders I had once trusted.

At the same time events unfolded at the church, I was in a graduate program for theology and my husband and I had to stay in the area, so we went across town to attend a church that was led by one of my professors. He listened to our story and held space for me as I mourned the loss of so many things. He offered to walk alongside us and hold us up until we could walk again. With those words, I saw my first picture of what a pastor really looks like. The people of that church let us in and began to show us what a church could be. We were only there for a year but during that short time, my professor became my advocate and under his leadership, the church board granted me my first Local License. Once again, I was pushed forward into my future, but this time with hope.

The following year it was my husband's turn to go back to school, so we then moved to Texas where we served under a pastor who had a gentle spirit, kind heart, and a desire to help us grow. He invited me to preach my first sermon, included me in all the conversations, and trusted me in leadership. I began to grow into myself as a minister. The challenges came as the people often directed serious questions to my husband. I often felt like a plus one. There was even a year when they Board Secretary was calling up the pastors to thank them and give them their annual bonuses when they called up my husband but left me off the list entirely. I received an apology but was left feeling that my call was, again, not affirmed by the church and my spirit was crushed

Thankfully, I was not left to despair as my husband and pastor both continued to encourage me. My pastor gently pushed me toward ordination and advocated for me, publicly stating why having women in ministry was so important to the church. This gentle push brought me to my knees in front of our district as one of our General Superintendents laid hands on my head and ordained me to do the hard work of pastoring, preaching, and leading in the church.

A few years later, we moved to Idaho where my husband was hired to teach at a private university. I was eventually hired as an Associate Pastor in a local church. It was a rocky season, both for me, trying to find myself as a pastor in a new city and church, and the church, as it had begun to decline with finances dwindling. I served for a few years in this capacity until our Lead Pastor resigned to become a church planter. I was soon hired as the Lead Pastor. It was fun, amazing, and a big deal both for me and the church.

The many people of our church now shape my life. I am part time, so I share many tasks with some fantastic volunteers. We have a preaching team of 5 ordained elders and 1 District Licensed Minister. They continually push me forward. They bring new ideas to the table and encourage me to think in new and different ways. The Associate Pastor to Young Adults was asked to stay on when I was hired, and we later added another minister to help with education and compassionate ministries. I have had 2-3 interns, and most recently a wonderful group of leaders was elected to our Board. These pastors, interns, and board members are all women. There was no purposeful planning to make this a reality; they are simply the people God has placed in my care and in leadership in the church. It is beautiful to be a part of this season in our church's life and watch as the people support each and every one of these women.

Every person who has pushed me forward in my journey to follow God's call on my life now has a part in creating a culture where women can lead without fear. They have enabled young students to see the model of a woman leading a church as I never did. Our board has been fully entrusted with guiding the mission and direction of the church, and they have begun to do so with grace, honest questions, a sincere desire to seek God, and competence only exceeded by their excitement to do the work.

Through gaping wounds and brokenness, God has been faithful. Those who have encouraged me and pushed me forward have been powerful conduits for the love of a gracious God. The same God who entrusted Mary Magdalene with the Good News of Jesus' resurrection has entrusted me to do the same, placing person after person in my life to help me grow, change, and step confidently into the future. I pray that I will continue the work of lovingly pushing others forward, providing grace and encouragement to those who are bold enough to step forward in faith.

MEET THE AUTHOR

I was born and raised in Oklahoma where I attended Southern Nazarene University and earned both my BS in Christian Education and an MA in Theology. I am married to the amazing Stephen Riley, my love, and am a mom to four inquisitive and energy-filled boys: Jonathan, Ben, Micah, and Gabe. I also pastor Real Life Community Church in Downtown Nampa, Idaho. My life is full and I wouldn't trade it for anything.

When Faith is All You Have

Merideth Densford Spriggs

Trigger Warning: Discussion of Suicide

The church is such a dichotomy for me. I was raised a third generation Nazarene. I am proud of my heritage. Yet some of the wounds I carry to this day have been inflicted on me by members of the church. I value the teachings of my faith, but I must confess, I remain wounded by its members. But I'm forever grateful because it made me a tough fighter with unshakable faith no matter what the odds are around me.

Proudly, I used to sit by my grandfather in church. When I visited other Nazarene Churches or attended district events, people knew my family and our reputation for service. That aside, my youth pastor and teens in the youth group would often bully me for my looks. It wasn't until I went to junior high camp that I would deal with my first mistreatment by a church leader.

"You are going to be a little slut. You need two of these buttons because you will be pregnant before you graduate high school." My sixth-grade camp counselor said in front of the whole cabin at our nightly devotions time as she handed me two buttons that said, "True Love Waits."

I sat down holding the buttons and was mortified as I looked down at them in my hand. I had just gotten my first boyfriend ever, and I was so excited when he held my hand during the service. I cried as my friends comforted me in the bathroom. Each time that week, my counselor saw me holding hands with my boyfriend she called out, "See, you need that button." Then to her daughter, loud enough for everyone to hear, "Look at how she dresses, I would never let you wear that." I looked down at my shorts. My growth spurt meant I was 90% leg and the shorts my mother sent me with were now a bit shorter than when purchased. Although hurt, I tried to have a good week at camp.

It wouldn't be until my freshman year in high school that I would date again. My first serious boyfriend was not a Christian, but he knew I was heavily involved in church. His parents encouraged him to try my church. He attended a few youth group events but was excited to attend his first youth group trip with me. On the drive through the night, everyone fell asleep. Being cold, my boyfriend and I had thrown a blanket over us. Dead asleep and drooling on myself I was startled awake by a youth leader who jerked the blanket off of us. "You two can't be trusted. No blankets for you. We don't know what you're doing under there."

All through my life, my mother and father reminded me that God does not live in one building. They told me he lived inside of me and I needed to be true to his voice in my life. My mother later told me she had talked to a pastor about the youth leader who had mistreated me. The pastor told her, "Maybe God is getting Merideth ready for bigger things. Maybe he is calling her to a life of ministry, and he is making her stronger. Because this whole time her faith has never faltered." Years later, she said she would check on me only to find me on my knees in my bedroom over an open Bible praying for those who oppressed me.

In spite of the way the church treated me, I felt called into ministry. I chose Christian Education as a degree. While attending Olivet Nazarene University, I was encouraged and challenged by my professors. I was blessed with an internship and served on staff at one of the then largest denominational churches. My senior pastor and an advisory professor encouraged me as a woman in ministry. "You're a real pioneer Merideth. You are blazing a trail," my professor would tell me. I would do a secret eye roll in my head. I had no idea what he was talking about. I was, after all, a third generation Nazarene that was super connected. I believed I could get any job I wanted, when I wanted it, based on my pedigree and my time on staff at the second largest church in the denomination

Feeling a call to seminary, I applied and was accepted at Nazarene Theological Seminary (NTS). There are three things I really enjoy in this life: Taco Bell, rap music, and fashion. I prided myself on keeping up with current fashions on a thrift store budget. On the first day of Seminary, I pulled up to the seminary eating Taco Bell, blasting gangster rap, and wearing a carefully picked outfit similar to a tear sheet from W Magazine. Excited and nervous, I got out of the car, and it was as if the record stopped. People scattered from the parking lot to the door. They stopped talking and stared at me. All eyes watched me as I walked up to the doors of the seminary. I said hello, and some nodded, but most followed me with their eyes, and they were not approving eyes.

"What are you doing? You are undoing all the good we have done here for women," one of the girls at the seminary hissed at me as she pulled me aside with another classmate.

"What are you talking about?" I asked in bewilderment.

"Look at what you are wearing. It's just inviting the guys to see you as a sex object. They can't stop paying attention to you." The other girl squinted, her eyes looking at my outfit from top to bottom.

"Wait, what? I thought I got here because I qualified to enter the course of study. I don't want any of these guys to hit on me. I'm here to learn and because God called me to ministry." I said.

I stood up to those that oppressed me and eventually won most of them over. I got hired at Olathe College Church of the Nazarene. I absolutely loved my time there. I worked under senior pastor J.K. Warrick and directly with Chris Launius. Chris gave me the freedom to be creative and write lessons, speak up front, and create fun events for the entire youth group.

Some of my closest friends became a random group of service industry workers, members of the LGBTQ community, KU cheerleaders, and Chiefs players. I loved that many of them wanted to hear my sermons or borrow my books from seminary. They loved bragging that they had a pastor friend. I remember sitting in my seminary advisor's office rambling on and on about how God had just called me to be a youth pastor. He listened and brilliantly responded, "Did you ever think that God has called you to be more than just a youth pastor. Don't limit yourself and don't limit God."

Another set of wise words that forever stuck with me came from the brilliant Dr. Paul M. Bassett. I said to him, as I paced back and forth in his office, "How do you deal with it? You are so smart, and people in the churches are so dumb. I can't believe they want to do a patriotic service." Dr. Basset did his infamous little giggle, then he settled down and looked me in the eyes, "Miss Merideth, do you think you are saved by grace?" He asked me.

"Yes," I replied.

"Do you believe you deserved that grace?" He asked his second question.

"No," I replied.

"Then why don't you extend that same grace to others? Grace that you were so freely given, grace so undeserved." He said folding his hands calmly atop a pile of papers.

I joke that I don't remember how I got out of his office that day. I may have crawled; the floor may have swallowed me up or I just melted into a puddle of humility. That lesson would help me through the next trials in my life.

After graduating from Nazarene Theological Seminary with a Masters of Divinity and having been passed over for numerous jobs in favor of my male counterparts, I happily jumped on a job offer in San Diego. However, when the stock market crashed in 2008, I lost everything. I lost my then job at Point Loma Nazarene University and my part-time job as a youth pastor at a failing church campus. As a result, I took on two part-time jobs in San Diego but couldn't afford to live indoors. I spent a year living in my car.

During the year of homelessness I experienced, only my faith kept me alive. There were times of desperation that I contemplated suicide, but time and time again, either through people or signs, God assured me he was with me. God gave me clarity and called me to homeless services. I didn't look like a typical homeless person. I realized I could have doors open for me and educate the public because of my unique firsthand experience. Caridad was created in 2010 in San Diego.

I moved to Las Vegas in 2013. Caridad was given a $40,000 donation by a good friend to get started in Las Vegas. We secured a contract matching that amount from the City of Las Vegas and later another from the Fremont Street Experience. I was the leader of a federal initiative for our community, and we helped end Veteran homelessness. I have pounded on tables and camped outside of lawmakers' doors until they would listen to me.

In September 2017, another call and email would change my life forever. I had been nominated and was one of three finalists for the American Heroes Channel Red Bandana Everyday Hero Award. My story was featured in People Magazine on October 18, 2017. The American Heroes Channel filmed me and ran a special about my homeless journey and the creation of Caridad. As painful as it was I shared how I almost committed suicide and how without a doubt I knew that God had saved my life and led me to my ministry, Caridad.

You would think that life should be easy now, but it's not. I continue to face opposition from social workers and directors of local agencies because I don't "fit in." I'm often mistaken for inexperienced because of my youthful appearance. Right now, I'm at a crossroads. The City of Las Vegas is treating the homeless inhumanly, including spraying them with water. Providers have come to me upset about the mistreatment of the homeless.

On April 17 after much prayer and after seeking with wise counsel, I organized a protest with my church pastor, volunteers, and the National Law Center on Homelessness and Poverty. The ACLU showed up along with three television station crews. Sadly, providers backed out fearful of the pushback from the City or Police. I wrote an open letter and posted it on my social media along with submitting it to local print editors. Feeling very alone, I took comfort in knowing God was with me. I have been getting private support from insiders from the City of Las Vegas and the police department. I'd like to think that the years of pushback from the church, based on my looks, has made me into the tough fighter I am today. By using the very thing I was criticized for, my looks, the television media pick up my stories more readily. Their belief that "I'm easy on the eyes," helps me advocate for those who are denied a voice.

For whatever reason, God has chosen me to fight for the homeless in Las Vegas. I'm so thankful God uses my organization Caridad and me. I truly believe that because of God and my faith, I am can do anything he puts in front of me. I pray daily:

> *God help me to go where you lead, and to lead with love.*
> *Help me to listen to a hurting world,*
> *and extend grace to those around me.*
> *Grace that was so freely given to me,*
> *even though I didn't deserve it.*

MEET THE AUTHOR

40-year-old Merideth Densford Spriggs graduated from Nazarene Theological Seminary with a M.Div. in 2004. She founded and currently is the Chief Kindness Officer at Caridad Las Vegas, a homeless outreach agency. Caridad's staff of eight helps homeless on the streets

of downtown Las Vegas. Caridad uses a customer service approach as they provide a con-cierge service to homeless guiding them to resources around Southern Nevada. In October 2015, the City of Las Vegas recognized Merideth and the work of Caridad and awarded her Citizen of the Month. Spriggs is also the federal lead for homeless outreach in Southern Nevada under the federal Built for Zero initiative.

BIOGRAPHY

"If my life and faith journey have shown me anything, it is that I can only glimpse those "clues to the spiritual potentialities" available to me when I listen for God's voice in the symbols that speak through story, song, and dreams. It is only when I pay attention to my whole world as if it is the mouthpiece of the Divine and notice every pattern, every dream symbol, and every sliver of light in the darkness, that I can see that I am in a deep relationship with the living God, who, at the Heart of the Universe, will transform my life and heart if I allow that relationship to be real."

SHERI

MY STORY STARTS IN CHURCH

Christina

My story starts in church. My Grandfather was a Baptist preacher in Florida, and our faith, as a family, reflected that commitment to the Baptist church. It was very common for you to find me in the front row of pews once on Wednesday night, and twice on Sundays. Having been raised in his small church, I often found myself volunteering in various positions in the churches I later attended. You could find me in children's church, tech ministry, or in the choir or worship team.

My parents divorced when I was young, and my mom moved me and my two brothers to Colorado. (That was where she was from originally.) We struggled to live on our own and needed to live in low-income housing.

With the support of my Florida grandparents, I attended a private school that was associated with the church I was attending. As in Florida, I was constantly at church in one way or another. Growing up in that lifestyle led me to have a very sheltered and narrow view of the world. I had some negative experiences in those churches, like being kicked off of the worship team so the leader could fill it with his friends. I still struggle to reconcile my conservative upbringing with what I believe today.

A few years after high school, I got married. We had some difficulties in the marriage, but the biggest struggle was his battle with mental illness. I grew up believing in miracles (and still do). As a good Baptist wife, it was my job to support him in any way I could. I supported my husband by getting him into doctors and getting him medicine. At the same time, I was praying to God for a miracle, using all the terms I had learned in the church: renouncing the illness in the name of Jesus, praying that the burden be given to me, and having the faith of a mustard seed. But he was never cured.

Because of this, my faith took another major hit. We attended a church that believed heavily in miracles. Seeing people healed for easy things made me start to become bitter because God wasn't healing my husband. I began to question why God wasn't answering my prayers. I tried to turn to my family for support. While they would listen and give me encouragement, they didn't have much advice to offer.

The marriage ended in 2016. After moving across the country to support my husband in a new job, he abruptly told me that he didn't love me anymore and that he had wanted a divorce for a while. I felt betrayed. I was now stuck in a new city with no support system or friends. When my marriage ended, I hit rock bottom. I felt that everyone in my religious circles would look down on me as a failure. People had talked about previous divorces, and I was afraid of what I would hear about mine.

In that church culture, the "in" thing was making sure your divorce was biblical. A pastor at a church where I went for counsel told me that since I was the one who filed for divorce, I had sinned and I would cause any future husband I might have to sin. It didn't matter that my husband had 'cast me out'. Because of all of this, I felt like a failure. Not only was I now divorced, but I was also jobless and living with my mom and step dad in their basement. I became depressed. I remember one day as I was crying in the shower, a voice inside of me said: "I need help."

However, what was meant for evil, God turned into good. God started to reveal himself to me. One of the deacons at my old church (that was associated with the school), told me about the love of God and that I did everything right. I began to believe that I was not a failure. God revealed to me that it was okay to lose the identity of being married. I also came to realize that jobs come and go, but that it was okay to trust that something better was coming. I felt I was ready to embrace this new chapter in my life. I finally believed that my divorce was not a sin and that God still loves me for who I am. I am starting to trust Him again. My faith is growing. I am excited to see what God has in store for me.

While I have made peace with God, I started to feel like I didn't belong in church anywhere. My views of the church were changing. I was attending 3 churches but felt like I couldn't find a connection in any of them. I was single, so I didn't want a young married class. I'm in my 30s, so I was too old for the college group. I don't have kids, so the mom's groups didn't appeal to me. It became clear to me that the church didn't have a place for me. It was nearly impossible to relate to anyone. It seemed that everyone was already happy and had found people to connect with for fellowship and support. But, if you are young and divorced with no kids, you are an anomaly.

Why is that? I am the modern day woman at the well (minus the cheating). Why does the church turn their back on me? After this experience, I have very little hope that the church will ever have a place for everyone.

It's sad that I had to go outside of the church to find a place that would accept me where I am in my spiritual journey. My boyfriend, Jeff, introduced me to a weekly group called Brew Theology, where quite a few people understand my struggles and have helped me grow in my spiritual walk with God. As I continue to participate in this community, I have found the support and friendship that the church failed to provide. I am glad to see God at work in the world in new ways.

MEET THE AUTHOR

Christina is an avid geek. She loves to watch movies and sports, play trivia/board games, and learn about new technology. She currently resides in Denver, CO with her boyfriend and dog, Ellie.

Jesus in the Boat

Tahmina Martelly

"You have to buy NUDE panty hose at the store. Do you know what PANTY HOSE is?" The nice lady spoke slowly and loudly to me in the church bathroom to make sure I understood English. It was my second week in church, in any church actually. I was marveling in the fact that men and women could worship together and my head did not have to be covered. It was so freeing. I wanted to fit in properly so I was wearing one of my few dresses and nice shoes, but I didn't know about this thing called pantyhose. The mid '80's in rural Idaho churches had a special dress code that I did not know. The first week of church, I made change in the offering plate because I had $10 in cash but wanted to give $5. Not making change inside the offering plate is also another rule. Somebody told me about that as well, although not in the women's restroom.

In my defense, I had arrived in the United States just two weeks earlier from Yemen. Our family had lived there for 8 years, though I had been born in Bangladesh. My whole family is Muslim so I was used to rules. Islam has a variety of rules: Halal and Haram about eating and daily living, and doing all the right things to get into heaven. It was those very rules that made me feel as though I would never be accepted by God. I used to ask questions and get into trouble for it as a child. One of the biggest questions I used to get into trouble for asking was, "How do I know God answers my prayers when I am praying in Arabic but I speak Bengali?" I used to worry that if I pronounced the words incorrectly, then God wouldn't understand me and accept my prayers.

So let me back up and tell you how I ended up in a church in Idaho. You see, I met Jesus in the middle of a boat while fleeing civil war. Our father wanted to take our whole family from the capital city of Dhaka during this brutal war, by boat, to my grandmother's remote village so we would be safe. My grandparents were with us on this rickety wooden boat with bamboo paddles. It did have a second "floor" with a thatched roof. We passed areas where there were dead bodies in the water and often tried to pass through the river as unobtrusively as possible.

One night, some people with bright lights and big guns boarded us. I was sitting at the edge of the boat against the bamboo poles holding up the thatched roof and holding my grandfather's hand with my left hand. I could hear my grandmother mutter some Suras under her breath. The men were asking my dad questions as they shone the light on us. Our boat rocked with the wake created by the other motorized boat. My heart was beating loudly in my chest. My grandfather squeezed my hands in warning to stay quiet. I looked to my right, at the edge of the boat, and suddenly I felt a Presence. I knew that God had shown up. I had prayed many memorized prayers from childhood, but this did not look like whom I had prayed to. When God shows up, he doesn't have to introduce himself. He didn't speak, he was just Present. I felt my heart rate slow down. When I looked to the left, everything was still going on like a drama, yet to my right there was this incredible peaceful Presence. I knew then that everything was going to be alright.

We were finally let go and went on to the village. We separated from my Abba for almost a year, but right after the war, we ended up moving to Yemen. Things were too uncertain in our country. My brother and I started attending an International School and my sisters moved to Canada.

Seven years later, some friends at the school invited me to a "Friday Club" held at the American Embassy. I knew my father would never let me attend with a bunch of foreigners, but somehow, to my great surprise, he gave his permission. The first time I walked into "Friday Club" (Fridays are weekend days in Islamic countries) room, I immediately felt the same Presence I had experienced seven years ago on that boat. When I looked around to see where he was standing, I couldn't see him. During that Friday Club, which was actually a church service, people began to tell me about Jesus. I recognized who they were talking about immediately. I had met him on the boat already; I just didn't know his name. I was given a Bible, which I began to read in secret at home.

I wanted to learn as much as possible to find out about this God who offers a shortcut to heaven, who comes to find you when you are scared on a boat.

It was about that time that my parents were moving again. My brother, who is younger than me, would stay with them. But there was much discussion on where I would go. I could continue education in a boarding school in London or perhaps another one in Greece. Then the American family who had invited me to Friday Club generously offered their home for me. They lived on a farm in Idaho. I thought there would be no chance that my Abba and Amma would allow me to live with a Christian family in Idaho. But after much deliberation, many warnings to not disgrace the name of the family, and with the directive to stay away from Christianity, I was allowed to go live in Homedale, Idaho.

I was so excited to arrive, to learn the ways of Christian people, and know more about this Jesus. In this little town and church, I was like a tootsie roll in a marshmallow factory. Most people didn't know how to interact with me but they were eager to teach me how to act properly in this new culture. That's how I found myself in church without pantyhose and making change in the offering plate. I quickly had my host mom buy me pantyhose and found out that "nude" pantyhose for white people were not "nude" on me. As I tried on all the church rules, I also began to read the Bible in earnest and Jesus began to speak to me. I was afraid of the repercussions of choosing Christianity. I knew I would lose my family, my friends, and much of my culture, because so much of my culture is tied to religion.

I finally heard Jesus' voice as clearly as he if he spoke out loud. "I will take every step, you must take one step." I remember clearly praying for Jesus to rescue me and make me His. The same peace I had felt in the boat 8 years before flooded my soul. When I made the decision to tell my parents, my father disowned me. The blessing of my family was deeply missed, especially as I entered my first year of college. When I would call my parents, they would often hang up on me.

I met my husband during my freshman year of college. He is from the Caribbean and a Christian. This decision further alienated my family. When we got married, nobody from my family came to give the blessing. Yet, during this time, the women in church surrounded me. I wore a borrowed wedding dress, shoes, and veil, and got married in the backyard of a professor's home with flowers left over from graduation.

The story of my journey with Christ is also a journey with the imperfect people of the church. As a woman of color and an English as a third language speaker, I often found myself on the receiving end of a LOT of instruction in church culture or church rules. There were so many unwritten things not found in the Bible, or in any other book, but followed rigorously by everyone. I have lived in the United States for 36 years now. I have practiced my English, completed my education, raised children, and even co-pastored a church startup in Salt Lake City, Utah. Throughout this time, I worked with refugee and vulnerable immigrants in a variety of ways, interacting with thousands of stories of grace and redemption.

All this time, I have clung to Jesus, the one who rescued me on the boat. He alone has steadied me and helped to separate out culture from His Word. I realize that often women can bring great grace to each other but they can also harm each other with expectations that nobody can meet. I gave up wearing pantyhose after one year because it was hot and my legs were already brown. I give whenever I can, whatever I can, even it means making change on the offering plate; and I speak grace to other women, especially if they don't look like me. I revel in worshiping with all kinds of people, even those who make remarks about my race or culture that can wound. We are on a journey together. I cannot give up on them because Jesus doesn't give up on me.

Not too long ago, a friend who was going to our church in Salt Lake City, a transgendered woman of color, called me from jail. She used her one call to reach out to me because she was so frightened to be locked up on the male side of the jail even though she dresses and looks like a woman. She begged me to pray for her so she could feel peace. I prayed for Jesus to show himself mighty on her behalf. I know he can show up in crazy places. That's what he does, even if the person doesn't conform to any church rules. Reconciliation can only come if we all hang in there with Jesus. He breaks all the rules.

MEET THE AUTHOR

Tahmina Martelly is originally from Dhaka, Bangladesh. Tahmina lived in Yemen before arriving at a farm in Idaho. A registered dietitian by education, Tahmina has worked with refugee and immigrant resiliency projects for the last 25 years. Most recently, she taught at the University of Utah, Division of Nutrition, and developed and taught computer

literacy classes at the Utah Refugee Education Center. Tahmina has been with World Relief Seattle since 2016. She oversees the new Resiliency and Empowerment programs at World Relief Seattle. She also serves as the Equity and Social Justice seat for King Conservation District in Washington State and was recently appointed to serve on the Board of Trustees for Northwest Nazarene University. She and her husband serve at Kent Hillside Church. https://worldreliefseattle.org/resiliency-and-empowerment

SOUL, STORY, AND SONG

Sheri D. Kling

When the Lord has given you the bread of suffering and the water of distress,
he who is your teacher will hide no longer, and you will see your teacher
with your own eyes. Whether you turn to right or left, your ears will hear
these words behind you, 'This is the way, follow it.'
Isaiah 30:20-21 (Jerusalem Bible)

In some ways, it is practically a miracle that I am even here today to write about soul, story, and song. I once heard mythologist Michael Meade say that sometimes a traumatic experience may initiate a child into the depths of what is more typically a midlife journey; if that is true, then I was plunged underwater by family pain and my father's suicide before I was ten years old. Rage seemed to lurk around every corner of my world, and whether it was the shame of acne and extra weight, my lack of athleticism or the bullying I attracted like flies, my body and its deepest feelings became unsafe territory.

By the time I was 23, I realized I was emotionally numb and relationally handicapped, and carted myself off to a therapist. So began a lifetime of interweaving the psychological with the spiritual to find some measure of wholeness and healing. What I came to see is that in the same way that energy ebbs and flows through the figure-eight symbol for eternity, my journey was buoyed by the influx of archetypal patterns found in the deep wisdom of myths and fairy tales while it simultaneously produced an outflowing of imaginal material in the songs I composed.

I began immersing myself in the work of such writers in the tradition of Jungian psychology as Clarissa Pinkola Estes, Marion Woodman, and Robert Johnson. Their illumination of the soul's journey through the patterns of myths and fairy tales allowed me to see my own small story as part of a much larger one. Myths are transformational stories that invite us into the hidden world — what I have come to believe is the inner kingdom of God — where we can experience the integration and reconciliation of matter and spirit. In this place, I am no longer just the victim of random acts of suffering. In this place, I can know both what Jung called the archetypal Self and my own life as filled with meaning, purpose, and a deep connectedness to God, to other people, and to all of creation.

In one of the tales in Estes' best-selling *Women Who Run with the Wolves*, the motherless Vasilisa finds in the doll that represents her intuition a constant companion and the resourcefulness to complete the seemingly impossible tasks that first reduced her to tears. Similarly, in Joyce Rockwood Hudson's interpretation of the story of Psyche and Eros found in *Natural Spirituality: A Handbook for Jungian Inner Work in Spiritual Community*, Psyche discovers the resources she needs even as she is in a state of emotional collapse. As a never-married woman, I regularly face seemingly insurmountable challenges alone — and these stories showed me that deep weeping and vulnerability are graces with gifts that I need not avoid. My original compositions "Shadow of Doubt," "The Wall of Why," and "I am the Lord Who Healeth Thee" reflect periods of deep pain and sadness, yet there are also hints of the secret hopefulness that urged me to call out to God for help.

By the time 2003 screeched a long career in software marketing to a halt with yet another downsizing, a new, more joyful path as a performing songwriter began to unfold. I felt especially drawn to the biblical story of Abraham following God's call toward an unknown future; after leaving my job, I spent a summer immersing myself in as much silence and nature as I could find. In this wilderness period, I clung to my call and to my faith even as temptations to abandon the path tried to trip me up from the sidelines. The images I composed in "Let It Unfold," "Into the Silence," "Coming Back for More," and "Working with Beauty" emerged from the story patterns of such trials.

I loved being a performing songwriter, speaker, and spiritual workshop leader. When I threw back my head and threw forward my voice — all the way to the "cheap seats" at the back of the room — I felt more present in my body than ever before. It was exhilarating. I prayed for God to use me as a channel for change, and poured my heart into every performance. My brain dreamed up new ways to reach new audiences even as I struggled to "sell" myself to those who made booking decisions. In the end, I gave my creative life all that I could, and yet it was not enough. In that season, I had offered my heart to two loves — music and an artistic man — neither of which fully returned my gifts.

Synchronistically, it was at this very time that I was introduced to the story of the descent of Inanna, a myth that emerged from the same Sumerian culture that gave us the epic of Gilgamesh. My own life seemed mirrored in this story of the musician, lover, and goddess Inanna who went to the underworld for wisdom and whose arrival there necessitated her being stripped of everything that identified her as royalty. My failure to achieve success in the music career to which I believe God had called me felt like Inanna's descent into the dark abyss. Like her, I felt stripped of everything familiar. I, too, seemed to hang in this state like a dead woman, and again, I had to allow myself to feel the rage, pain, and abandonment of that dark place before a new life could be born in me yet again.

Whether the story is one of feminine descent as told of Inanna and Persephone, or of the hero's journey through dragon-slaying trials and abysmal failures as experienced by Perceval, or of Christ on Calvary's cross, the protagonist always winds up in the hellish underworld where all is lost. But the good news — the *gospel* — is that the pattern shows us clearly that the story *never ends in the darkness*. Resurrection *always* has the final say. This is the good news of God: that even in the darkest place, when the despairing abyss has become our bed, the light — new life — is always there, working its way toward transformation.

But now, this is what the Lord says —
he who created you, Jacob,
he who formed you, Israel:
"Do not fear, for I have redeemed you;
I have summoned you by name; you are mine.

When you pass through the waters,
I will be with you;
and when you pass through the rivers,
they will not sweep over you.
When you walk through the fire,
you will not be burned;
the flames will not set you ablaze.
For I am the Lord your God,
the Holy One of Israel, your Savior . . .
This is what the Lord says —
he who made a way through the sea,
a path through the mighty waters,
who drew out the chariots and horses,
the army and reinforcements together,
and they lay there, never to rise again,
extinguished, snuffed out like a wick:
"Forget the former things;
do not dwell on the past.
See, I am doing a new thing!
Now it springs up; do you not perceive it?
I am making a way in the wilderness
and streams in the wasteland.

(Isaiah 43: 1-3a, 16-19, NIV)

This is the message that ached to move through me in "It's Time," "Light the Fire Tonight," "Crack in the Door," "Train to Metaphor," and "Last Link in the Chain." You see, these stories and the archetypes beneath their surfaces are not simply children's fairy tales. They are not just "myths" of long-lost cultures who could not possibly understand our modern lives. No, these are the life-giving patterns at the base of human experience that show us what is possible within the soul depths of human life.

In the same way, that Estes' storytelling audiotapes are a banquet for the ears, *Joseph Campbell and the Power of Myth*, a series that debuted on PBS in the late 1980s, was a feast for the eyes and ears. Within that series of interviews with Campbell conducted by journalist Bill Moyers is this telling exchange:

MOYERS: So, myths are stories of the search by men and women through the ages for meaning, for significance, to make life signify, to touch the eternal, to understand the mysterious, to find out who we are.

CAMPBELL: People say that what we're all seeking is a meaning for life. I don't think that's what we're really seeking. I think what we're seeking is an experience of being alive, so that the life experiences that we have on the purely physical plane will have resonances within that are those of our own innermost being and reality. And so that we actually feel the rapture of being alive, that's what it's all finally about, and that's what these clues help us to find within ourselves.

MOYERS: Myths are clues?

CAMPBELL: Myths are clues to the spiritual potentialities of the human life.[4]

How many of us can say we experience the "rapture of being alive"? If my life and faith journey have shown me anything, it is that I can only glimpse those "clues to the spiritual potentialities" available to me when I listen for God's voice in the symbols that speak through story, song, and dreams. It is only when I pay attention to my whole world as if it is the mouthpiece of the Divine and notice every pattern, every dream symbol, and every sliver of light in the darkness, that I can see that I am in a deep relationship with the living God, who, at the Heart of the Universe, will transform my life and heart if I allow that relationship to be real.

If I have what might be called a "signature" song, then it is surely "Waking Woman of the Heart." Women have told me that this song helped them in their own journeys, and I know that it continues to teach me years after I wrote it.

---

4. *Joseph Campbell and the Power of Myth*, episode 2, "The Message of the Myth," interview by Bill Moyers, aired June 22, 1988, https://billmoyers.com/content/ep-2-joseph-campbell-and-the-power-of-myth-the-message-of-the-myth/.

Waking Woman of the Heart

Standing barefoot on the shore, the black of the sky and the black of the sea,
I only came to find some peace, But now I'm frightened of this space
And rooted to this place, rooted to this place.
Waking Woman of the Heart, I climbed to the edge, and journeyed within.
Flying kites and grounded shoes, How can I see for miles and still feel so blind?

Always reaching and always searching; Never knowing that I was going too far,
Too far away from home.

Now I'm free to laugh and free to cry, Free to smile and not say why
Free to stay and free to go, Free to stand on things I know
I'm free to fall and free to dance, Free to touch and take a chance on love
Of the heart . . . Waking Woman of the Heart.

I wonder just how many times
I've pulled back the reins for fear of the race?
So many chances never played,
How many lovers and how many friends?
Stop the talking and start the listening
Stop the walking and start the living again.
Living my own life.

Now I'm free to laugh and free to cry, Free to smile and not say why
Free to stay and free to go, Free to stand on things I know
I'm free to fall and free to dance, Free to touch and take a chance on love
Of the heart . . . Waking Woman of the Heart.

Time to listen and time to dream
What I'm living is what I've seen in my mind.
I've seen it in my mind.

Now I'm free to laugh and free to cry, Free to smile and not say why
Free to stay and free to go, Free to stand on things I know
I'm free to fall and free to dance, Free to touch and take a chance on love
Of the heart . . . Waking Woman of the Heart.

What is your story? What is your song? What are the patterns winding their way through your life that are your soul's way of speaking of the depths of your own being and calling you to the rapture of being alive? Wherever you are in your journey, know that the living God offers you healing and transformation. In the light or in the dark — listen, and then sing.

MEET THE AUTHOR

In addition to being Executive Director of the Beecken Center and Associate Dean of the School of Theology, The University of the South, Sheri D. Kling is a theologian who works in the interdisciplinary space where worldviews, beliefs, and practices can create either dis-ease and suffering or psycho-spiritual wholeness and common flourishing. Drawing from process philosophy/theology, Jungian psychology, and mystical spirituality, Sheri focuses on communicating theological ideas and practices that positively impact humans' relationships with God, self, and world, especially the use of dream work as a spiritual practice for a divine encounter, personal integration, and widening our relationship to creation. She holds a PhD from Claremont School of Theology and earned a master of theological studies at the Lutheran School of Theology at Chicago. She is a faculty member of the Haden Institute, a visiting lecturer with Palacky University (Czech Republic) in Social and Spiritual Determinants of Health, and a singer, songwriter, guitarist, and essayist.

LOVED AND LOVING WELL

Anonymous

*"After that hard winter, one could not get enough of the nimble air. Every
morning I wakened with a fresh consciousness that winter was over. There
were none of the signs of spring for which I used to watch. . . .
There was only — spring itself; the throb of it, the light restlessness,
the vital essence of it everywhere."*
— Willa Cather, *My Ántonia*[5]

I live in Chicago, where spring just isn't all that warm. The sun will spill out,
bright and alluring, but you can't trust it. There's always the chance a sharp
wind will pick up and you'll get goosebumps all over again.

Recently, I was walking along the mall in Washington, DC, with the man
I married nine months ago. It was warm. No hint of a breeze. No need for a
jacket. Just pure, luscious warmth. Having just flown in from Chicago, it was a
joyous surprise. It wrapped me up in its embrace and relaxed me. It reminded
me of how it feels to be loved. Not in spite of who I am, not because of who I
am, just loved. No hint of the biting wind of judgment.

Since my divorce five years ago, I have been impressed by people who can
do that — who show true love, with no other agenda. I would love to be like
that too. If I went through all the pain just to learn that, then it was worth it.

---

5. Willa Cather, *My Ántonia*, Sentry Edition 7 (Boston: Houghton Mifflin, 1954), 119–2.

My ex-husband had a big secret. He had kept it from his family. He had kept it from the church. He had kept it from me. But he finally blurted it out one night, many years ago.

"I'm attracted to men," he said.

Our little kids were tucked into bed. We were standing at the kitchen counter in dim lighting. He had been to therapy that day and I had asked him how his session had gone. He suffered from an anxiety and panic disorder and was finally getting the help he needed. He had a tendency to laugh when anxious, so he said it with a big grin, his cheeks turning a deep pink. His therapist had figured I would not be surprised. He had been trying to decide when to bring it up. My question had given him the spontaneous courage he needed.

I don't remember what happened next, but suddenly everything made sense. Was it relief? I knew there was something amiss but didn't know what. Homosexuality was not on my radar. I said something like "that's okay" and "I'll always stay with you." That's what I was supposed to say. I was a Christian and Christians don't divorce. I had no choice. It was the noble thing to do. I'd be upright before the Lord. The faithful wife.

Besides, I'd already made that choice — on my honeymoon. I realized right away that I'd made a mistake. He was a friend from church, a buddy. We had fun going out and doing stuff, usually with a group from church. It seemed natural for him to ask me to marry him. And though I was reluctant, it seemed right at the time. Besides, all sorts of people from church were urging me to say yes. He was from a "good Christian family." If only I'd trusted my gut.

He did not cherish me like I thought he would. I was devastated early on. But now I had an explanation for my pain. And for what I would later realize was his pain — unbelievable pain that had begun when he was young.

He grew up thinking he was flawed and that he needed to hide it or change it. He couldn't change it, so he hid it. I can't imagine what it is like to believe who you are is wrong and sinful. No wonder he suffered such anxiety.

I stayed with him, like I said I would — for another decade. One of our children had autism and often had pneumonia. I had larger concerns. I did not have time to deal with it. But it took its toll.

If you were to ask me to talk about it today, I'd probably start shaking and lose my appetite. It's the feeling I got while lying in my living room one night shortly after he told me. I was talking with his mother on the phone. She could tell something was wrong and asked me point blank, "Is he gay?" She had suspected it for years. She went on to tell me that his dad cross-dressed and wore makeup. I couldn't believe what I was hearing. I started to shake uncontrollably.

I told a good friend soon after, once again lying on the carpet in front of my fireplace. I don't know if my little girl, not yet three, overheard, or if she was just intuitive, but she asked, "Do you not love Daddy?"

No, I did *not* love Daddy. I never had. (Of course, I tried to hide that from her and assure her all was well.) But I suddenly realized I hated him. Not because he was gay. But because I was so wounded. I was so trapped. How shameful for him if the church found out. How shameful for both of us if we divorced. It was against the rules. Divorce was out of the question.

And yet he felt free to hurt me. He wasn't trying to, but he hurt me deeply. He would tell me about men he was attracted to. He asked why I never wondered why he loved to do our daughter's hair. He had many feminine traits and was finally free to tell me why. He was so happy to be "out" that he was oblivious to how horrible it made me feel. How unloved and unwanted. How desperately lonely. I was married to my "girlfriend," and he was okay with it.

Once he asked me on a date. I was to go downtown and meet him after work. I dressed up and was looking forward to a good dinner. But he had a surprise. He took me to a demonstration by a famous chef that he was infatuated with. He stood so close to the table that I was embarrassed and stood at the back. Afterward, he tried chatting with the chef. Instead, the chef looked at me and said, "Your wife has a beautiful smile." After that, I expected we'd go to dinner. But he made a beeline for the train. He'd never planned to take me to dinner. His big event was over.

I despised him. But on the outside, I pretended. Especially at church. We were a "happy couple" and attended Bible study. I enjoyed that because I liked some of the ladies, and it brought some normalcy to life. But his homosexuality or "same-sex attraction," as he referred to it, weighed heavily.

Rightly or wrongly, I blame the church for a lot of his pain. And for how I dealt with my own.

There is a lot of selfishness wrapped up in Christianity. In *distorted* Christianity, that is. It's easy to trample other people's feelings in the name of Jesus. Christians feel free to tell you what you should do. It is the "loving" thing to do. I was given all kinds of destructive directives in the name of godliness. It was so ingrained in me to make church people happy, that I let them tell me who to marry. Then I let them tell me not to divorce.

My parents were missionaries. I was constantly watched. My personality is such that I cared what people thought of me. And rightly so, because it directly affected my quality of life. I knew what happened to people who didn't follow the rules. They got talked about. Shamed. Worse yet, they were headed for hell. There were the "good people," and then there were the "bad people." The sheep and the goats. Christians were good, and the people who drank and didn't go to church were bad — but they were "ministry opportunities." There were those who you thought were good but then made some bad decisions, which they never got to live down. And the people who were bitter and angry — they were bad too. Definitely bad. Never mind compassionately finding out what pain they'd endured.

I didn't want to be one of the bad ones. Or one of those missionary kids whose parents had to leave the field to take care of. I followed the rules. That allowed me to fly under the radar and be whoever I wanted to be when I was not being watched. I actually had a wonderful childhood and loved growing up in South America. I even liked boarding school. But church does not rank high on my list of things I miss.

I'm not sure when I became aware of God. But I've always talked with God. That's why I was confused at the age of five when my dad asked if I'd ever "asked Jesus into my heart." That question ruined a perfectly good day. My two older sisters were at boarding school, and I was alone with my parents, "helping" my dad build a vacation cabin. It was located in a remote area near a river in the foothills of the Andes. I helped by handing him nails and sitting on boards to steady them for sawing. My dad announced it was time for a break and had me sit down. He sat to my right. The sun was bright. I was suddenly intensely self-conscious. He seemed overly excited to ask me this all-important question. My mom was inside a tent nearby. I knew she was listening to every single word.

I didn't want to have this conversation. But I knew I'd better go along with it and repeat his prayer. That would get it over with faster. But I never did get over it. I don't tell the story, but my dad does. To this day, he shares the story of my conversion with anyone he feels like bragging to. It's his story. A notch in his spiritual belt. How many times do we as Christians violate other people because of our own spiritual agendas? My dad ignored how I was feeling that day. He trampled my tender feelings and reinforced my view of the church: do it this way or else . . .

The same thing happened when it was decided I should be baptized. I was nine. I was told on Christmas Eve that I'd be baptized the next day in the river. I was not thrilled. I would be ogled at again. I remember having to change into dry clothes with my mom holding a towel around me, a crowd peering through the trees. That baptism had nothing to do with my spiritual life. I was going through the motions. I would be a Christian on my own terms, privately, thank you very much. I would pretend for them, but I'd have my own vibrant faith, whether it was writing to God by flashlight at boarding school or singing from the top of a tree.

That private faith is what I held onto years later, or maybe it held onto me, when I was unhappily married. I was not constantly unhappy. I had learned how to deal with stuff I didn't like (like the continual goodbyes to my parents from second grade onward). I knew how to redirect and busy myself. How to get my mind off of the pain. The one aspect of married life I enjoyed was spending time with my three children.

But the pain was eating away at me. I thought of my husband as one of my kids. His anxiety caused him to make poor decisions, and I had to take care not to upset him. He had a good job, supported us, and was conscientious about doing what was expected of him (which helped him hide his secret). But he was a shell of a person. Eaten up by his pain. We were not a healthy pair. Our marriage was not a marriage. I remember thinking, you can break up with a boyfriend or quit a job, but you can't end a marriage. I found myself dreaming he died in an accident and feeling free. I know this is horrible. But that's how trapped I felt.

I desperately needed out of that relationship. It was a hard decision to make, because I knew there'd be a difficult road ahead. Finally, one of my sisters accompanied me to a lawyer, and I filed for divorce.

The responses I received varied.

The first to respond was my pastor. He was sympathetic and said that he was surprised I'd lasted so long. (Wow. If I'd only talked with him sooner.)

Many others thought they were being loving by beating me over the head with Scripture and judgmentalism. My neighbor hugged me goodbye when I was moving, and when I said, "This doesn't have to be goodbye," she said, "Yes, it is." She was sure I was making a sinful choice and felt she could no longer be my friend. Another friend pulled out her pink iPad Bible and read to me about how I was not allowed to divorce. When I refused her offer to watch my kids for the summer so I could "work things out," she started to cry and said it was just so sad. *Of course, it was sad!* On so many levels. Who gets married hoping for a divorce? I have shed buckets of tears for my kids. But the list of sad events had started years prior.

I was told not to be selfish, and I was tempted to believe that. But a trusted friend pointed out that I'd already been unselfish for a long time. I hadn't put myself first. But now I needed to if I was going to heal. If I was going to be a good mother. If I was going to survive. I needed to find my own voice. I needed to get out of an emotionally abusive relationship, regardless of what those church friends thought.

Amazingly, most of my family supported me. I had been worried about that. In part, it was because they thought that I had biblical grounds for divorce (my ex had been into porn, which to them meant he had been unfaithful). And according to church rules, this made divorce tolerable. Nevertheless, their love and support helped sustain me at a difficult time.

There were those who supported me, *despite* everything. They disagreed with me, but felt it was their duty to love me in the hope I'd repent and turn back to Jesus. Conversations usually revolved around my divorce. Despite my requests to do something fun together, they refused and felt like they needed to discuss my pain. My divorce defined me, in their eyes. I had to set some boundaries because time with friends should be refreshing, not draining.

I could be bitter about people who have been unkind, but I can't point my finger. I was one of them too. That's how I was brought up. But last I checked, I think our goal should be to love. To treat each other with dignity. Not to define each other by our differences or deficiencies.

A few friends stand apart from the rest. Being with them was like stepping outside the airport in DC and being enveloped in that warm spring air and by the man who truly loves me. It took a few seconds to register that I didn't have to brace for a cold wind. And then my shoulders relaxed. I smiled and might have whooped with delight. It was warm, and I hadn't thought to expect it! No hint of cold. It was the same with those friends. I braced for judgment, and instead was enveloped in healing, restorative love. It appeared effortless, but I believe such love was a choice they made. In some cases, it was born out of personal pain. And in other cases, it was simply a direct result of taking Jesus seriously when he commanded us to love each other.

They have been Jesus to me. And that's now my goal. To be a warm-spring-day to others. Not for the sake of being like Jesus. Not to put notches in my spiritual belt. But simply because love is amazing. Being loved well is amazing. And selflessly loving is freeing. If your heart is full of love, there's room for nothing else. No judgment. No agenda. No cold breeze. Just the calming warmth of love. The love of Jesus.

MEET THE AUTHOR

I work from home as a copyeditor and proofreader of nonfiction books for a Christian book publishing company in the Chicago area. I have three kids (19, 17, and 12), who bring me lots of joy. I was born in Argentina to missionary parents, attended boarding schools, and graduated from college in 1992. I settled in the Chicago area and worked in magazine editing and then freelancing once my children were born. I was married last year to the love of my life who I knew from boarding school thirty years ago. We live in separate states and look forward to the day we can live under the same roof!

A Survivor

Chelsie O.

Survival has been a theme in my story for a far back as I can remember. Being born to an alcoholic mother and father, neglected and abandoned by all the adults who were supposed to protect me, being in a relationship with a narcissist for 17 years, and losing the only adult who ever loved me on this earth to cancer, are just a few of the major hardships that still impact my life today. As a very faith-driven person since childhood, I have always believed that God walked beside me and protected me from the "monsters" of life. I believed that the bad things I endured were a combination of God's plan for me, and learning how to deal with bad people in the world who can inflict harm upon me. Through all of my struggles, I still felt God protected me from the horrible stuff, and that my situation could always be worse.

My faith allowed me to believe that. I thought that one-day things would get better, that I was strong, and that I was put on this Earth to triumph over these struggles as a part of God's greater plan for my life. It wasn't until my marriage fell apart that I began questioning his "plan." As I looked back on my life, I started to feel that things were never going to get better. There were glimpses of things being okay for short periods of time, but it seemed my life was filled with one tragedy after another. I started to question God, his plan, and even my very own existence. I wondered why he would put me on this Earth and allow me to experience all of this pain. At 33, I found myself feeling alone, unloved, abandoned, and confused. I was never one to have a "woe is me" attitude or ever to feel entitled — that the world or God owed me anything — but I knew that I was exhausted with how my life was going and I was beginning to feel defeated. I felt like I was a boxer way past my prime, and I was tired of fighting.

My relationship with God has been rocky all my life. My relationship with the church is now non-existent after some devastating events happened to make me completely lose my faith in humanity. I was baptized at The Heritage Christian Center in Aurora, CO where I attended Sunday and Wednesday services, went to every Christmas and Easter play, and just all around loved the church. I enjoyed attending Heritage because it was very diverse with people from all walks of life. We didn't have to dress up if we didn't want to because the pastor's famous saying was "come as you are." I loved the pastor because his sermon delivery was so down-to-earth and easy for even the young people to follow.

I attended Heritage for four years when the church received devastating news — the pastor had embezzled money from the church, and it would soon be closed. I was so sad and confused. How could someone who claims to live by such a higher power do something like that? It's one thing to do wrong in your personal life, but to steal from the church and the members who trusted him to guide them in their faith; it was unfathomable. I quickly concluded that church people were just humans like me and they could not be trusted any more than all the other people who disappointed me in life. I quit going to church and decided my relationship with God was between him and me, and I didn't need those deceitful human middlemen to help me have a relationship with him.

Fast forward 20+ years and a friend invited me to the church, Potter's House, for Women's Day, to hear the pastor's wife speak. It was a few weeks after I had left my ex-husband and I felt this was a good time to try and reconnect to a church community. The pastor got up to introduce his wife and began to tell the story of how they met. He said they met at the age of 14 and 16, had dated all through high school and college, and then married and began a family. She was currently working on becoming a pastor herself, and he just glowed as he spoke of her. He seemed so proud of her success and growth as a woman. As I sat and listened, I cried my eyes out as their story was so similar to mine; my ex and I met at 14 and 16 and grew up together. While he never seemed proud of me and I had never seen him look at me the way the pastor had looked at his wife, I felt like it was divine intervention for me to be there that day. It was beautiful to see how someone is supposed to treat the one they love and to see that look in his eyes; it seemed so genuine.

As the pastor's wife got up to speak, he stood next to her clapping profusely with pride as she delivered a powerful sermon. He was her biggest fan, standing on the stage sideline, cheering her on. Not having any positive role models in my life, this was the first time I had seen such pure, true love. After her sermon, I had goosebumps and felt like maybe I could give the church another try. I decided I would join Potter's House after the little league season I was coaching and my Sunday mornings would free up again. However, disaster struck before that could happen.

A month after attending Women's Day a story broke stating that the pastor had cheated on his wife. To make matters worse, the woman he was cheating with was a newlywed. He was the pastor who married her and her husband. He had also given the woman a clerical job at the church, and they had many rendezvous inside of the church!

I was devastated. It ruined my image of true love that I thought actually existed. It made me question my judgment as I thought what I witnessed was genuine love that he had for his wife. It left me completely devoid of faith in the church. At this point in my life, I have no interest in attending church and will not step foot in one. I feel like as long as my faith is strong, I pray and believe, then I can get to Heaven without the church.

While I would love to close this out as a happy ending, that is not the case. I still struggle daily with depression, abandonment issues, anxiety, and the feeling of being unlovable. While I have some days that I am not happy with God, I still believe. My hardships have impacted my faith in a huge way. But I also believe that he has been there for all of my successes as well.

I encourage every woman who is struggling to keep believing. Talk to him daily and keep an open mind on what his plans are for you. I still am trying to figure out what his plan is for me but I hope when he finally reveals it, IT WILL BE AMAZING!

Xoxo
Chelsie O.

MEET THE AUTHOR

My name is Chelsie O. I'm a 34-year-old Data Analyst. I scrapbook in a planner during my free time. I'm an introvert who enjoys my alone time. I have no kids or pets. I'm the oldest of 4 sisters. (I helped raise my sisters because my parents were alcoholics.) I grew up in foster care and currently am the founder of a non-profit named, A Good Place to Start, where I help underprivileged youth transition to adulthood by teaching a free life-skills workshops. The content I use for the workshops comes from the curriculum I self-published titled What to Do Before You Move Out. *If interested in seeing what services I offer, please visit my website at gpsdenver.org.*

RELIGION IN EVERYTHING

Liz

Raised in an extremely fundamentalist Christian church, I learned at an early age that my significance and value to the church was limited because I was female. Only men were allowed to be pastors, deacons, Bible study leaders, adult Sunday school teachers, and ushers. Women could teach children's Sunday school (but they couldn't teach teenage boys), attend women's missionary prayer groups, and make and serve food at church potlucks.

Wives were expected to obey their husbands and submit to their decisions without balking or complaining. Women who were unlucky enough not to find a husband could be foreign missionaries, as long as they were under the spiritual authority of a male leader. Our church believed that Christian women didn't have gifts from the Holy Spirit that involved any kind of leadership skills — the word "leader" automatically implied a human who had a penis.

As I started middle school, I became extremely aware of the sinfulness of my female body. It was the mid-1970s, and short shorts were in style (think Chrissy on *Three's Company*). I had to wear cut-off jeans that went to my knees, instead of shorts, so that I wouldn't cause a man or boy to have lustful thoughts about me. A very popular, well-dressed girl in my class called me John-Boy because I looked like John-Boy from the then-popular TV show, *The Waltons*.

During my sophomore year, I attended a local Christian school instead of the public school. There was a modesty-based dress code for girls — our blouses could be no lower than two fingers below our collarbones, we couldn't wear sleeveless shirts, and our skirts had to be below the knee. There weren't modesty-related rules for the boys — apparently, good Christian girls weren't capable of lusting after boys' bodies!

As the youngest child in the family, I watched my older brothers and sisters go off to Bible College — the boys to become preachers, the girls to become pastor's wives or elementary teachers in Christian schools. The standard joke was that a female Bible college student was getting her "Mrs." degree.

As a teenager, I rebelled against almost everything I was taught. I was the only sibling to attend a non-religious university. As an adult, being a feminist was — and is — an ingrained part of my identity. But for many years I attended evangelical churches that didn't allow women to be pastors. Why? Because a part of me still believed that only men should have that role.

As a child, spiritual growth was only supposed to come through the Bible, in a church building under a preacher's tutelage, or as part of a church community. I am in my 50s now and that no longer fits me. When I want to get in touch with my soul, I go to nature — whether that means a walk in the mountains or sitting on my patio and feeling the sunshine on my skin. The 19th-century poet John Ruskin sums it up for me:

There Is A Religion In Everything Around Us[6]

There is religion in everything around us,
A calm and holy religion
In the unbreathing things in Nature.
It is a meek and blessed influence,
Stealing in, as it were, unaware upon the heart;
It comes quickly, and without excitement;
It has no terror, no gloom;
It does not rouse up the passions;
It is untrammeled by creeds . . .
It is written on the arched sky;
It looks out from every star;
It is on the sailing cloud and in the invisible wind;
It is among the hills and valleys of the earth

---

6. John Ruskin, "There Is a Religion in Everything around Us." June 10, 2012, https://naturalpantheist. wordpress.com/tag/john-ruskin/

Where the shrubless mountain-top pierces the thin atmosphere of eternal winter,
Or where the mighty forest fluctuates before the strong wind
With its dark waves of green foliage.
It is spread out like a legible language upon the broad face of an unsleeping ocean;
It is the poetry of Nature;
It is that which uplifts the spirit within . . .
And which opens to our imagination of world of spiritual beauty and holiness.

You Can Be Both

Emily Burke

My identity as a woman never stops me. That's what I would have told you when I was little. While the culture around me wasn't always pro-female empowerment, I didn't care. I didn't let it stop me.

Even at the age of seven, when my heart was set on being a missionary, I pushed against gender roles and norms. I would tell people that when I grow up, I'm going to be a missionary. And when I was a missionary, I was not going to stay home and watch the kids. I wasn't going to be a secretary, while my husband went off and had adventures. I would go out and have adventures, too. I even told my parents that I was going to move to China one day and start schools/churches/orphanages all across the country. I was nine years old when I declared this plan.

My heroes growing up were Nina Gunter (a former leader in the Church of the Nazarene) and Condoleezza Rice (former Secretary of State). I looked up to these women and knew that I could do great things, too. Being a girl didn't stop me from anything. It didn't stop me from leading in my church. It didn't stop me from moving to South America right out of high school. It didn't stop me from pursuing a calling to ministry. Being a woman didn't stop me, but being a queer woman almost did.

For many years, I ignored my sexuality. When I couldn't ignore it, I would go for a long drive and think about the choice I had made. In my mind, there were two options: me or the Church. Choosing me looked like freely accepting my sexuality as part of who I am. It meant a different career path. It meant a brand new university. (My university was and is not open or affirming.)

Choosing the Church meant choosing to pursue a life as a pastor. It meant following the path to ordination. It meant remaining in a community that I had known my whole life. It meant being connected to people and opportunities. But, it also meant repression, denial, and shame. And when I say shame, I mean waves, upon waves, of shame that crashed over me with no end in sight.

Me or the Church? On these long car rides, I would remind myself that I only had one real option: the Church. That was my choice, to sacrifice me at the altar of the Christian community. What an ironic dichotomy I had made for myself back then.

What I didn't know then was that I could choose both. That in fact, I needed both in my life — being a queer woman and a Christian — in order to be an active part of the Church. They were both deeply knit into me. The longer I tried to divorce those parts, worshipping at the altar of faith, while ignoring my own reality, the more I suffered inside.

I have always had trouble accepting that God loves me. I can get behind the idea of God as love. My theology is based in that. But when it came to me as an individual, I didn't think that God was a fan. God wasn't in my corner. God wasn't rooting for me. If anything, God was disappointed in me. And if God was disappointed in me, then so was everyone else.

Long before I came out to myself or anyone else, I had a theological conversation regarding my views on sexuality and gender. Sometime during college, I stopped believing that being gay was a sin. I discovered strong theological arguments that gave room for non-heteronormativity. And I wasn't afraid to share these new convictions with close friends and professors.

Yet, when it came to myself, I wasn't allowed to be gay. Instead, I kept choosing the Church over and over. I convinced myself that by doing that, I was choosing God. I was doing God's will. My obedience would gain the love and respect of God and those around me. I didn't want to disappoint God, and I especially didn't want to disappoint all of the Christians in my life. So, the only person who knew about my "attraction" to girls was my counselor.

Ignoring a huge part of my identity was not sustainable though, and after graduating from college, I came to the point of real decision. I finally gave myself an actual choice. At first, the choice still seemed black and white: me or the Church. Yet, through the guidance of friends, a counselor, and I believe God, I realized that I had invented a false dichotomy.

Coming out as gay would affect my relationship with my current denomination, but it didn't mean that I couldn't be part of any church. Being gay didn't mean that I couldn't pursue graduate studies in theology. Being gay didn't mean that I couldn't minister in the Church. Being gay didn't have to end my personal faith, either.

If I'm honest, coming out as queer was the best thing for my faith, my ministry, and my theological endeavors. When I accepted myself, I finally accepted God's personal love for me. When I accepted myself, I was more healthy within myself, so I could better serve and love other people. When I accepted myself, I was introduced to so many new theologies and theologians who expanded my views.

Accepting myself didn't come without consequences. I left the denomination that raised me. I gave up having met almost all of the qualifications for ordination in that church. I left a great local church where I served. I gave up opportunities within that denomination. I gave all those things up because they gave me an impossible choice. They were asking me to choose myself or the Church. They made a false dichotomy whereby if I chose myself (which included personal health, self-love, and wellbeing), I was choosing sin.

The denomination of my birth believes that that actions outside of heteronormativity are sin. They don't think it is a sin to feel attracted to a girl, but the moment I ask that girl on a date, I'm sinning. The sad reality was that if people in that denomination even knew I was attracted to women, roadblocks would have been put in my way. Even if I never asked a girl on a date, if I outwardly and proudly identified as bi-sexual or a lesbian, my personal faith and ability to lead in the church would be suspect.

In their minds, if I chose me, it wasn't just their denomination I would be leaving. I would be turning my back on God. Choosing the Church, or at least this specific group of churches, didn't seem to be working out. The self-loathing, the hiding, the shame. None of that seemed to be from God. It didn't line up with the message I was preaching to the women, the kids, and the teens that I worked with in my local parish. It didn't line up with who I believed God to be.

So, before that denomination could kick me out, I chose to leave. I chose to be an out and proud queer person. I chose to be part of a different denomination. I chose to continue to profess the Christian faith. I even chose to continue to be a minister and pursue my theological studies. I chose me, and in choosing me, I chose everything I am passionate about and believe in, including the Church.

There are times when I still feel like a walking contradiction. A queer woman who is also a Christian and a minister! How can that be? It's sad that I and others around me even ask that question. It points to a failure of the Church truly to accept people who fall outside of the norm, whether that be women or the queer community.

I'm thankful that through this all of this I have been able to separate the judgement of some Christians and the love of God. I don't judge anyone who decides not to attend Church or even believe in God because of how Christians treated them. I wish I could say that the Church is a safe place now for those you who have been pushed out because of your race, gender, sexuality, or state of being, but I can't guarantee that. While I see some denominations and some individual congregations making great strides toward true acceptance and equality, it's not universal, and that breaks my heart.

The denomination I grew up in told me I had to choose between myself and the Church. They acted like self-acceptance and self-love were from the devil himself. I have learned though, that when I truly accepted myself, I could finally accept God.

A God of love. A God of acceptance. A God of community. A God of relationships. This is the God I believe in, and this is the God I want others to see. It's this God who told me "well done good, faithful, *female, lesbian* servant" (Matthew 25:23).

MEET THE AUTHOR

Emily Burke is a youth and family minister at an Episcopal Church in Kansas City. She is also pursuing her MA in Theological Studies. She enjoys reading, learning about different expressions of Christianity, and trying to find intersectional ways to live out her faith. She hopes to one day teach theology.

GENDERFUL

by Lē Weaver

G ender is a fiction.

Gender expectations, gender roles, gender anything is fruit of the "poisonous," fictional tree.

Fiction.

I understand. There's no reason for most people to look into gender. It's a concept as pervasive as the blue of the sky. The only reason most of us spend any time at all thinking about whether or not gender is an actual necessary and functional concept is if that concept stopped working for us.

Like it did for me.

It never would have occurred to me to think about gender if I didn't have to. I would have gone right along with everyone else and picked a side.

I got the same blinding indoctrination as every other person growing up in the sixties. I believed in gender because there was absolutely no dissension. I believed in it because the way it was presented — by everyone, everywhere, all the time — left no room even for curiosity.

We miss so many chances this way. Because we are fearful creatures, hard-wired to believe we risk death without social acceptance, we love neat and tidy categories and rules. Our survival once depended on our ability to join with and maintain connection to groups of other humans, and now we are stuck with the need to create and reinforce systems in which we can constantly reassure ourselves that we "belong." This makes us overlook, ignore, and suppress evidence that might offer opportunities to expand our understanding of our own potential.

The idea of gender, in its present prevailing binary form (tied to the appearance of external genitalia), is extremely limiting. It chokes off an avenue of creative human expression and it eliminates some important learning opportunities.

The fictional nature of gender has remained invisible for so long because patriarchy requires the gender binary. Patriarchy is an adversarial system in which one clearly defined side of the binary requires the acquiescence and subjugation of the other clearly defined side of the binary. If the absolute distinction between the two classes is somehow compromised, the model that relies on the exclusive notion of two classes becomes much less relevant.

In other words, patriarchy becomes irrelevant in a society in which there is a belief in and acceptance of a *genderful* understanding of human biological and psychosocial orientation.

But even if something is a fiction, when everyone believes it to be true anyway, fiction or not, there's hardly any difference.

The new tights were lacy. Not just the plain ones like I usually had to wear. There were little raised patterns, and differences in the weave that allowed more skin to show through some places than others.

It wasn't cold, the sun was out, the snow was melted, and it kind of smelled like mud, like it does when the world is waking up from winter. I wanted to go outside to play.

"Okay, but don't run, and don't get your beautiful dress dirty," Mom warned me.

Beautiful dress. I think it was blue, and it was lacy, too. The shiny black patent leather shoes completed the look. I was dressed up for church.

I tried to push it out of my mind. I hated dresses. I hated lace. I hated girl shoes. But since hating all that was bad and bothered Mom, I just tried not to think about any of it. Being all dressed up seemed to make everyone else happy. And I was quickly discovering that making other people happy was what mattered.

The aluminum screen door was held open for me and I ran outside — down the two steps, over the little sidewalk, and onto the blacktop driveway. The door slapped shut behind me.

I jumped around with my arms up toward the sun. A little breeze was blowing over the greening grass. I just wanted to get the sunlight all over me.

I don't remember how I fell. I was little, though, so I probably just tripped over my own feet. The feet in those stupid, shiny shoes. The thing I remember is looking down to see the skinned and bleeding knee and the big hole in the new tights, black around the edges from the driveway.

I started crying. It wasn't the sting of my knee; it was knowing that Mom would be sad because I ruined her pretty outfit before anyone else saw it.

My experience as a trans kid growing up in the sixties meant I endured deep personal rejection and invalidation everywhere I turned. There was no one to reassure me that the suffering this caused would pass. There was no one to soothe the pain, because no one could even believe the pain was real.

Everyone knew that tomboys grew out of it. Everyone knew that, after a time, all tomboys would begin to play along with the religious and cultural expectations of femininity. There was no knowledge or example of people who did not grow out of it and, thus, no reason even to think that was a possibility.

So the job fell to all the women around me (in the sixties, men were not very involved with children) to work unrelentingly in an effort to indoctrinate me into the cult of femininity. Adopting a practice of femininity seemed to have some dire importance that I simply could not comprehend.

This work of theirs, making me into a nice young lady, necessitated all manner of coercion. I was gently and cheerfully instructed, I was bribed, I was shamed, and, sometimes, I was threatened. But worst of all, I believe, now that I look back on it, was the emotional manipulation. Though I felt embarrassed, even humiliated, by the "pretty clothes" I had to wear to church and school, wearing them never failed to provoke my mom, grandmothers, and other peripheral women into expressing satisfaction and happiness. I wanted to please these people, as does any little kid.

"What a beautiful outfit!"

"How pretty you look today!"

"Oh, the dresses your grandmother makes for you are so adorable. You are so lucky!"

"Don't you just feel so pretty?"

I was confused about how my perceptions could be so far removed from the perceptions of everyone else. I couldn't help but know something was fundamentally wrong with me and, sadly, I could already tell it was something immutable.

It was an impossible problem for a kid's brain to solve. What I knew of myself was completely at odds with what everyone else seemed to know about me. The only way around the confusion was to stop letting myself think about it. And as I got better at not thinking about it, I found I could distance myself from the feelings of shame and humiliation, too, just by letting go of my body.

I had found a way not to have to feel anything.

You may not have noticed, and most women have never really thought about it in this way, but we're afraid of men.

It's one of the first things we are taught. Before we know much else, we know that they can be dangerous. We know to be careful when we are alone with them. We know they don't always have the best of intentions. We know they are allowed anger and that anger can lead to trouble. We know they are allowed power and that power can lead to a sense of ownership.

We are taught to appease them, to be quiet and accommodating, to "honor" them, in hope this will keep them calm and prevent them from harboring ill will toward us.

When I was four or five years old, an adult man I didn't know wanted me to get into a car with him. I knew enough about men even then, as a tiny child, to run. I had already learned to fear them.

I never thought of it as "their" church. The men. They just worked there. They came and went. They did some things, sure, like go to meetings and stand up in front of the congregation on Sunday to explain the Bible, God, and the rules of being a good Christian. But from what I could tell, the rest of the time they mostly stayed in their offices.

On Sunday mornings, of course, there were more men around for a couple hours. There were some in the choir. The deacons who seated people and served communion were all men. There were always lots of men seated in the congregation and, later, tapping their feet in the fellowship hall as they waited for their wives to quit talking so they could go home.

But to me, Sunday mornings didn't have that much to do with church. Sunday mornings sometimes felt like a performance or, maybe, more like an invasion. People filling the place up, wandering around, people all dressed up, people who didn't know those of us who were there all the time. It was always nice when they left and things got back to normal.

Church was actually quiet, interesting, and safe, with an endless array of places to explore. Church was a place where, every day but Sunday, I could count on people being nice to me. I think church felt like this because the only people around, most of the time, were women. There were secretaries, receptionists, sewing circle and service guild members, choir mothers, Sunday school teachers, cooks, housekeepers, childcare workers, and librarians. And in my mind, the church actually belonged to these women (and maybe to a few of us kids who were there a lot, too).

It seemed to me that we were the ones who gave it life. Without us, it was just a giant, empty building. A dead thing. But all week long, the women and kids moved through the church, sustaining it, like blood moves through vessels and keeps a body alive.

At school, I felt like an outsider, looking from the margins in toward the normal kids. I wasn't like them. Just wasn't. They knew it. I knew it. Very few of them even talked to me. I knew some of them laughed at me behind my back. I just tried not to think about it.

At school, there was another person who was supposed to be a girl but wasn't, like me. Debbie something. We never spoke to each other. We never had classes or activities together. But I watched her. I heard the rumors. It was said she went on a date with a younger girl who didn't know she was a girl. I didn't really believe it. Everyone else did, though, and called her a freak. As I watched her, I wondered if people saw me the same way they saw her.

I always tried as hard as I could to be nice. I wondered if she did, too.

But things were different at church. Everyone talked to me, and I could tell they liked me. I was there all the time. I knew a lot of people. I belonged.

It felt, in a way, like the church was my safe place. The walls were arms around me, keeping me safe from harm. The building itself became a sanctuary from all the confusing things that happened on the outside.

I wasn't sure why people were so much nicer to me at church than they were at school. I felt like I was the same person in both places. But I figured it probably had something to do with God, Jesus and all that.

At one point, a new youth leader was hired at church, a man who was quite active in Young Life in our area. When he set up the first meeting of a new youth group, I felt kinda excited.

On the Sunday afternoon of the first meeting, I arrived early and was already seated as the other kids began arriving. A lot of them were from my school. Normal kids. Popular kids. Kids whose parents belonged to our church but who I'd only seen there every now and then, on Christmas and Easter.

Finally, I thought. *Finally, they will see me in a place where I belong. They will see that I am not just some freak. And maybe it will help how they treat me at school.*

The meeting started. There were sixty or seventy kids there. The leader and his helpers played guitars, and we all sang from Young Life songbooks. Then came the talking.

After a few words, the new youth leader asked, "What do you see when you think of God?"

I put my hand up quickly. I was happy to help get this conversation started. I didn't want him to have to stand up front awkwardly while all the kids just sat there looking at each other. I wanted to be helpful.

He pointed at me.

When I was a little kid, I'd had a picture of the statue of Zeus at Olympia on one of my View-Master reels, and the image dovetailed nicely with all the Sunday school lessons I'd heard and the hymns I'd sung about God. I saw this picture in my mind when I thought of God.

I dropped my hand to my lap and offered brightly, "I see an old man with a long beard, sitting on a throne."

There was no thoughtful pause in which he looked closely at me and considered his response. Instead, he simply threw back his head and laughed uproariously. On cue, all the other kids exploded in laughter, too. No need for them to laugh behind my back this time. Now they had been given permission to do so right in front of me.

It was so unexpected, it was so impossible, that the outside of me froze. Not so, the inside. Heat flushed through me; I felt like I might throw up. My thoughts raced, trying to make some sense of what was happening. I'd never been humiliated at church before. I didn't think it was possible.

I felt myself start to cry and inwardly screamed at myself to stop. That was certainly not the correct response. I didn't know what to do. What would a normal person do? I looked at the laughing youth leader. The kids' laughter rang in my ears. And suddenly my body remembered what to do. I let go of my body so I didn't have to feel anything. And then I laughed, too, like I was in on the joke.

The meeting went on, and my awareness returned. I coaxed the tears out of the space right behind my eyes and funneled them deep inside me. (They would remain contained for decades.) I assured myself that there would be an opportunity to redeem myself. This was my safe place. They were all just visitors who would be leaving soon. It would be okay. It would be forgotten. It didn't mean anything, really.

After this experience, the first of many to come, church, my safe place, become a little less safe and a little less *mine*.

The women were still there, and I still felt I belonged when they were around. But as I got older, I found I had to interact with the men more often. And try as I might, I never really trusted them.

It would be another five years before a couple other male pastors finally finished the job this one had started, and succeeded in destroying the illusion that church could ever be a safe place for me. And just in case I had any lingering intentions of sticking around with God, Jesus, and all that, they succeeded in destroying my awareness of faith, for many years to come.

We are hardwired to look for belonging. But belonging is not found by swimming in great oceans of imposed similarity or by subjugation of anyone else's authenticity by imposition of power or pain.

Belonging blooms from the knowledge that there is no discernable distance between us. That each of us, just as we are and all together, is the lifeblood flowing through this strange and wonderful Holiness.

I've gone on to find faith again, and I found it through and within the company of women. Those people we label "women" in this culture, even with all their misguided efforts, still come closer to practicing something very important, something that is, perhaps, easier to learn from a life of subtle fear and subordination. How to *embody* Love.

MEET THE AUTHOR

Lē Isaac Weaver is a non-binary writer, musician, and feminist spiritual seeker. Lē's work in the world is primarily focused on drawing attention to and mitigating the ongoing violence directed at women and LGBTQI people. They (Lē's preferred pronoun) believe that acceptance of a genderful understanding of God is necessary toward that end. They dream of a cultural/spiritual awakening which will encourage each of us to move deeper into a practice of non-violence and embodied love.

FAITH
TRANSITIONS

"As we seek equity for women and men in our world and our churches, we would do well to acknowledge and celebrate the masculine and feminine traits that God embodies, as we are all made in God's image. If we begin to think of God as having both masculine and feminine traits, perhaps we could see the potential for us all to possess those traits. If we see God's strength as feminine and God's care as masculine, it becomes possible for men to be caring and women to be strong."

ELISE

Don't Label Me

Jen Fulmer

religious structure of my childhood held nothing but anxiety for me for
           concept of god and faith was completely wrapped up in my father the pastor.
about 20 years after their divorce I couldn't walk into church without much anxiety and fear
My second iteration of faith was packaged in the concept of romantic love of
                expectations put upon it
marriage and partnership and physical intimacy. The first person I had sex
           All I want is to be kissed and snuggled
My first boyfriend did not love me well but I had bought the ticket so I had to go. My first
  In the death of god, never be an abuser, God will never force anything on us, that is the
entire reason for all heartache ever, god knows we must choose. . . . ohhh loaded statement!
god is found.
myself to Spain, Turkey, Colombia, Peru, Ecuador, Bolivia, and Chile. I
             know people far more adventurous than me
   no idea how I like to travel, no idea about any of it. And I had so
  had built space that tells a story it was not lock myself into a tight itinerary, any more, the
    done so much research and preparation but I couldn't quite manage to
       opinions are of night was in a hilton, my mom had booked the room for me and from
another man describing was actually process theology
  and then overheard a conversation in which a guy described
    "needing to dry out" spiritually and he said he followed a yogi who said "
        that he was wrong. Was he wrong objectively? I don't know but subjectively
theology conference I was so excited to talk to a bunch of dudes about

naïveté and innocence are something that needs to be burned away before
  this, he was so comfy in this structure this or that and he would say that was,
his statements were like a polar opposite of every experience I have ever had
  doing, I do not speak the language, I do not read the language. I have
explain to me that what I was   But every
    conversation I had felt like it was with an idea and not with a person
  aligning myself with groups, I am afraid of commitment I don't like group,
        I'm like a bad healthy
   But through the act of discussion
  thoughts and a couple definite meetup points but a lot of vacant
 I would like to learn how to cultivate that. How to force people to stop
lecturing and stop reciting and just talk and listen and learn from what are my experiences
they think, and women are way better in my experience at accessing
    Kinda the opposite of theology or philosophy.
I feel the same if theology, a structuring and boxing of god seems to make her
       on time on budget and on point
   no not women, not smaller gender pronouns make god smaller.
    Straight lines make god smaller.
I used to dress like the things my mom liked
    Then I tried to dress like the me. . . . I know.
   I spent all day avoiding words. Doing all the unhealthys. Not being
Faith feels like the first hit of a cigarette when all that trying releases for a
   home and struggled for an hour to squeeze two pages out of my heart and
best self but doing all the things that allow me to feel ok with being less
  than my best. Because if I do them then maybe I'll at least be good enough.
   there it was 14 days of ?????????????????? so i got there, i got to the
 the first morning as the jet lag makes the waking up inevitable so when I remember the night
before i left i had
   Just lost everything i typed while pooping, no idea if it was brilliant or
  But the first stop was Japan. with obligations and I booked a trip that schizophrenically
popcorned from LA
   Yet I spend thousands of dollars in
  to Japan, to Spain to Turkey to New York and back to home.
have the perfect vortex of free time, savings, and utter lack of financial
  hotel, I knew that the fish market tuna auction was something to see
   Reading Matthew I got Mary.

In the death of self you find self
and
All the should make me smaller
today I found a dress in a Theological problem
and I said "I'm not comfortable with labels"

MEET THE AUTHOR

Jennifer grew up the daughter of a pastor and has continued a faith centered worldview which has ever been evolving with the life she experiences. She studied theatrical design at UCLA and works as a set decorator in Los Angeles. She is always seeking new ways that we can more deeply connect with ourselves and others and spaces where our messiest most imperfect selves can be known and loved.

A Dinosaur Shaped Hole

Anonymous

ACT I

How about you, princess? Do you want to do something important? Or are you going to go do cartwheels and make friends with a bee? — Lillian from *The Unbreakable Kimmy Schmidt*[7]

It is difficult for me to approach this project. My 'faith' now is nearly nonexistent. I believe in God, but I have no spiritual practice. I feel that I am becoming more centered, more integrated, and more authentic, which could be called spirituality. However, that process of "becoming" is more about knowing myself than about knowing God. I have spent the last several years searching for . . . something. The search has included some sexual and emotional promiscuity, exploration of broader belief systems, embracing a 'fuck it' attitude, letting go of some moral high ground, pulling away from my family, and drinking more whiskey.

I now realize that faith (and its crumbling) is messier than I ever imagined. I recoil from statements of absolute truth or anyone who deigns to teach me about spirituality. Whatever I have in the present moment has become intensely personal. Sometimes I worry about the consequences of my flight from

---

7. *The Unbreakable Kimmy Schmidt, Season 2, Episode 10, "Kimmy Goes to Her Happy Place," directed by John Riggi, aired April 15, 2016, on Netflix.*

"the narrow path." My current view of a broad, immensely gracious, and understanding God could actually be wrong, and he (or she) could be a concrete, black and white judge who will count my myriad of sins against me. The notion of eternal misery is daunting, yet the notion of ordering my life around fear of that fate is repulsive. On my braver days, I think I would rather be struck down by lightning than succumb to the shame and fear-driven groveling of my past. I simply can't go back.

Midwestern Evangelicalism taught me that I, as a woman, am responsible for the choices, feelings, and eternal destiny of everyone around me. I learned quickly that my value was based upon how well I performed my role. I, as a woman, was "called by God" to be nice, be gentle, make people comfortable, make people food, and share the good news of Jesus (and by extension, the bad news of sin and hell) with any who would listen (including those who wouldn't). The logical reverse of those expectations was to repent of any feelings that were not nice, gentle, or may make anyone uncomfortable (i.e., anger, desire, ambition, etc.).

I became an intuitive genius, capable of reading another person's emotional state almost at first glance. Not only could I intuit the moods of others, but I was also adept at subtly ascertaining how their mood could be improved and then adapting my conversation and presence to achieve that goal. In doing so, with the idea that I was not only responsible for their mood but also choices, I developed the skill of gently advising those who had attached to me as "that person who always makes me feel better." I offered "wisdom" and advice to guide them to greater compliance with the moral code I believed to be absolute.

Being nice is not bad. Feeling and attempting to improve the emotional situations of others is not bad. Offering advice to those who want it is not bad. The part I resent is that in that paradigm there was no room for me. My being was consumed by the existence of others. I did not learn to take up my own space. I did not learn to identify and defend my own needs. I did not learn that I mattered independent of what people think of me. I did not learn to advocate for myself. I did not learn that I had a unique voice that was defined by my unique humanness, not just my Christian womanness.

Because of this, I did not realize that my youth leader was misogynistic. I did not realize that he regularly mistreated myself and the other girls. Rather, I accepted the abuse as an accurate assessment of our value and intelligence. I played piano on the worship team because, while I was not musical by nature, it was better than childcare. I regularly repented for the attention the boys showed me because obviously, my "flirtation" (i.e., friendliness, eye contact, and ready smile) was causing them to stumble. My journals (starting from 10 years old) are filled with heart-rending expositions of my daily failures, and pleadings for God to forgive and right my oh-so-wrong self.

ACT 2

We have a world full of women who are unable to exhale fully because they have for so long been conditioned to fold themselves into shapes to make themselves likeable. — Chimamanda Ngozi Adichie[8]

I think that the role, identity, and value offered by traditional Christianity to its adherents are far too limited. The church offers what could be imagined as a two-dimensional shape to its members. A square, perhaps. A person gets to belong in the institution if only they are able to fit themselves within the shape of the square. The square is marketed as a part of a beautiful mosaic. Perhaps it is described as a beautiful, unique expression of the person God made you to be. And perhaps that is not inaccurate. But it is still a square. You are still expected to conform to this 'unique,' 'custom made' shape that fits within the larger mosaic. Worse yet, it is stamped with God's seal, reinforcing that a square is all you're destined to be and any sanctioned self-expression or self-actualization needs to fit within that shape. Diversion from that shape is labeled 'sin' or 'rebellion' from 'the will of God'.

Maybe we are not designed to be two-dimensional. Maybe we are actually three-dimensional blow up beach toys with all kinds of shapes and forms. Maybe we're inflatable dinosaurs. Maybe the universe has a unique, me-shaped hole that requires my specific constitution. If that is the case, the two-dimensional shape handed down by the church is a sad, under-representation of what we actually could be. It may sound like the three-dimensional, dinosaur-shaped hole in the universe is equivalent to the two-dimensional, square-shaped hole in God's mosaic, but here is the difference: you don't know what shape your

---

8. Chimamanda Ngozi Adichie, *Dear Ijeawele, or a Feminist Manifesto in Fifteen Suggestions*, 37 (New York: Alfred Knopf, 2017), 37.

dinosaur is until it is. No one tells you what shape to fill. The shape morphs and changes as it fills with air.

What if each time we choose to show up, to be vulnerable, to be authentic, to challenge the status quo, to be brave, and defy expectations we are opening the valve and letting air in? What if the choices we make to step away, to speak up, to take up space, to say "hell no" to abuse and repression, add form to our space in the universe? What if God's kingdom is less about people who conform to a preset shape and more about pinching open the valve and waiting to see what happens?

ACT 3

I shall become, I shall become a collector of me. And put meat on my soul. — Sonia Sanchez[9]

As it all turns out, I am deeply angry. I am angry at a system that tells people who to be and what to do. I'm not angry at the people in the system, nor am I angry at God. I don't think that the real God is who I thought he/she/they was/were when I was growing up. That God resembled an unstable, manipulative, and insecure parent. It makes sense that the people who follow that God respond like children of that sort of parent.

So here we are. Here I am. Anger is new to me. I do not know how to resolve it. Somehow agreeing with some of Christian spirituality feels like assenting to all of it. It does not seem possible to be partially compliant. It seems to be all or nothing. At this point, if that is the case, I choose nothing. God forgive me.

---

9. Sonia Sanchez, *Wounded in the House of a Friend* (Boston: Beacon Press, 2012).

A RELUCTANT CHRISTIAN

Helen De Cruz

When I was six years old, I was preparing for first communion. My grandmother warned me, "When you receive the host, you will hear Jesus speak." With great anticipation, I looked forward to the day I would hear Jesus' actual voice. Church was boring; it was mystifying to me why adults kept on going there week after week to hear our priest drone on, and even more baffling that they insisted I should be there too. Now I would finally taste and hear why they went there.

On that day of first communion, I was dressed in a silken, white, drag-on-embroidered dress (recycled from the fabric of my mother's wedding dress), and received the wafer with great solemnity. But though I listened intently, I did not hear Jesus speak. When I questioned my grandmother about this, she said, "Well, I never meant he would *literally* speak. I meant he would speak in your heart." If I have to pinpoint a moment where I first got interested in the philosophy of religion, it was then. I was burning with questions: what does it mean to hear someone speak not literally, but in your heart? My grandmother could not answer those questions; neither could anyone else.

I grew up in a very white and culturally homogeneous village in Belgium, a predominantly Catholic country, (at least culturally speaking). I am of mixed parentage: my mother a Belgian, my father from Malaysia (both are Catholic). As a result, I could not pass as white, especially in the months after the summer holidays, when my mother put me in summer camp and the sun was merciless. The other kids would ask me all the time: Where was I from? Have I ever been to Malaysia? Also, of course, there were racial insults and abuse — being physically attacked, or having my property destroyed by fellow classmates, merely for the colour of my skin. I didn't feel like I belonged; and felt awkward and out of place at school and elsewhere.

I never ended up having a Eucharistic experience of hearing Jesus, but singing in the local church choir came close. When I joined the local village church choir and the youth church group, aged sixteen, I finally felt I belonged somewhere. The Saint Gregory Choir, a former men's choir, but now led and populated by women due to collapsing interest from male members of the congregation, was sometimes unsympathetically described as a bunch of quavering elderly ladies' voices. All parts were sung by women; our women basses could hit a low F. I was just one of three young women who could read music. Together we bravely held up the alto part; always a rather unspectacular musical line squeezed between the agile tenor and the soaring soprano. Funerals were the most moving experience. We worked closely with the next of kin to give the dead a dignified send-off, and we would sing, sometimes with tears in our eyes, as we knew the deceased, the Latin mass of the dead. As the notes of *In paradisum* died away, I had a sense of closure, even though I did not (and even now scarcely) dare think there is such a place as paradise.

As I went to university, I did not leave my parental home, and just commuted to the nearest town (Ghent). But many of my friends from choir and church group left to other university cities, in Brussels, Antwerp, and Leuven. I slowly drifted away from Catholicism and Christianity. I didn't like the power structures; I didn't like the misogyny; I didn't like the whole package deal of Catholicism, which struck me as rigid and unaccommodating.

I recall vividly how my best friend (like me, aged 18) asked our priest whether it was permissible to have an abortion if — in spite of her best efforts to avoid it — she became pregnant. His reply was full of condemnation for even daring to think such a thing: she should just refrain from having premarital sex, and it would be unforgivable to kill an unborn child. To make matters worse, our local church was, at that time, beset by a series of scandals, including a chaplain accused of pedophilia, and a teacher at the local Catholic school on whose computer child pornography was found. Perhaps the most heartbreaking was a nearby boarding school for disabled children, where the priests had been abusing boarding children for years. The church responded with its usual lack of transparency and lack of accountability.

What ultimately led me to embrace the label of 'Christian', albeit still with some hesitancy, was working in the philosophy of religion. I stumbled onto the philosophy of religion by accident through a workshop in the cognitive science of religion that I took while a grad student in Oxford in 2009. I take great intellectual joy in puzzling over philosophical questions about God and religion more broadly. Intellectually, I remain quite skeptical; for instance, I recently published a paper that argues that the evolutionary origins of ritual should give us reason to doubt we are really interacting and engaging with God. I am also wary of arguments that say that religious belief is wholly unproblematic. I do think the standard arguments against religion have considerable force, and remain sceptical about several aspects that seem to come as a package deal for Christians: the belief in an afterlife, in an omnibenevolent God (or at least an omnibenevolence we would recognize), and in salvation through Christ alone.

A few times, I have felt God's presence clearly. One time — I was at my third postdoc position, and I was at a point where I despaired of the job market and a string of failed interviews — *I got this distinct sense that Christ is with us, and nothing else matters. With him by our side, why should we worry?* Now, God obviously did not promise me a tenure track job (that would be quite something!), but it brought some perspective. I've experienced something similar a few times more, and it has helped to give me courage and stave off hopelessness and cynicism.

Church structures, unfortunately, still don't work for me entirely, and I probably won't find one that will not disappoint. To give one example, in the Church of England parish close to where I live, young children are not welcome except in special "family services." Children go to Sunday school, and parents — especially mothers — of children under five, are expected to accompany them to the special separate children's service held in the churches' adjoining rooms, where the leader sings Taizé songs, where we all do crafts together and eat grapes and small pieces of baguette (the former in lieu of wine). Although I am the mother of a young child, I do not particularly enjoy doing crafts (at home or during church) and would much rather be a part of the bigger church communities. This is one of those subtle ways in which the church excludes younger women, or rather, polices what they can be part of and what they can do. Flowers and cakes are fine, being a lay preacher, not so much.

While academic philosophy of religion has its problems, in my experience it is far more welcoming and gender-equal than the church communities I've been a part of. It is still common to be the only woman who is invited as a key-note speaker, or (one of the) only woman audience members, but there is nevertheless the space to engage with religion that is much less constrained by gender expectations. There is also an increasing effort to engage with female voices in religion, including female mystics in Christian and other traditions. The Society of Christian Philosophers, of which I have been a long-time member, makes efforts to increase diversity and to be welcoming not only to women, but also to LGBTQ philosophers, and philosophers of colour.

However, philosophy of religion and its practitioners are not isolated from church communities. I am glad never to have seriously pursued a calling to priesthood, for what I have heard from several senior women in the philosophy of religion who did (both those who succeeded and those who failed), is that this is an arduous journey whereby one must prove oneself as a traditional woman before one can even begin to think of being trained as a priest. While it is proper that people called to priesthood go through a discernment process, it seems unwise to use gendered norms to shape expectations about what hoops people are expected to jump through before they can begin training, for what is (in the Church of England at least) an unpaid position.

On balance, I find philosophy of religion a meaningful way to engage with religion and perhaps would go as far as to call it a kind of religious practice. Whereas ritual is a way to engage the senses, philosophy of religion is a way for me to involve the intellect in religion. I am not interested in philosophy of religion for apologetic purposes, or even as faith seeking understanding — I work in it as a purely intellectual exploration of something that is of personal significance.

Recently I have been working on a short monograph on religious disagreement for Cambridge University Press. Work on this has made me think of ways we might engage with the intellectual needs of ordinary religious believers in a way that does not infantilize them or trivialize the questions they have. Many ordinary religious disagreements focus on topics that have their academic counterparts, such as the problem of evil, the problem of religious diversity, or who should have the burden of proof. I found, however, that the Catholic school I attended, or the churches I attended, did not sufficiently engage with such questions and were perhaps too quick to dismiss them.

One particular example of how it can be different: When I was in Amsterdam, I attended a Reformed church, where the very talented minister talked about the terrorist attacks on Charlie Hebdo and the #jesuischarlie campaign afterwards. He warned that Christians should not pile on and further alienate another a population that is already quite vulnerable, namely Muslims in Europe. He drew on a Pauline epistle to make parallels with very early Christianity, and the duty of care we have towards people to different faiths (and none). I recall the distinctly uncomfortable shuffling of feet of the congregation, but also how extensively we discussed this sermon afterwards during tea. In my experience, at least, churches will often underestimate the intellectual needs and capacities of their audience.

I long for a church I can belong to that doesn't shy away from taking risks, or treating their members as adults. In the meantime, I am just an unaffiliated Christian; grateful I can intellectually engage about religion with fellow philosophers. I call myself a reluctant Christian, because I am still quite unsure whether I belong.

MEET THE AUTHOR

I am a senior lecturer (associate professor) in philosophy at Oxford Brookes University, with specializations in philosophy of religion, philosophy of cognitive science, and experimental philosophy. My work is concerned with higher domains of human cognition, including art, science, and theology, and seeks to explain why and how we engage in these endeavours. In my spare time, I enjoy playing my Renaissance lute, drawing and painting, and spending time with my family.

ONE STRANGE NIGHT

Anonymous

The first week of January 1986 was one of the strangest of my life. I had spent the previous summer in Nashville, interning at the Baptist Sunday School Board. While there I won a radio contest — a trip to Los Angeles, a New Year's Eve party with one of my favorite bands, and a premiere showing of their new concert album. A few days after Christmas, I landed at LAX and got on a rowdy bus with other winners from around the country. I was 20 years old, in the middle of my sophomore year in college. Nothing like this had ever happened in my sheltered, Southern Baptist, girls' prep school, teetotaling, morning-in-America existence.

The trip was a whirlwind of tours, parties, meet-and-greets, and a few glimpses of celebrity. I flew back with my head abuzz, sleep-deprived, and star struck, and drove back from the airport late at night. Mom was waiting up. "Your dad's left us," she said. "He's at a hotel with Becky."

I couldn't make heads or tails of it. During my year and a half at college, eight hundred miles from home, I had come to relish my independence. I almost never called home. That fall semester my mother, a licensed pilot, had started to ask more frequently whether she could come up and visit, or fly over and bring me home for a long weekend. I brushed her off; she was bothering me, getting in my way. I never felt curious about what might be behind her insistence. Now I understood — Dad was drifting away, and she was desperately looking for some way to hang on to her family.

Becky and her husband were my parents' best friends. They met through flying; the husband piloted a sweet King Air (nicer than Mom's Cessna). For a few years, they did almost everything together: parties, tennis, golf, and vacations. Absorbed in my own adolescent dramatics, I hadn't the faintest idea that Dad and Becky had anything more to do with each other than that.

That January night in 1986, Mom stayed on the phone into the wee hours. She called our pastor. She called the retired pastor who baptized me in the only church I'd ever known, where Dad was a longtime deacon and treasurer. She called the televangelist in whose ministry Mom worked. Anyone who could plead with Dad to come home.

He did. I was blearily brushing my teeth, about to fall into bed, when the garage door opened. Dad awkwardly hugged me. "I'm sorry this happened," he said.

That was more than 30 years ago. Mom and Dad left that church, and their entire social circle with it. I suppose too many people knew. As soon as my younger brother went to college, they moved to the coast and left our hometown behind for good. Now Mom is frail, slowly succumbing to dementia, entirely dependent on Dad as her caregiver. I've never spoken to him about that night.

My parents were role models of faith, privately and publicly. Every day started with a devotional and prayer at the breakfast table. Our family was well known in our large and prosperous congregation. Every Sunday morning, Sunday evening, and Wednesday evening, we were there. My older brother preached on Youth Sunday; I taught an adult Sunday school class as a teenager and sang in the choir. Mom and Dad led the singles ministry, taking the members under their wing, showing them what a godly marriage looked like. Mom flew that televangelist around the country to conventions and events, and I spent evenings answering the prayer line when his show aired on a fledgling Christian network in the early days of cable and satellite TV. I never heard Dad curse or call anyone a worse name than "dingo." As far as I know, neither of them have ever smoked a cigarette or tasted alcohol.

So when I was blindsided that night by Dad's affair with Becky, it was like he'd been replaced by an alien. I had no framework of understanding into which to fit this stranger who had the capacity to be unfaithful. It's not just that I idolized Dad, although I was much closer to him than Mom. No one who knew him could ever imagine him doing such a thing. He was such a model

Christian, not in the sense of being ostentatiously pious, but in being genuinely Christlike. Gentle, thoughtful, a servant to others, steady, and morally upright. How could his thoroughgoing life of faith square with leaving us for another woman, even for a few hours?

I was too self-absorbed, I'm afraid, to think much about it at the time. But it was later that semester that I switched my major from English to religion, the first step on the road to my career as a theologian. The conscious trigger was the exciting new ways of thinking about Christian doctrine and scripture that I was encountering for the first time in the classroom; I felt like the doors of my Sunday School religious education had been thrown open, and a whole new world awaited. Now I wonder, though, whether an unconscious thread of bewilderment, rooted in my father's inexplicable betrayal, runs through that decision as well.

Because what this episode revealed is that faith wasn't what I'd been told it was. I didn't — I couldn't — come to the conclusion either that Dad had failed to have enough faith, or that his faith had somehow failed him. Instead, I discovered that faith doesn't function as a prophylactic for moral lapses. I was taught to use my faith to bolster myself against temptation, to stay within its confines to avoid falling into error. The metaphor was of a zone of safety, outside of which were pitfalls (error) and enemies laying siege (temptation). Much of my Christian education consisted, in retrospect, of a familiar chant: "Build that wall!"

Seen from the outside, Dad's affair didn't appear to stem from shoddy construction, or "straying" outside a protective boundary. It wasn't that he didn't know enough, believe enough, try enough, or pray enough. Becky didn't come to him as a snare or stumbling block. What Dad experienced, I believe, didn't feel like temptation. It felt like love.

In my career as a theologian, helping undergraduates understand the traditions in which they were raised and grapple with the world in which faith plays out, I've come to appreciate the outsized influence Paul (as opposed to Jesus) wields in the Bible Belt. It's Paul who urged us, in a passage I memorized for the quasi-military Bible Drill competitions of my youth, to "put on the whole armor of God" (Ephesians 6:10-18). "Take up the shield of faith," we were exhorted. But what led Paul to think about faith this way?

Scholars of Paul, such as John Dominic Crossan, point out that (perhaps because of his own psychology or key experiences) Paul conceived of himself as beset by all kinds of unseen antagonists; we wrestle "against principalities, against powers" who surround us waiting for an opening to strike. These seem to be quite literal for Paul. Striding through the Agora (marketplace) of a Hellenistic city purpose-built for imperial expansion and glory, one of the dozens of such cities that he visited in his travels all over the known world, he moved amongst invisible spirits crowding the air, circling, screeching, and conniving. The way I was taught, this is the reality. We don't so much live in the world to enjoy it, as we are in the world to fight it, tooth and nail, every step of the way.

Many evangelical kids, much like me, emerged into a world full of beauty (both natural and created), and we were instructed to appreciate it as the unsullied work of the divine. This applied to humans too: their work, lives, creativity, emotions, and intimacies. That beauty doesn't completely submit to moral categories. The same emotional bond that enriches two people that it connects, can damage another person that it excludes. What makes human life so vivid and precious can't be neatly sorted into categories of good and evil, blessing and temptation. Often we can only make such judgments in retrospect, and even then, they will differ depending on whom you ask.

We have a word for people who are confident in making those judgments ahead of time and with absolute certainty: fanatics. My dad isn't a fanatic. But the faith he taught me, the faith of our church and its inexhaustible universe of supporting materials, was the faith of fanatics. Living in a reality that is true and right, simple and clear, this faith says: that's the way God sees it. Our job is to see through God's eyes, and then all the confusing nuance will fall away.

When Dad ran off with Becky, even though they didn't make it through the first night, he showed me something different. He would probably say he showed me failure. But that wasn't what I took away from that wild night. What he did was reveal the end of the line, as far as I was concerned, for a faith of simplicity. It was like that whole edifice was revealed as an inflatable castle; all that was holding it upright was everybody blowing as hard as they could. Shouting, chanting, repeating, asserting, and claiming. One pinprick of reality — messy, irreducible, unavoidable, tragic, awful, wondrous human reality — and it collapsed. The shield of faith was a husk protecting a void.

Did I lose *that* faith? Yes, I did. Not from that one incident, but I did.

Did I lose faith? No. Because also in Dad's life was a faith that inspired me. It was the faith of responding to the world, not keeping it at bay. Faith that meant taking the world as it comes and asking how to honor the humans within it, as Jesus did. There's bedrock to that faith. It's built of sturdy stuff. It stays upright no matter my failures and no matter what changes around it. A faith in justice, in healing, in human dignity, in seeing the risen Christ in every single person. Walking in the light isn't being bathed in purity, but moving towards wholeness for anything and anyone in this broken world.

I think about that night often. I wonder if Dad does. I suspect that, like I do with what I perceive as my worst moments, he tries not to — and can't help doing anyway. I wish he knew that the failure of his faith opened my eyes and gave me my life's work.

REMEMBER WHO YOU ARE

Rebecca Berciunas

Trigger Warning: Rape

I was raised in the church — a 'PK' — a Pastor's Kid. However, in this strict environment I didn't learn about *faith*. I learned about *church*. I learned church routines, church culture, and church expectations. I was the youngest of five children, and my early childhood memories were of the older siblings supervising the younger ones while our parents were away doing church work. They would be gone long hours visiting people and running long board meetings. As a young 'PK,' church became a second home. Naps were taken on pews while we waited for meetings to end, pews were detailed with Liquid Gold on Saturdays, and bulletins were folded with precise technique while we inhaled the smell of ink from the mimeograph machine. It was definitely a family endeavor preparing for Sunday mornings.

My parents were devoted, dynamic, and charismatic pastors. They both worked full-time jobs and pastored churches successfully. They had a clear calling that they responded to at a young age and they carried it out wholeheartedly. I admired and respected how they worked together. Their work ethic was impeccable and I deeply respected them. They were our first teachers, and they instilled in us a strong, responsible work ethic, physical discipline, and a fear of God.

Yet, I felt something was off or missing. I sensed things and had feelings I didn't understand. I remember having horrific nightmares, always evil in some form and me battling demonic forces. I was always fighting in a good versus evil scenario. I didn't understand why I wasn't being protected from these dreams since I lived in a Christian home, prayed to God, and did devotions. *Why weren't the dreams going away? Why wasn't I protected?* I would tell my parents about these nightmares and that they were happening nightly. They would tell me just to pray and would dismiss me from their room, (or their bed if I tried to sneak in). What I needed was for them to pray with me and reassure me with tenderness. They didn't. I was confused and hurt, feeling unloved, and emotionally abandoned. This may sound harsh, but it is what I felt. I couldn't figure out why they were incapable of entering into my feelings with me.

Along with this, we were expected to participate in family devotions, which my siblings and I dreaded. I resented this strongly because this it did not feel warm or loving. We had a huge white, large print Bible that smelled like mothballs, and we were expected to take turns reading out loud and then praying out loud. It felt very forced and unnatural. To me, we were just having church at home. This was not building faith or relationship. We weren't asked about what we wanted to pray about or how we felt or what we were going through as kids. It was like my parents were trying to making sure we were saved. *Were we supposed to have relationships with Jesus and the church, but not real family relationships with our parents and each other?* There was no freedom to ask why we were doing what we did. There was an expectation to perform, and this made me more resentful.

In the midst of continued nightmares, mandatory devotions and church life, I learned to soothe myself with crying, prayer, sneaking into my sister's bed, singing all the hymns I could think of that had the words — *Jesus, Blood, Power, Victory* — and the Lord's Prayer. Strangely, these early years were the beginning of learning about God's presence in my life. How I sensed Him in my own spirit. I didn't understand what was happening, but I felt the Holy Spirit's presence. This was more real and spiritual than devotions. God felt real, but the way I was experiencing him seemed wrong to me. *There must be a reason for this. No one will ever understand that God is showing up in my times of fear.* Even so, I felt a heaviness, a seriousness, a confusion. I still had nightmares and I accepted my experiences as my 'hauntings.' *What was I supposed to learn?* I couldn't talk about it, so I didn't. If I tried, I was told that my faith in God is enough, and to put those thoughts aside. This didn't help, but I decided to put my mind on growing spiritually.

As a teenager, I was fortunate to have positive, healthy youth leaders that welcomed me and my fears. This was new to me. I was so grateful and relieved when they said they didn't have all the answers. It was refreshing to be in a place where I wasn't scolded or judged for having questions. In fact, I was reminded that there will always be questions. I was learning that questions, fear, and doubt can build faith. That relationships build faith. That love builds faith.

I started experiencing faith on my own, in my own personhood — my talents, creativity, work, and relationships. I started asking: *Who am I and what am I doing here? How is this supposed to happen? What is my identity outside of being a church kid? Is this all I am ever going to be? Was there room and permission for other goals and dreams?* I am thankful that I had loving and honest spiritual mentors who gave me a strong foundation as I grew into adulthood. It gave me a base that I could go back to. One of my mentors, Ed Robinson, taught me a song I will always remember: "I am crucified with Christ therefore I no longer live, Jesus Christ now lives in me." This song was special. It gave me meaning, identity, and reassurance, even if I still did not understand it all. I learned that Christ is always with me.

During this time, before college, I was hopeful for a while and felt like God was showing me the possibilities of life beyond high school. However, college was scary, and I was not prepared for what happened. A professor blindsided me emotionally by scolding and shaming me in a rehearsal studio, in the presence of an accompanist who was a friend from church. I was humiliated. What made the criticism feel worse was that this was a Christian college where my expectations were high. *Professors could talk to me like this? Christians could talk to me like this?* I didn't expect to be addressed this way. I didn't deserve the lashing. I shut down. I felt the way I did when having those nightmares — powerless, frozen, cold, and afraid. This event affected me profoundly, and I left college feeling like a failure.

I went home and couldn't get the over the embarrassment and shame for a long time. I was depressed. I was overwhelmed by these feelings and stepped away from God. I didn't attend church or sing for a couple of years. I was grieving the loss of personal dreams and hopes and the loss of identity. I felt disapproval from God in the same way my parents disapproved of goals and interests I had. If I didn't use my talents for God, then they were meaningless. *Where was my faith now?* I didn't know where I was or who I was supposed to be. *What was wrong with me?* Where were the people to speak the words of Christ into my life?

Eventually, I went back to school and explored other interests. I was introduced to new people and new experiences. One person specifically took an interest in me and took advantage of me by sexually abusing me. This was the worst nightmare of all, which left me numb and feeling locked out of my body. I felt broken, betrayed, and ashamed. *How could I be so reckless to let this happen?* I felt like I was breaking away from Spirit. This was such a breach of contract with my church, parents, and God. I had betrayed my instincts, my body, my knowing, and my way of being. I was raped, dirty, and abandoned. It was my fault, and now I was different.

I hid this experience on the back shelf of my mind for a time, and it haunted me into my marriage relationship. All the ugly hurt and shame got projected onto my husband and family. Scary dreams came back, and the cycle of coping began again. Compounding these feelings of confusion and hurt, my husband was called to ministry. He grew up *unchurched* and had a meaningful salvation experience as a teenager. This was a stark contrast to my faith journey and caused even more conflict. It was difficult for me to accept being so involved in the duties of a church again. Even though I had admired my mother's ability to fulfill her role as a Pastor's Wife, I respected and loved her more for just being a strong woman, my mom. I wanted to be a strong, Christian woman, but didn't feel called to play the role of Pastor's Wife. I wanted my faith to be about more than fulfilling duties. Also, I did not want my children to experience church and God in the ways I had. I wanted them to experience authentic and vulnerable faith. I wanted to create generational change.

About ten years later, we followed God's calling to ministry and moved our family from the West Coast to the Midwest. It was clear that we were starting fresh, taking a risk, and really living out faith with every aspect of our life: home, children, jobs, seminary, church, and more. It was overwhelming to start over with three kids and no family around, but we were willing to be obedient. Thankfully, we connected with a wonderful church and met other couples that had moved to start seminary as well. Our church family was a place where we felt welcomed and cared for. This was a new beginning, and we built an altar of faith on the lyrics of, "Come Thou Fount of Every Blessing":

Here I raise my Ebenezer,
Here by Thy great help I've come;
And I hope, by Thy good pleasure,

Safely to arrive at home.
Jesus sought me when a stranger,
Wandering from the fold of God;
He, to rescue me from danger,
Interposed His precious blood.

During this time, my husband and I had a wonderful and transformational experience. One of my husband's seminary classes planned a visit to St. John's Abbey/Monastery in St. Cloud, Minnesota. The class was on Spiritual Formation and the Early Fathers of Faith. I was thrilled when they extended the invitation to spouses. Little did I know that this trip would be the beginning of healing and a place where a deep shift would take place within me.

A journal entry from October of 1994:

As we drove up to the campus, the Bell Tower was so architecturally striking and what rang within me was that for now, these few days would be a time to come and rest, and drink and eat in the midst of my desert journey. I immediately sensed that this was the place that God has been preparing for me to be — to encourage my faith. In a way, God was saying I will give you proof of things that have been and things that are to come.

As we arrived, we were greeted with open arms by Father Fran, the monk in charge of guests and hospitality. We sat and lingered in the lounge area for a while, chatting, and getting acquainted. The pace of life suddenly slowed down.

There was a new awareness of presence and intentionality, of looking at one another and listening deeply. It was a safe place, and I was mesmerized by the beauty and love I saw in Father Fran. Being there made me realize how much I wanted my faith and belief to be renewed. Learning the history of the ancient fathers and the history of the monastery helped me see that my faith had been so small; yet, my small faith was connected to so many others before me. I felt connected to their faith and their desert experiences. I was able to identify with souls and stories of those before me. I didn't feel so alone or ashamed. I felt understood. I felt safe and loved.

While at the monastery, bells beckoned us to early morning prayer with the monks, and I remember being so ready to go, sit, and hear the scriptures being sung. I melted into love, peace, and rest. It was a healing balm for my soul. I wept. I received validation that all the hard things that had happened to me were real, hurtful, and destructive. I felt the assurance that I was God's personal concern. I was able to receive God's love in the midst of a tender community of believers that knew how to listen, love, and comfort a fellow sojourner. I was being cleansed, healed, and transformed. Similar to what Richard Rohr calls, "cleansing the lens"; by setting aside hurts, feelings, expectations, and plans, I was able to love again.

It has been about 20 years since this transformational event. In those years, my husband pastored a few churches, and we have certainly had our share of positive and negative experiences. We focused on raising our children and making generational changes in the way we were a family. This meant being intentional in our relationship with God *and* each other.

In the midst of all of this, we renewed our marriage vows as a sacred act, symbolic of redemption and healing in our relationship. This was as profound to me as my experience at the monastery because both represented a shift, a shift into **identity.** Faith was teaching me who I was: *surrendered, changed, beloved, and free. Surrendered:* not in a passive way of giving up, but actively receiving truth. *Changed:* Purity was restored. *Beloved:* I was God's personal concern. *Free:* No longer a slave to fear. Faith was teaching me that my *soul-identity* is sealed with Christ!

A Journal entry from June 1997, a song "Blessed Are" by Wayne Watson:

"Blessed are the poor in spirit God has faithfully revealed,
That the riches of the kingdom, with their souls in Christ are sealed."

I am the poor in spirit. Christ has faithfully revealed this to me. This song says to me that I am blessed no matter what condition I am in. I am blessed because of Christ's faithfulness for me. He is faithful for me when I cannot be.

I have spent years diving deep into my conflicted feelings and cycles of shame and guilt to rebuild faith and identity. I now have a better understanding of why I have always been attuned to spirit energy and things that are happening around me. This has led to seeking creative ways of self-care through spiritual and physical practices that have helped me to express faith. I have become mindful that when I allow myself to get lured into being someone that I am not, I step out of my soul-identity. When I hold on to a victim mentality, I step out of my soul-identity. When I step *into* my soul-identity, I have clarity, intelligence, patience, and love. I am in the recovery process daily, learning to let go of fear and *being* what Christ has revealed in me.

The most powerful lesson by far was letting go of my mother, Sarah, as she died from Alzheimer's disease in 2014. Intellectually, I had come to terms with the fact that she would die, but had not processed the fact that I was the only one of her five children she no longer recognized. Saying goodbye was not the painful part; the pain was in her not identifying me as her daughter. The woman who gave birth to me; the human root of my identity was leaving without knowing me. Faith was telling me, *"Let go. Remember who you are; come and die."* This became my mantra, my prayer. I began to let go which helped me to see that mom was teaching us how to look at death without fear. She was literally experiencing *her* faith in death.

We held a Holy Vigil as a family in the hospital for seven days as she passed. The presence of the Holy Spirit was very real as we sang, shared stories, laughed, and wept. As I watched, my dad often held Mom's hand in comfort as if ushering her to a destination. I was witnessing a deep love. I was witnessing a strong partnership. In those powerful moments, gaps in the emotional connection that I thought existed in my relationship with my parents were filled with the indescribable power of Love. I realized that everything I needed from them was always there. Faith was saying, *"Receive it."* What could have been the most fear-filled nightmare turned out to be the most profound.

Life *is* the faith experience. Step into it — with or without fear. Only God's power and redemptive love drives out our fears and leads us to freedom.

> *What does faith tell me now?*
> *You are loved.*
> *Remember who you are.*
> *Come and die.*
>> *Come thou fount of every blessing,*
>> *Tune my heart to sing thy grace;*
>> *Streams of mercy never ceasing,*
>> *Call for songs of loudest praise.*
>> *Teach me some melodious sonnet,*
>> *Sung by flaming tongues above;*
>> *Praise the mount I'm fixed upon it,*
>> *Mount of thy redeeming love.*

MEET THE AUTHOR

Rebecca Berciunas lives in Kansas. She and her husband Harold have three adult children and three grandchildren. As a Body Coach in the wellness and healing arts, Rebecca's passion is helping people identify and work through physical and emotional pain. EMOVERE' emotion in motion.

GOD OUR MOTHER

Elise L. Overcash

My feminism arose from a toxic church situation in which I was discounted because of my gender. Yet long before that church, the seeds that would turn into full-fledged and quietly passionate feminism were laid in subtle ways.

I entered the world loved and cherished. I grew up in a white, middle class, Evangelical Christian family that adhered to very traditional conservative Christian values. We were very involved in our church and attended at least twice a week. Our typical ways of being were heavily influenced by our Christian faith. It determined every value we held and often everything that we did. Since our lives revolved around our church, it became the social reality that I recognized as I grew up. I was generally sheltered and surrounded by people who looked like me and thought like me. I had examples of strong women and men in my life and felt secure in my relationships and in my church. As I grew older, I began to notice the different ways boys and girls were treated, but I did not yet know anything different.

As a child growing up in the Evangelical church, I learned all the male-centric names for God. It was never acknowledged that we could think of God in any other way. Though it was not explicitly discussed, leadership positions were not available to women in my childhood church. This subtle lessening of the value and impact of women affected me, though I would not realize it until later. I attended an Evangelical Christian college and the sexism that persisted throughout those years began to build up within me. I made the conscious choice to move away from that denomination, and I unconsciously became more open to the possibility of seeing feminine traits in God.

I spent my twenties attending and leading a church that tried to be open and progressive, where everyone was welcome. It was there my idea of spirituality began to widen and shift from the rigid formula I had been fed in my younger years. I connected with the music, with the people, and with the new ideas being cultivated. However, after a few blissful years, cracks began to show. Rumors of dissension emerged, and a sense of concern grew. Over the course of a year, this little church that had become the largest and most important part of my life began to crumble. The environment became toxic, and the church began to lose its authenticity and sincerity. As we went through that year, I felt myself questioning my faith. I questioned God and if I should even call myself a Christian.

Adding to this confusion was the fact that I had been experiencing sexist microaggressions perpetuated by the pastor, which led to my own questions about my judgments and feelings. I could not find my voice: it was being silenced and disregarded, and I began to distrust it. I sat through meetings where I was prevented from speaking simply due to my gender. Where the only positions of leadership I could hold were alongside my husband. Where I had to fight to pay a livable wage to the women on staff. Where I watched the leadership disregard the women in their lives and families, and where the only acceptable position for a woman was in the home with the children. Where my confidence was eroded day after day, week after week, month after month.

I began to believe the lies. Maybe they were right. They were, after all, the ones in positions of power, the ones proclaiming that God had spoken to them. If that was the case, maybe I was in the wrong. I began to distrust men in pastoral leadership. The male images of God I had grown up with began to overwhelm me. Yet instead of falling prey to the damaging messages being spoken over me in the name of God, I decided perhaps I could no longer call myself a Christian. I wanted no part in such a religion and certainly no relationship with such a God. This began my journey of identifying more as a feminist than as a Christian. These are now concepts that I strongly believe can and should be held in tandem, though at that point in my life it was not clear that was possible.

It has only been since I left that church that I realized I could think about God more expansively. I could not turn my back on the heart of my childhood religion, nor on the spirituality that I held dear: instead, I needed to separate my idea of God from the male examples I had had all my life. I began to seek out female voices and pastors. I cautiously and quietly replaced "he" with "she" in my private prayers and spiritual readings. As I began to think of God with feminine traits, I saw God in a completely different light. The first time I thought of God as a mother, tears instantly sprang to my eyes. It felt right and safe, and I began to see God in a different light that started to heal the hard things I had experienced in the Church.

God as a mother is a completely different image than God as a father, as a king, or as a lord. The only masculine image of God that comes close to a mother is a shepherd, which still falls short. Using feminine pronouns for God is often controversial. In the Catholic tradition, the role of mother is filled by Mary, the mother of God. In most Protestant traditions, however, linking the Divine to the feminine is frowned upon at best. God is Shepherd, Father, King, Lord, and Son. It is often never suggested or even considered that female pronouns or metaphors could be used for God. Other religions have goddesses, but the prophets we recognize are almost exclusively male. There are feminine and motherly metaphors throughout the Bible, such as in Isaiah: a comforting mother, a woman in childbirth, and a mother drawing her child to her breast. However, contemporary churches often ignore the use of these metaphors, which leaves out half the world and severely limits our ability to express and appreciate the full spectrum of human experience.

Mother Earth is a widely used and recognized metaphor for the earth, though not often used in the Christian tradition. Churches that prioritize earth care may use this metaphor to connect God to earth, but my experience is that these churches are few and far between. Perhaps this is changing, but some Evangelical churches in the United States still reject the idea of earth care and have historically been hesitant to link God and the Earth. If we were to connect the trinity of the Divine, humanity, and the Earth, we could bring the Mother Earth metaphor into mainstream church vernacular. This would serve to create an openness to caring for the Earth and help us begin to see the feminine traits of God.

God as a mother is caring, peaceful, and loving. I see God as a mother in a dimly lit kitchen, baking bread over a fire hearth. It smells of yeasty bread and burning wood, and She is there, lovingly tending the hearth. She offers me a glass of deep red wine and a hunk of warm, crusty bread; ensuring that

I eat my fill and am satisfied. Somehow, the communion elements in this setting mean more than in a brightly lit auditorium or even the sanctuary of a church. She cares for my physical needs as well as my spiritual needs. I see God as a mother in a lush forest that smells earthy and moist like the woods of the Pacific Northwest. Taking a deep breath there fills my lungs with verdant air and my heart with peace. The sun is dappled on the forest floor, the birds are singing, and the wind is whistling softly through the trees. When a storm rolls through, and the trees begin to creak and sway, and raindrops wet my face, I am not afraid. I know that Mother God will guide and protect me. I look ahead and see Her hand reaching back toward me; I take it and let Her lead me into the unknown, and back home. She loves and gives grace, no matter how far I have traveled from Her. The overwhelming feeling I have is that She is safe: there is nothing I could do to travel outside of Her grace. She is like a mother hen, gathering her chicks under her wings.

As I look forward to being a part of a church community again, I know that I can draw on this new image of God that is dynamic, diverse, and wide-ranging, and I do not need to rely on my church or my church's leadership to set these images or metaphors for me. It is empowering to see feminine traits in the God that I worship and serve; traits that I see in myself and can emulate. As we seek equity for women and men in our world and our churches, we would do well to acknowledge and celebrate the masculine and feminine traits that God embodies, as we are all made in God's image. If we begin to think of God as having both masculine and feminine traits, perhaps we could see the potential for us all to possess those traits. If we see God's strength as feminine and God's care as masculine, it becomes possible for men to be caring and women to be strong.

My feminism came out of a painful and life-altering season. Yet it led to a more beautiful and expansive view of God and faith that impacts my life and my work. I have discovered the simple joys of connecting with God through nature and solitary study instead of in a corporate church setting. I still struggle with trusting my instincts, but I know that I must. As the years go on, I see more evidence every year of my own trustworthiness and must continually remind myself of that fact. As I begin to trust my instincts, I have found myself actively seeking female pastors and theologians. I was deeply impacted by the works of people like Rachel Held Evans and Sarah Bessey, and I began exploring other ways to think about God. My hope is that more people who could relate to and find healing in the feminine traits of God are able to do so, with the support of the Church. May we eat the bread fresh from the hearth, run through the forests, and rest in the loving arms of God.

MEET THE AUTHOR

Elise L. Overcash is pursuing her license as a Marriage and Family Therapist. She seeks to live wholeheartedly through reading copious novels, expressing joy through laughter, experiencing her body in nature, sitting with people and their stories in therapy, and learning to appreciate both the sun and the rain. She lives in Seattle, Washington, with her husband.

EVERY WORD IS A PRAYER

Jen Fulmer

I am totally capable of carrying heavy things   But I seek
lightness
> *faith as a spiritual practice brings us back to our innocence it is*
> *A stripping away. An act of living naked.*

Faith looks like revealing something I am scared of sharing
something unformed and squishy and tied to my most unconscious
associations because I know being unsure and vulnerable makes space for
others to be the same.
I'd rather ask questions that inspire conversations than answers that
inspire pedestals
> *Answers make god smaller.*
> *Seeing the wisdom that rests in everyone around me.*
Seeing so many people trying to hard to do faith better, seeing a
> *There is a brokenness you cannot heal from on your own.*
You need other people's brokenness to heal. You need other people's wholeness

I learned my current experience of faith in moments   where I could not anymore
> *the character of God, which I know intimately.*
> *Feeling seen   transformed me from a person who complied*
> *it made me a subject of my own life.*

A space where i am surprised by the strength of my opinions and that i
resonate so much better with   strong intuitive stances
Knowing a yes.
Intuitive
Internal congruency as faith.
so much more wisdom inside how I know God.
can hear it wrong but   this innate wisdom   it's
so much softer so it can handle big changes
and course corrections without batting an eyelash because   i am what
remains, when all the stripping away happens I am still here and I am
is still here. And here is all we ever get to be.

so I walked. And I learned the faith practice
that i have been trying to implement in my life ever since, being
present for the gifts that are here right now. That is my faith,
this time, no one else had any say in this relationship
Faith feels like a sigh of relief and release.
Knowing god and being known is one of the most joyful things in my
life, and yet i forget, and have to learn all over again, over and over
again.   Like a new morning,
that is what faith
One thing at a time.
know. God will heal.

stay thirsty my friends

BODIES

"My body became something external to me, something I hung clothes on as if they were selves, as if they could transform me from the outside in, into the person evangelical Christianity told me I should be."

CHRISTINA

A Womb with a View: Feminine Consciousness Reborn

Kate Sheehan Roach

In the silent stillness there is no knowing. Only being.

Do you remember? Do you recall the essence of your being as you experienced it before you were born? Most of us forget. But a part of us can remember if we clear away the cobwebs in our minds.

When little children ask their parents where babies come from, I doubt many of them expect the dreaded anatomy and physiology lesson. They're more likely remembering the place they inhabited before they took this form and simply want to reminisce with a fellow human being. But after shocking descriptions of Daddy's sperm swimming into Mommy's eggs, they learn never to ask *that* question again. (Mommy has eggs in her? Does she have chickens in there too?) And so, our inner awareness defers to outer knowing and our faith becomes an intellectual pursuit — often controlled by theologies and philosophies handed down by the powers that be — bypassing the soul wisdom that is our birthright.

The musings of female philosophers and theologians, had they been recorded, codified, and studied over the millennia, may have reflected a very different view of God than the tomes produced by (supposedly) celibate males upon which most of the world's religious traditions have been built. But, you may say, women didn't have access to the universities and seminaries where classical philosophy and theology were developed. If I may venture to guess, I'd say female philosophers and theologians had developed their wisdom lineages well before universities and seminaries existed.

The ancient and evolving feminine consciousness has long been at the forefront of our understanding of God. Maybe it's because the birthing of babies, which sparks images of God's birthing of us, has long been held within the feminine jurisdiction. But this is not to say that only those who have borne children or witnessed the birthing of children have experienced this parallel; every person has access to this same wisdom by virtue of our very own birth. Our natal and prenatal memories can serve as a skeleton key that unlocks the divine mystery and reveals the essence of who we really are.

Swimming in the spaciousness of whatever cosmic sea our souls occupy before landing in our chosen body, do we know we're about to be catapulted into a physical dimension? Do we volunteer to go? Or are we drafted, given a bad haircut, and sent marching to the front lines of incarnation? Imagine your original self, engaged in a blissful backstroke through a boundless channel of space on a gentle current of time, completely aware of all that matters, when suddenly you experience form emerging from formlessness. Whereas you were once pure consciousness, you now have being. And your being finds itself contained in a bloody sack.

Initially, the womb might not feel all that different from the cosmic plasma — fluid and dark and warm. But gradually the walls start closing in as we grow in size and begin to feel our mother's incarnation pressing in on ours.

As our *in utero* living quarters get tighter and tighter, we begin to think we're nothing more than the body that's feeling the squeeze. And then, when contractions start crushing our head and the only way out is a tiny tunnel we had never noticed before, things get stressful. Under this literal and figurative pressure, most of us forget about our origins as pure consciousness and begin to identify solely with the body. It's different for everyone, but especially in highly clinical births with a lot of medical intervention, the soul tends to get lost in the shuffle. While some babies settle down quickly after the trauma of birth, others lose all sense of the oneness they came from and spend the first few months of life in an absolute panic. We all experience the birth process with varying degrees of trauma, and we all spend our entire incarnation trying to find our way back to the blissful place from which we came.

In my late twenties, I was told I would never bear children — that is, without the help of modern science. A fertility specialist told my husband and me that even with the $25,000 treatment he suggested we start right away we only had about a two percent chance of conceiving a child. But even as those dreadful words crossed the specialist's smug lips and hovered in a cloud over our heads, unbeknownst to any of us at the time, I was actually already pregnant with our first child — having received no medical treatment whatsoever.

Tremendously grateful to God and fully aware that every life is truly miraculous, Randy and I prepared our home and hearts for the arrival of this long-awaited child. We went to Lamaze classes, read all of the trendy books, and talked things through with our Birkenstock-wearing California doctor who promised to facilitate a natural childbirth. Having previously had a bad reaction to anesthesia, I was determined to deliver this baby without narcotics.

Twenty-four hours may not seem like a long time when you're on vacation, but when you're in labor, it feels like years. Not knowing how long the agony would go on, I just took it one contraction at a time. Thankfully, the nurses let me walk laps around the hospital halls all through the night, which is what my instincts were telling me to do. Feeling very much like every other mammal who must wait and watch while the birthing process progresses, I found myself stomping my heel rhythmically on the hard tile floor each time a contraction wrapped itself around my middle like a boa constrictor. I later learned from a reflexology chart hanging on a waiting room wall that the heel contains pressure points associated with the uterus. (The ancient woman in me must have known that!)

As the pain intensified and the hours rolled on, I hunkered down in the dimly lit labor room as if seeking shelter from the storm brewing on the horizon. My focus turned inward — not only physically, but spiritually as well — as I settled into a place I later came to recognize as my *inner sanctum*. I must have been to this place before, but I experienced my very own spiritual womb in a new way that day. It wasn't just a feeling or an idea. It was an actual place.

So this was my intensive introduction to superconscious meditation. Never one to sit still long enough to calm my soul, and rarely surrounded by enough silence to quiet my mind, the only inner life I had cultivated up to that point was that of the intellect. Herman Melville, Henry David Thoreau, Walt Whitman, Emily Dickinson, Antoine de Saint-Exupéry, Madeleine L'Engle, and Anne Morrow Lindbergh had taken me on many guided tours of their inner lives, but I had not yet fully explored my own.

With Randy by my side throughout the labor ordeal, my consciousness actually left my physical body and entered the mystical realm. Initially more a function of pain management than spiritual transcendence, I inadvertently discovered a new way of seeing. Like one of those deep-sea creatures with no need for eyes, I surrendered the need to know. The third eye (about which I knew nothing at the time) became a portal by which I entered the wormhole of superconsciousness. Just as the cervix opened up an escape hatch for my daughter and the birth canal became her passageway into a new dimension, I took off on a parallel course within myself. Neither I nor she had any idea where we were headed, yet we allowed the miracle of birth to carry us forth like the perigee moon pulls the spring tide.

In the throes of childbirth, I remembered my own birth and revisited the hidden place from which all life emanates. I sympathized with my daughter as the pressurized chamber she inhabited flattened her nose, pressed down on her shoulders, and bound her arms to her sides. She writhed and bucked as my body insisted she leave the premises. But she couldn't get out. She was trapped. That's when the ObGyn discovered another water bag — a separate entity that had pinched itself off from the main amniotic sac and had thus not emptied when my water broke — blocking the already narrow passage. Once Doctor Birkenstock ruptured that membrane with what looked like a crochet hook (while wearing what looked like a welder's helmet — *did she think something might explode?*) Charlotte made her grand entrance. What a relief it was for her to be out of that vice grip! I instantly remembered having felt the same way myself thirty-one years before.

The birth of our son Jonathan was remarkably similar, albeit an early arrival with a few complications. Having moved to a different city while I was just a few weeks into the pregnancy, we were lucky to find a wonderful midwife to aid in the delivery. I knew Beverly Jacks was a special person the first time I met her. Her commitment to natural childbirth was clear, not just because of my concerns about narcotics, but because she understood that birth is a spiritual as well as a physical passage. Beverly not only understood, she shared my desire to be fully present in the process.

I went into labor almost six weeks earlier than expected, so the hospital assigned an MD to monitor the delivery. Thankfully, the ObGyn on duty was much more interested in the basketball games on the doctors' lounge television than she was in my twenty-plus hours of labor, so she mostly stayed away. Beverly remained with me almost the entire time, tag teaming with Randy pressing on my feet through each contraction. (This hospital wouldn't let me walk the halls as my instincts begged me to do.) With Beverly and Randy standing watch over my body, I was able to go even deeper into superconscious meditation than I had during Charlotte's birth. But every few hours, that clueless ObGyn would barge into the labor room, completely unaware that she was disrupting a sacred ritual. "Oh yeah," she'd blurt out. "I forgot this one insists on no drugs." Beverly somehow managed to shoo her away, saving me from the caesarian section the hospital surely would have mandated had they known the umbilical cord was wrapped around the baby. Beverly was confident she could free him from it safely, which she did quite dexterously as he emerged. I will be forever grateful to her for allowing me to hold my baby boy for just a few minutes before the medical team whisked him away as they tend to do with premies.

Following Jonathan's birth, Beverly and Randy and I huddled together in a celebratory embrace as if we had just walked on the surface of the moon (which, of course, we had!) That's when the ObGyn revealed her true ignorance. Was she actually a sensitive soul, jealous of the bond we shared with Beverly, or was this physician just an insensitive jerk? I was inclined to think the latter as she glanced at Beverly and said, "No matter how many times you assist in delivering a baby, you'll never know the wonder of childbirth until you physically experience it yourself." Knowing that Beverly didn't have children, I wanted to jump up and give Dr. Clueless a physical experience of her own right then and there. Thankfully, Beverly handled the situation. I remember exactly what she said: "I may not have had a child come through my body, but I am keenly aware of the miracle I witness each time I help bring a baby into the world."

Awareness really has nothing to do with being female or male, maternal or paternal. It's more a function of consciousness than gender. When we're attuned to feminine consciousness, we can experience direct communion with God in the miracle of birth. And birth is the one thing we all experience at least once.

So why is it that most people don't give their own birth passage a second thought? Entire religions hinge on doctrines related to life after death, but what of life before birth? I'd like to suggest that there might be greater balance in this and other theological and philosophical questions if the people who were fully present and engaged in the birth process had been more present and engaged in the birthing of the world's religions. The fact that men have historically excluded women from conversations on theology, philosophy, and religion — and the inexcusable reality that male voices continue to dominate in many religious traditions — has created (among other idiosyncrasies) an undue obsession with the afterlife. The beforelife is actually much more accessible and relevant to our relationship with God.

From the vantage point of incarnation, both the afterlife and the beforelife are pure mystery. But the feminine inclination toward apophatic experience — as opposed the more masculine leaning toward cataphatic knowledge — allows us to imagine either end of life's mystery without needing to master it, package it, and deliver it to the masses. The same is true with things of God. I love how in the Vedic traditions the Sanskrit phrase "neti" (नेति नेति), which, roughly translated, means "not this, not this", accompanies any attempt to describe God. Indeed, Hinduism with all of its feminine deities could be seen as yet another would-be monotheistic religion that simply recognizes that God can't be reduced to one anthropomorphized (usually male) character. "Neti neti" reminds us that all attempts to define the undefinable are destined to fail. And so, apophatic inquiry brings us closer to God while humbly confessing that God cannot be captured or contained.

There is no knowing when it comes to faith. Distinct from knowledge, our faith informs our knowledge and our knowledge informs our faith. But ultimately, there is only not-knowing — or "unknowing" — in the phrase coined by the anonymous 14th-century Christian mystic who wrote *The Cloud of Unknowing*. This auspicious text exalts *via negativa* as it instructs us to seek God not through the intellect but in the deepest recesses of the heart.

By the time I first encountered *The Cloud* I was a self-professed intellectual in my late twenties. Having developed a successful academic life based largely on hard-earned masculine consciousness, I was baffled by this feminine perspective that had (sadly) become somewhat counterintuitive to me. Perplexed by the idea of "unknowing", I tried to circumvent the process by scrutinizing the text, whose authorship remains an enigma to scholars: "No one has succeeded in putting a name on him, though many attempts have been made. . . . so successful was his desire to remain anonymous."[10] Years later, after falling in love with this mysterious book, I developed an inkling as to why its author is so enigmatic: *maybe he was a she.* Why not? Julian of Norwich — one of my very favorite female mystics — wrote her *Meditations* around the same time *The*

---

10. William Johnston, *The Cloud of Unknowing* (New York: Doubleday, 1973) p 29.

Cloud was written. Could it be we've just stumbled upon another great female Christian theologian hiding in plain sight?

Whether female or male, this unknown author's feminine consciousness was clearly intact, as *The Cloud* speaks directly to the apophatic way. Or perhaps the author of *The Cloud* had reason to remember the essence of being that transcends gender. Again, maleness and femaleness are not necessarily determining factors of which way our consciousness leans, nor have these identity markers ever been etched in stone. But experience does shape our psyche, and the fact that women's lives have historically been controlled by dominant male cultures has forced womankind to develop strong apophatic skills. Perhaps the greatest example I know is the young Palestinian Jew named Mary who "pondered these things in her heart" after some scraggly shepherds told her the word was out that her newborn son was no ordinary baby. Women and men like her have been on the receiving end of miracles for thousands of years by virtue of their willingness to embrace the unknown. Conversely, when Jesus tried to show Nicodemus the way by encouraging him to be "born again", Nicodemus's cataphatic addiction to logic prevented him from receiving the teaching. "How can someone be born when they are old?" Nicodemus asked. "Surely they cannot enter a second time into their mother's womb to be born!"[11] Mary's receptivity to miracle and mystery versus Nic's inability to grasp the meaning of Jesus's illustration speaks volumes.

There are many more examples, both ancient and modern, that we might explore as we consider the roles of feminine and masculine consciousness in religion. But let's take our cue from Mary and ponder them in our hearts and not in our heads like Nicodemus. Heart-centered inquiry is, in my experience, a better approach to theological and philosophical questions. The dearth of feminine influence on the world's religions over the past several millennia has had such far-reaching damaging effects on how God is perceived intellectually, just about everything we think must be rethought. This ongoing lopsidedness has especially crippled Christianity — in terms of the scriptures themselves, the interpretation thereof, and the commentary thereon. But thankfully, all along, feminine consciousness has been gestating in *via negativa*, continually birthing the fullness of God in our hearts in spite of any imbalances we perceive.

---

11. As translated in chapter three of the Gospel of John in the New International Version of the Bible.

It's time we reconsider not just what we think about the mysteries of God, but how we ponder them. According to Jesus, the best place to start is by returning to the womb.

MEET THE AUTHOR

Born into a big Irish-American family in an ethnically and religiously diverse suburban neighborhood, Kate learned from an early age to appreciate, experience, and value multiple spiritual paths. She studied history as an undergraduate at Mount Holyoke College and then as a pre-doctoral fellow at the University of Connecticut. After working in the teaching and publishing fields, she served as founding editor of Contemplative Journal *and, later, a managing editor at Patheos.com and consultant to ContemplativeLife.org. Kate has the honor of working with some of today's great spiritual teachers in the capacity of developmental editor, podcast host and moderator, education director, and (holy) ghostwriter. She is a certified Centering Prayer presenter with Contemplative Outreach and serves on the national leadership team of 12 Step Outreach. Kate lives on the edge of Philadelphia with her husband, children, and animals.*

Running Ragged: Spirituality and the Demands of Caregiving

Andrea Hollingsworth

Wild and Unlikely Places

In the late 1920's, Minnie Tallulah (Grant) Walker, mother of Pulitzer-prize winning novelist Alice Walker, ran away from home to marry a sharecropper named Willie Lee. By the age of twenty-five, she had birthed eight babies. Walker describes her mother as a "large, soft, loving-eyed woman who was rarely impatient in our home."[12] Each day, from dawn to dusk, Minnie made quilts, grew vegetables, plowed fields, and tended to her many children.[13]

Walker says that although her mother's spirit, like the spirits of so many black women, was muzzled and overworked, there was a vibrant creativity, an intense spiritual expressiveness, which burst forth in "wild and unlikely places."

What places, you ask?

[M]y mother adorned with flowers whatever shabby house we were forced to live in. And not just your typical straggly country zinnias, either. She planted ambitious gardens — and still does — with over fifty

---

12. Alice Walker, "In Search of our Mothers' Gardens," in Alice Walker, *In Search of Our Mothers' Gardens: Womanist Prose* (New York: Houghton Mifflin Harcourt Publishing Company, 1983), 231-243, at 238.

13. Ibid.

different varieties of plants that bloom profusely from early March until late November. Before she left home for the fields, she watered her flowers, chopped up the grass, and laid out new beds. When she returned from the fields she might divide clumps of bulbs, dig a cold pit, uproot, and replant roses, or prune branches from her taller bushes or trees — until night came and it was too dark to see.

Whatever she planted grew as if by magic, and her fame as a grower of flowers spread over three counties. Because of her creativity with flowers, even my memories of poverty are seen through a screen of blooms — sunflowers, petunias, roses, dahlias, forsythia, spirea, delphiniums, verbena . . . and on and on and on.

[. . .]

I notice that it is only when my mother is working in her flowers that she is radiant, almost to the point of being invisible — except as Creator: hand and eye. She is involved in work her soul must have.[14]

I begin with the story of Minnie Walker's tenacious insistence on being "involved in work her soul must have" because my goal in this essay is to ask the following question: *What does the spiritual journey look like for women juggling the multiple and ever-proliferating responsibilities that go along with intense caregiving?*

This is a profound and personal question for me. As I will soon explain, caring for dependent family members at both ends of the life-spectrum is the current backdrop of my faith journey. This little essay, then, is written for women like me — women whose search for God takes place amidst a cloud of physical and mental exhaustion. Women who, immersed in the labors of the daily and the practical, refuse to ignore the call of the Holy that beckons them in the midst of the overwhelming stress. Women who, although they feel pressed by societal expectations to "do it all" — to be an attentive mother, loving partner, successful career-person, supportive daughter, resourceful homemaker, and to look good doing it all — nevertheless manage to turn their hearts and faces toward the light of divine grace, and to seek solace and wisdom there.

If such descriptions apply at all to you, then I'm guessing that your way of pursuing spiritual sustenance is a bit different from, for instance, the methods Richard Foster describes in his well-known *Celebration of Discipline*: meditation,

---

14. Ibid., 239, 241.

study, solitude, and the like.[15] Instead, it might look something like the watering, pruning, and replanting practiced by Minnie Tallulah (Grant) Walker.

RUNNING RAGGED

Or, to take a personal turn, it might look like a contemplative diaper change. You might be chuckling, dear reader, but I'm being entirely serious. In her book, *Elevating Childcare*, parenting educator Janet Lansbury describes watching a diaper change that made her cry:

> It was a scene from a film about The Pikler Institute, the highly respected orphanage in Budapest, Hungary, founded by a pediatrician and infant expert Dr. Emmi Pikler. The camera focuses on a 3-week-old new arrival being welcomed with a diaper change. We hear the caregiver speaking slowly and see her gentle touches. The subtitles read: 'Now I will lift your legs. I will move the diaper under you.' She pauses after she explains each action, giving the infant a few moments to respond and anticipate what will happen next. Several minutes later, the delicate task completed, the caregiver says quietly to the tiny, trusting person: 'I think you will like it here.'[16]

Deliberateness. Love. Attention. Aren't these the ingredients of pretty much every spiritual practice you can think of?

I grew up in a Christian tradition in which the Bible nourished my spirit. (It still, for the most part, does.) As a formerly avid runner, I've long found illuminating the Apostle Paul's comparison of the spiritual journey to a race that's run in the face of anxieties and obstacles. Moving ahead with this metaphor, I ask: Doesn't a deliberate, loving, attentive diaper change count as a step in the race toward the goal of the divine call (Phil. 3:14)?

Absolutely it does. I've fully embraced diaper changing as a spiritual practice. I've needed to; I'm in a life moment in which prayer, meditation, and worship are not going to happen unless they happen in the midst of everyday life.

---

15. Richard Foster, *Celebration of Discipline: The Path to Spiritual Growth* (New York: HarperCollins, 1998).
16. Janet Lansbury, *Elevating Childcare: A Guide to Respectful Parenting* (N.p.: JLML Press, 2014).

I'm running all right, but I'm running ragged, and I need new and creative ways to tread the track of faith.

My raggedness comes from my place in what's called the "sandwich generation." I'm the slice of salami between a new baby over here, and a very ill father (and full-time caregiving mother) over there. I'm also attempting to maintain a professional identity with some part-time teaching, writing, and preaching. This is a sea change from the life I was living just a few years ago as a busy tenure-track professor in Boston, with no time even to call my friends and family, and no space to provide care to anything except my writing projects and lecture prep. I chose to leave that life so I could be available for a family that sorely needs my physical and emotional presence and support.

Believe me when I say I'm happier now. This is true from the depths of me.

That said, studies have shown that the stress of being a sandwich generation caregiver causes premature aging, and can take as much as 20 years off a person's life. The stress comes from, as one research summary recently put it, "simply not having enough time in the day to accomplish [the] multitude of responsibilities."[17] (Other recent research reveals that the sky is, indeed, blue.)

Sandwiched caregiving, and the fatigue to which it gives rise, is mainly a dilemma for women. Despite changes in social norms and despite the fact that men are doing more caregiving than ever before, caregivers of all kinds are still more likely to be female. And so today, as ever, women bear the brunt of the depression, loneliness, financial hardship, and career curtailment that comes with caregiving.

I am lucky to have a spouse who is sandwiched right along with me, and who shoulders a ton of childcare and parent-care responsibilities on top of his full-time job. If I'm the salami, he's the cheese, and we're both feeling the smother.

But even with the massive amounts of help my husband provides, it remains the case that when I recently came across Cynthia Bourgeault's beautiful instructions for centering prayer, I was crestfallen at the first line: "It's very, very simple. You sit[.]" Sit? Hmm. Okay. Can there be a pulsing breast pump involved? What about a moving vehicle with groceries in back? My despair was

---

17. https://www.aplaceformom.com/blog/10-05-15-what-is-the-sandwich-generation/ Caregivers also report financial hardship, depression, and changes to jobs and/or careers (usually in the form of scaling back). http://workplace.care.com/5-things-you-need-to-know-about-the-sandwich-generation

complete by the time I reached the conclusion: "You do this practice for twenty minutes, a bit longer if you'd like, then you simply get up and move on with your life."[18] Would that I could sit for twenty minutes, "maybe a bit longer," in prayerful silence! On a good day, I can seize five or ten.

It's more, though, than just being unable to find time to "fuel up" (in conventional ways, at least) for my spiritual race. It's the embarrassment of being asked 'what are you reading or thinking about lately that's life-giving?' and needing to dredge up stale insights from the sole book I was able to read, *last summer*. It's the colossal effort it takes to move from the choppy surface of dishwashing and laundry folding to the cool, clear undercurrents in my mind where thoughts of God, life, truth, death, meaning, beauty, and love flow gracefully. It's the shame that attends the exhaustion-driven choice to cruise Facebook, Quora, and Zillow during my seven free minutes instead of [insert spiritually/intellectually virtuous activity here].

Could it be that women throughout history have been deemed sub-par thinkers and spiritual leaders simply because they're constantly pulled in a hundred directions except center, and because when they are able to find center, they go straight to sleep (as well they should)?

PRESSING ON

So what does pressing on in the spiritual race mean for sandwiched women? For exhausted caregivers more generally? For ragged runners everywhere?

First, as I've mentioned, there's a huge need to think anew about spiritual practices. Here is my advice from the trenches: Take one everyday activity, and do it with deliberateness, love, and attention. Boom. A new spiritual practice has just been born.

Second, if you are a ragged, breathless runner, you must pause for self-care. You must get a break to attend to your spirit. There is no substitute for soul-rest, and if you neglect it long enough you'll look up one day and find you've wandered far from the track. It's often said that self-care is crucial, and it is. But here's the other true thing that rarely gets mentioned: As a stressed-out caregiver (or overwhelmed person in general), my self-care is somebody else's

---

18. Cynthia Bourgeault, *Centering Prayer and Inner Awakening* (Lanham, MD: Cowley Publications, 2004), 6.

other-care in which the other they are caring for is me. Most caregivers, especially sandwiched ones, have a very difficult time figuring out how to recognize and meet their own needs without dropping the ball on one or more major caregiving responsibilities. And these are balls that cannot be dropped. You can't *not* pick the kids up from school. You can't *not* cook the parents their dinner.

If the caregiver is going to get respite, then one of two things has to happen, preferably both: (1) the caregiver seeks out helpful souls; (2) helpful souls notice the caregiver's predicament and go out of their way to provide assistance. To return to the biblical metaphor of the race of faith, other runners must gather round the limping, parched, stymied runner. As they tape her sprains, quench her thirst, and remove her obstacles, she'll soon remember how to walk, then run, the race set before her.

I close with a personal story that illustrates exquisitely both the point about spiritual practices and the point about self-care. About six weeks after my son was born, I found myself needing, yet again, to nurse him in the gathering room just off the sanctuary during Sunday service. (I've no qualms about nursing in public, but the sanctuary seats at our church are unbearably uncomfortable for this particular activity.) That particular Sunday, the sleep-deprived loneliness was intense. I was desperately hungry for community. Yet even having made it to the same building where so many of my friends were also present in the flesh, here I was again, alone with my baby.

Our church does communion once a month, and it was a communion Sunday. If I close my eyes, I can still feel the heartache of hearing the musicians begin to softly sing and play as people lined up to receive the elements. My baby still had a long way to go with his meal, and I needed to stay put.

After several minutes, I heard gentle footsteps. When I turned, I saw a young couple walking toward me and my baby with the bread and wine. They had noticed me slip away during the sermon with my crying son, and had come to find me. There I was — weepy, lonely, and quite exposed. They approached me without hesitation and served me the elements. As I received the bread along with the words, "Christ's body, broken for you," and then the cup along with the words, "Christ's blood, shed for you," I fixed my tear-filled gaze on my son. My son born just weeks prior in a wash of my own blood. My son was now eating and drinking from my own body. And this even as I ate and drank of Christ's body, even as I was being served by members of the church body, even as the worshippers sang a song called "Drink You Deep" softly in the background. In that moment, Christ was made real in a way I've not experienced before or since.

Such embodied love, given and received, is the entire point and end-goal of the race.

I close with a prayer for exhausted caregivers:

God, we're running toward you, and we're running in you,
for you are both the goal and the way.
But some of us are out of breath. Some of us have lost the path.
Others are chapped and parched. Still others are facing major roadblocks.
A few are about to give up.
For weary runners, I ask that you make us attentive to your presence
in the wild and unlikely places of our journey.
And I ask that you come and give us what we need
so that we can take the next step toward the life to which we're called.
Amen.

MEET THE AUTHOR

Andrea Hollingsworth, Ph.D. is Theologian in Residence at First Covenant Church of Minneapolis and teaches at United Theological Seminary of the Twin Cities. She has held numerous full-time teaching and/or research posts, including at Boston University School of Theology (Boston, MA) and the Center for Theological Inquiry (Princeton, NJ). As a scholar, Andrea's focus and passion is spirituality; she loves teaching and writing about the work of the divine Spirit, dynamics of human spiritual development, spirituality, and science, and the historical writings of various mystics. She has an existential bent, and keeps coming back to the question of how struggle, suffering, and unanswered questions factor into spiritual transformation. Andrea's husband, Ryan, and son, Bennett (born May 2017), are the great joys of her life, and her favorite place to be is sitting on the rocky shores of Lake Superior, contemplating God's mystery and infinity.

ON BECOMING A MOTHER

Hannah Stevenson Doornbos

My daughter was baptised in the Church of England nearly two years ago when she was four months old. While I was brought up in a faith culture that doesn't recognise infant baptism, my partner was. It was therefore important to him that our children were christened, and so we had them both baptised in the first few months of their lives.

With our son, I was most excited that he'd be able to wear the family christening gown, made by my late mother-in-law from the train of her wedding dress, and last worn by his dad in 1976. The service itself was beautiful, and I was glad we had done it because of the opportunity it gave our families to celebrate together. But when it came to my daughter's baptism a couple of years later, I found myself caring far more about the symbolism of what we were doing than I had done with my son.

The idea behind infant baptism is beautiful — at least, my understanding of it. That we are all created unique and are deeply loved by God, our Creator, is a beautiful reason to celebrate and to declare value and worth over a new life. But watching my daughter in the family gown be christened in the church, I could only feel a rising anger. How can this symbolic act of God's love and holy creation be truly meaningful if it is performed by a church that does not recognise my daughter as equal? While attitudes are beginning to shift in the Church of England, equality between men and women continues to be a battle. If my daughter could grow up to be the Archbishop of Canterbury, the words of blessing and love over her would be equal in meaning as they were over my son. That she is not recognised as worthy of the highest leadership within the church because she is female, to me makes a mockery of a church practice that is designed to celebrate God's unique creation in all children.

I carry heavy baggage as a woman experiencing faith. I imagine that most women with a consciousness of privilege and discrimination have a good hold on the same baggage as I do if they too have grown up in a church setting. I long to meet women who can say that they don't. I fear that these women are still a generation away, and I hope that it is only one generation.

I did not grow up in the Anglican Church, but in a charismatic evangelical church with roots in the House Church Movement and influenced by Brethrenism. The church believed in the inerrancy of scripture, and as such, I was taught that women were created to be helpers of men; that submission and obedience were key qualities for women to embody; and that women were ultimately inferior to men by God's holy design. Women were taught to cover their heads to honour God. Women were not allowed to lead or preach, although they could (and should) organise the food and cleaning rotas, contribute to the music, and teach the children.

Finding a husband and having children was painted as the ideal path in life. Many of the single women in the church were missionaries (it is a whole new area of horror to consider the theology that allows women to lead people of other ethnicities but not their own). My sister, brother, and I, between the ages of about 4-8, would 'play' church. There are family photos of the three of us doing so. In them, we are all holding either red or blue 'hymn' books, and my sister and I are both wearing headscarves tied tightly under our chins, while my little brother looks on confused. If I try to inhabit the mental space of my childhood experience without cynicism, it was a church environment in which I felt very loved, made lifelong friends, and had a strong sense of Jesus as my friend. But through the gaze of my adult self, I can see the damage of that belief system through two things I carry from my childhood experience of faith: a deeply rooted fear of a God understood as a discriminatory, angry, and wrathful father figure; and a subconscious belief in my inferiority as a woman. I feel both will take a lifetime to get over.

When I was a toddler, my mum planned to organise a coffee morning for other stay-at-home mums of young children in the church so that they could share and encourage each other during the week, when they would otherwise be at home with their children. One of the male elders of our church visited my mum in our home to tell her that this would not be possible unless a man was present when the women met. He said that when women meet on their own without the oversight of a man, they can too easily lead each other astray. This was one of many examples I can share of ways in which value, power, and control were exercised over females in the church.

Despite this, I developed a strong sense of independence and a deep determination that my life would be more than the pattern that was expected of me. I politely declined prayer that I would find a husband, and I felt a genuine disinterest in children and the idea of having them myself. I also came to the point in my twenties where I could no longer reconcile the values of justice that I had begun to hold so strongly with the discriminatory father figure of the Christian God that I had been taught. In addition to this, I started to work in research for human rights policy in countries affected by conflict and extreme poverty. My career took me to some of the world's most fragile and violent countries, and I was devastated by the enormous gap between the promises in the Bible that I had grown up believing, and the reality of life lived by millions of children in our world every day. This tension between what I had been taught and what I was increasingly believing is a turmoil I continue to live.

Ironically, motherhood has been the turning point in my life back towards faith. I was lucky to find a life partner who had had a similar faith experience and recognised mine. We were equally uncertain about growing our family with children and had decided to wait a while to see if we would feel more strongly either way. It was in this waiting time that I became unexpectedly pregnant with our son. It's important to say that his arrival has blown my world open with only beauty and happiness, but on discovering he was on the way, I was devastated. I felt that discrimination/patriarchy/the church/'they' had won; that I could only ever be what was expected of me as a woman, however much I might try to be more. Luckily, I have since learned otherwise, and my journey to becoming a parent was the grounds for this lesson.

I experienced the birth of my son as a deeply spiritual experience after years of feeling as though God couldn't care less about me, and feeling that I too could no longer pretend to be interested in 'him'. During the birth, I felt a presence of power around me and in me that I had never felt before. It was different from the ecstasy of worship music or the sense of God's presence that I thought I had felt before. For the first time in my life, I felt that my body and my self had power and value. I was birthing this child; God could not take the credit, but I also felt God's presence and joy in the moment. It was a deeply empowering experience after a lifetime of faith messages hammering home 'my' original sin, my inadequacy in life without submission to a male God, and my inability to find my own salvation without the man Jesus' conditional help. My journey to motherhood was not just the first time that I felt of value; I felt that my life and actions as a woman must surely, in the truth of their experience, be an expression of God's love.

The beginning of reimagining God for me started with the birth of my son and continued with the arrival of my daughter two years later. My second pregnancy was fraught with physical and mental health issues, and I spent much of it immobile, hobbling around on crutches and weeping with pain, nausea, and depression. After a truly miserable 41 weeks, my daughter was born in 45 minutes in our bathtub at home. I had an immediate and major hemorrhage, and blacked out after losing two-thirds of my blood onto our bathroom floor. The miracle midwife who arrived just in time told me afterwards that my body tried very hard to leave this Earth. My memory is very hazy, but I recall the presence of a spiritual comfort with me in both my consciousness as I was aware of the danger and in the darkness to which I descended before the paramedics brought me back to daylight. I felt as though I had retreated deep inside myself to a place of strange existence, or non-existence. I had an overwhelming feeling of regaining consciousness that something had been there with me, keeping me safe, and talking with me in the darkness.

Since the arrival of my children, I have been trying to articulate the spirituality of my introduction to motherhood, without much success. Recently, however, I came across a poem by Allison Woodard named *God Our Mother*. It both took my breath away and gave me the words to articulate what I felt. *'To be a Mother is to say, 'This is my body, broken for you,' And, in the next instant, in response to the created's primal hunger, 'This is my body, take and eat.'*[9] In all my experiences of faith through the church, I have felt consistently and negatively *less* by being female. Allison Woodard's words took a phrase which I have uttered hundreds of thousands of times through my life — one which paints a picture of a male God on the cross — and she made it female. In doing so, I felt that she gave the feminine both power and value, challenging our inequality. For the first time,

---

19. Allison Woodard, "God Our Mother", October 2017, http://www.allisonwoodard.com/god-our-mother-poem/

I felt I could connect with the anguish and the meaning of the words. I feel as though my soul cried '*Me too!*' in the experience and because of that, '*me, too*' in being of equal value, and of God.

I still cannot reconcile the God of my childhood with the essence of holiness which I have come to believe exists in everything around us and in all that we are. I am still stumped by the overwhelmingly male imagery and language commonly used in church worship, prayer, and teaching which ultimately excludes anyone who doesn't identify as male. I have seen safe spiritual space created by leaders who use female pronouns to describe God, who are not afraid to embrace the feminine God, and who intentionally seek to redress the gender balance in church leadership. I find it strange that this is not more common, considering that most churchgoers in Britain are women.

Now, my faith finds freedom in embracing the mystery I know I will be understanding in new ways for the rest of my life. I have been confused that my journey into motherhood has been the route to rediscovering a faith that I rejected for so long, but which I find is still deeply rooted. Yet I am still unable to walk through the doors of most churches. The shame and worthlessness I felt as a child in church still holds a power over my life which I refuse to pass on to my children. I find this deeply sad because I know that my children will lose out on the sense of community and commitment to each other that I grew up with. But the majority of that loving community still considers the idea of a feminine God as deeply profane at worst or irrelevant at best. I know that the issue is in personifying God at all; that to conceptualise God as essence, breath, source, life, love, peace, and nature are surely more truthful to the limitless mystery of who or what God really is. But wouldn't it be great if the metaphors we use to try continuously to understand God actually related to the truth of our diverse world?

My partner is a gift to me in so many ways. Both having a son and sharing life with him has taught me so much, the least of which is how much the patriarchy wounds both men and women. It is a fight worth having for the sake of us all. I often say that my partner is more of a feminist than I am, in that I am still becoming conscious of the small and minor ways in which I perpetuate inequality because they are so deeply entrenched in me. He, on the other hand, has never believed it to be true. He, too, is determined to teach our children that all created things are made in the image of our parent God. For now, the practices of faith that feel most like Truth to me are raising our children to recognise and respect our beautiful creation; to challenge shame in themselves and in others, and to recognise instead the unique holiness of God in who we are all made to be; to fight against injustice and inequality; and to have kindness, courage, and gratitude.

MEET THE AUTHOR

Hannah Stevenson Doornbos is a freelance writer and researcher in international development. She is a mother of two preschoolers and partner to a red-haired Canadian who works in humanitarian aid. Her published writing includes advocacy reports on children's rights in conflict, harmful traditional practices that particularly target girls, and the current refugee crisis in Europe. She is passionate about celebrating all things great and small, is addicted to podcasts, and plays basketball with her local women's team. Hannah lives with her family in the Thames Valley in the UK.

FLOWER PETALS AND FEMALE BODIES

Sarah Lane Ritchie

Flower petals. Who would have imagined that flower petals could become such a symbol of shame? Perhaps you know the youth ministry gimmick I allude to here: A Good Girl stands at the front of the church, holding a single flower (daisies or roses work best, I've noticed). Holding her single, beautiful stem, she is approached by a teenage boy — a boy we implicitly know to be Bad News. Good Girl is seduced by Bad News, who subsequently rips a single petal from her flower and walks away, leaving her quaking, alone, and reduced to an imperfect flower. Boy after boy follows suit until Good Girl is left ashamed and alone, with nothing but a worthless, petal-less flower stem.

The message is clear: Your worth, your lovability, and your goodness are dependent on absolute purity. God has a beautiful plan for your life and has chosen the perfect, godly husband for you (before you were even born, no less!), but this idyllic future is dependent on you avoiding all sexual activity (including kissing, of course), praying away desire and lustful thoughts, and hiding your body under layers of clothing in order to prevent your brothers in Christ from falling into sin. But, don't worry! Even though you must spend your first twenty years being ashamed of your body and afraid of the dangers of sex, these emotions will magically disappear on your wedding night, when all these entrenched cognitive frameworks vanish — and you experience the joyful bliss of giving your unadulterated body to a man who will protect, lead, and order your life from here on out. He will have headship over you, as Christ himself is the head of the church — your body will be his (you were designed for this!), and he will make you whole.

If this sounds like a cynical view of girls growing up within a conservative evangelical faith community, that's because it is. It's also an accurate description of the lived realities that so many girls and women experience in the Church, many of which are never discussed or examined in the bright light of day. It is a tragic truth that for many women, shame and sexuality are not only related, but inseparable. It is even more tragic that the resulting self-hatred and shame are not only engendered by toxic doctrinal commitments and abusive dynamics within faith communities, but so often result in a silent implosion of self-destruction: self-harm, unsafe, or abusive relationships, eating disorders, and addictions. The result? Women who are either consumed with silent shame but continue to don the obligatory smile and serve the church in love and humility, and women who shun the faith altogether, seeking health and wholeness in other communities that acknowledge and respect their experiences. My life has wavered somewhere between the two.

I am an academic. Working in the area of science-and-theology, my days are structured by teaching, research, admin, and writing papers. My mind is my career; my work is entirely dependent on my ability to be analytical and critically to engage questions lying at the interface of theology and neuroscience. In other words, I have chosen one of the most disembodied, cognitive career paths possible. On one level, this has worked out well for me: I love what I do, and have found deep meaning and purpose in the vocation of theological education and research. On another level, I am aware that my career path has been driven by a pressing need to answer questions that are deeply personal and vulnerable. Questions like: Is there a God? Am I lovable? How can I make myself believe in God, when God's love is not something I feel? If I am perfect, if I achieve all the things, then will I be "ok"? Of course, these are disparate questions that require different sorts of answers; but when I scratch the surface of my career path, what I recognize is a deep need to drive away shame, to escape the complexities of my embodied history by throwing myself headlong into a life of critical thinking and cognitive engagement. What I recognize is that seemingly intellectual questions and crises of faith are often driven by something far more raw and vulnerable.

It is perhaps not a coincidence that my struggle to believe in God began at a crucial time in my cognitive and physical development — those early-teen years when girls are particularly vulnerable to implicit and explicit messages about their worth, their bodies, and their identities. The faith community I grew up in was one of extremely conservative evangelicalism. In some ways, the community was absolutely wonderful — kind, loving people who truly cared about one another and had a real grasp of divine love. However, there was a dark side. Women in my church were extremely limited in what they were allowed or encouraged to be and do. Women could not teach, preach, or do much of anything other than run the nursery and facilitate potlucks. As a budding intellectual, I struggled to come to grips with my deep questions about faith, in a context where any doubt or challenge to the faith was viewed as extremely threatening and sinful. I wanted to be perfect; I had learned that if I was good and perfect and achieved all the right things, people would affirm me and show me love. This approval was intoxicating. My doubts and questions about faith thus seemed threatening to me, a secret that I must keep if I were to retain the love of my community.

At the same time as this intellectual struggle with faith was beginning, I began to experience another powerful, all-consuming emotion: shame. Having a body, being a body — by my mid-teens, the fact of my embodiment had become a deep source of pain for me. Early experiences with men involving compromising power dynamics; the deeply entrenched narrative that my future lovability lay in my purity; the strong impression that God was, above all, a male authority figure; an ingrained sense of disgust toward sexuality in general; a sense of shame that I was a threat to men: these led to a complicated cognitive and emotional knot that made it nearly impossible to address questions of faith in isolation. Humans are holistic, embodied creatures — it is impossible to separate spiritual questions from issues of the body and mind. What I took to be a merely cognitive lack of faith was driven by deeply problematic messages about my embodied self — my femaleness.

The effects of such messages are manifold. For me, body shame led to a long and excruciating struggle with eating disorders. For others, the outlet is unsafe sexual behaviour, overachieving in the workplace or church, or self-harm. In the classic words of the Goo Goo Dolls, there are times when "you'd bleed just to know you're alive." Indeed.

BUT. But. I would be remiss and inauthentic if I painted a caricatured picture of faith communities or my own experience in them. Every faith community has its flaws and blind spots, and I am so thankful to have come from a particularly close-knit group of people who taught me how to love. I am also deeply thankful for the life of the mind for which I have the opportunity to pursue. The winding, sometimes-unhealthy paths we take do not invalidate the meaningful and redemptive lives which we build. In fact, I wouldn't change the fact that the sorts of academic questions I pursue and the sorts of classes I teach are driven by existential questions, and embodied experience. It is this union of the academy and personhood, cognitive ability and the willingness to feel, that lie at the heart of my vocation. See, it's not just about me. The most meaningful and teachable moments I have in my career come from the times when I can enable a student or colleague to feel known, accepted, and valued. It is when the person — the whole, embodied person — is affirmed that true insights are experienced. But it is difficult to lead others on this path of holistic theological exploration if we ourselves are unwilling or unable to examine, embrace, and redeem our own complicated pasts.

Lest we stray too far into abstraction, I would like to close with some specific suggestions and warnings, both for faith communities, and for women grappling with embodiment and faith:

1) Be wary of the toxic implications of some theological stances, such as, "you are nothing without Christ," "you were born an evil sinner deserving eternal punishment," and "nothing about you is good unless you believe." While important theological debates underlie each of these overstated positions, it is vital to consider how destructive such messages can be to girls and young women — many of whom are already struggling with a sense of worth. Emphasizing their depravity or linking their value to belief in God is deeply problematic.

2) Change the conversation around sexuality and purity culture. Be aware of the historical and theological contexts around traditional stances on sexuality, and avoid treating sex as a taboo topic within faith communities. Linking sex to shame or being "dirty" will only be destructive. It is not enough to tell girls to save themselves for marriage; not only does such language undermine their personhood, but it is unrealistic to suggest that the cognitive pathways of shame and fear around sex will magically disappear on a young woman's wedding night.

3) For women who are struggling to heal from unhealthy sexual dynamics and entrenched feelings of shame, I encourage you to explore embodied

spiritual practices. It can be extremely difficult to change our thoughts around sexuality, shame, and our bodies — engaging in embodied practice is a gentle, non-threatening way to open yourself to God's presence and healing. For example, begin a meditation practice. Breathe — sit and breathe.

4) Spend a day alone in the forest, practicing mindfulness of your surroundings and the sensory environment in which you are immersed. Explore spiritual practices — such as the Lectio Divina — and liturgies that invite contemplation and receptivity to God's presence, rather than overly cerebral engagement with the faith.

Dare to speak about your experiences. You are not alone.

MEET THE AUTHOR

Sarah Lane Ritchie is Research Fellow in Theology & Science at the University of St Andrews. She holds a PhD in Science & Religion from the University of Edinburgh, an MSc in Science & Religion, a M.Div. from Princeton Theological Seminary, and a BA in Philosophy & Religion from Spring Arbor University. Her research interests involve all things science-and-religion, but her work focuses primarily on topics at the intersection of theology and neuroscience. A Michigander by birth, Sarah has found her true home in Scotland, where she loves running, forests, and doing anything vaguely life threatening.

SHINING LIGHT ON VEILED LESSONS

Christy Gunter Sim

Trigger Warning: Sexual Harassment, Domestic Violence

Some days, more than anything else, my faith feels like a war.
A battle with myself and all I was taught over the years.
A daily fight to pull back all the layers of my own internalized misogyny
and step into my value, dignity, and beauty.
A combat with those who assume I am stupid or undecided
because of my gender.

Every day we see obvious inappropriate communication and blatant messaging about women. This is clearly repulsive and we label it as such, with passionate outcries. This happens in our cultural and religious landscapes. Often people declare women's contributions to the faith "less than." Many times, we see arguments that women are mere objects and claims that the feminine body is to be used for men's pleasure. These are the *macroaggressions*.

But there are also the hidden, behind the scenes, inferences to a women's perceived weakness and lack of value. This is the kind of communication that slowly eats away at our sense of agency, choice, and power to influence the environment around us. This is the scariest messaging of all. These are the masked implications and suggestions that sneak up on us and often remain just outside of our awareness while it subtly changes our beliefs. These are the *microaggressions*, doing incredible damage to women's views of who we can be and what we can do in the world.

Deep inside myself, I am kinesthetically aware and know I am powerful. My body has given life. My breasts have sustained life. I am woman. To give and sustain life is very powerful. My very body exhibits and emits this power.

However, I also spent my entire life trying to push away the *microaggressions* that quietly stack the evidence against my perception of power. I spent my entire career trying to act like I have that power anyway: To speak. To guide. To lead. All while silencing the stealth messaging that I should just sit down and shut up like a good girl.

Here are some snapshots of various moments in my life to shine light on that which is often hidden or just outside of awareness. Perhaps by telling my story, others will become aware of their own internalized misogyny as well.

I am 15 and shopping with my mom. I found an amazing dress and when I put it on, I feel beautiful. I spin and admire myself in the mirror, loving it on me, when an older man looks me up and down and tells me I am hot.

I don't get the dress. I can't feel beautiful. Because of the men.

I learn:

- I have to cover myself and tone down my looks in order to protect my body.

- Keeping men's eyes off me is more important than feeling strong and beautiful.

- I must hide who I am. It's not safe.

I am a young person attending church. Every pastor in my church is male. I'm sure every pastor on the district is too. Every book we study is written by a man. Every great leader who visits is also male. And every woman I see speak has her husband alongside of her.

I learn:

- Men make the great contributions in the faith.

- Women don't offer anything worthwhile without male guidance and support.

- Men make excellent leaders, writers, and teachers. I will never be a man.

I am 17 and on a trip, having fun, when a boy decides to touch me. He runs his hands up and down my legs. I'm not even dating him and I don't even like him or want to be with him.
He didn't ask. He just took.
I try to move him off. He comes back. All over me. His hands.
I feel gross. I wait for it to be over. I wait for it to stop. It seems like forever.
I learn:

- My body is a plaything and what I want is irrelevant.

- The most important thing about my body is to give men pleasure.

- I am an object for men's use.

I am a student in seminary and the school is passionate to declare women's voices matter and that women can do anything a man can do. I revel in it.
But the practical everyday implications are saying the exact opposite. The syllabus is full of male voices, they dominate the conversation. Most of the professors are male, they hold the positions of power. Nearly every book I read is written by a male.
I learn:

- We still aren't allowing women's voices to take center stage.

- My voice probably can't take center stage either.

- Maybe I should just shut up.

I am a pastor and on a team planning a camp. It is a lot of fun. I am creative and I get to use my gifts to the fullest. I laugh a lot and enjoy being on this team with other pastors.

Two of us come to the meetings from the same town. We should ride together and save the church gas money. We do this several times and we sharpen each other's passion and ability to minister with our heartfelt conversations on the trip.

But I can't now. Not anymore. I'm a girl and he's not. Something could happen and he has to protect himself from me. Because, as a beautiful woman, I would obviously reciprocate anything he might do.

I learn:

- My body and anatomy is a problem that is solved by getting shut out and ignored.

- I can't be alone with males because I'm too tempting.

- My ability to say "no" and reject him doesn't get factored into this decision at all.

I am in my first pastorate and it is election time on the district. I am excited to be an ordained elder and take part in the voting process.

But the District Superintendent has other ideas. I have to watch the kids while the others are voting. Someone has to do it, he says. And traditionally it has always been the responsibility of whomever is in my role.

I learn:

- My gender throws me in with the kids while the big boys make the decisions.

- I'm not good enough to get full voting rights like an ordained man.

- The church might ordain women but when it comes down to it, we aren't good for much more than childcare.

I'm searching for another position as a pastor. The District Superintendent recommends me to a church of about 50. He tells them I would be a great fit and that I'm smart and gifted.

But the church board says no. They just can't imagine a woman leading them. The District Superintendent fully supports their decision and I am left to deal with it. That's how life is.

I learn:

- My gender creates a barrier to my talent.

- My gender is not something to affirm or value; it's more of a problem. I am simply not worthy because of my anatomy.

- Women can't lead everywhere a man can.

I am in a serious, committed relationship and trying so hard to be happy. We fell in love and I adored him.

But he tells me I'm disgusting. He accuses me of things . . . like being a lesbian or having an affair. He threatens to have his own affairs with women offering themselves to him. He lays on massive amounts of shame. I feel afraid often.

He makes me have sex with him. He deserves it, he says. I hate it. I'm usually just waiting for it to be over.

He keeps me up at night. Usually to yell at me about how pathetic I am. I'm tired all the time.

He won't let me leave a room when he yells at me. I sit there. Trapped.

I try to be better, make him good meals, and do what I can to help him be happy. But it's never enough. I can't ever be enough.

Do I leave him? Do I get out of this situation?

No. Why would I?

Didn't you just see the long list of things I learned throughout my life both in obvious messaging and the hidden implications?! Didn't you see what society and the church have taught me?!

- I have to hide who I am and cover myself up.

- I'm not enough and don't get to make decisions.

- My body is a problem.

- I'm not worth fighting for.

- I'm not valuable or worthy.

- I'm a problem.

- Women's voices don't take center stage.

I finally get out of this toxic relationship anyway, even with all the messages that tell me I deserve otherwise, and I battle with myself to deconstruct all the things I learned. It takes so much time and effort to believe I am valuable. It is hard work and wears me down.

And unfortunately, as I fight, I only get more messages.

I am in my doctorate program. I am working hard and writing millions of words and reading dozens of books. I am becoming an expert in violence and developing a theology of healing.

A male pastor is inappropriate with a survivor of violence who I'm helping (and with her blessing) I stand up to him. I tell him she deserves better and he cannot treat her like this.

He invites me to his house and refuses to meet with me in a coffee shop . . . where I feel safe from the way he just treated another woman. Only his house, he says.

I have it, there in black and white on my email screen. His words, his solicitation to have me at his house.

I send it to the District Superintendent. I talk about how inappropriate his behavior is. I tell them what he did to me and another girl.

No action is done. There is no legitimate response to my cries.

I see the obvious message from the male pastor and call it out. Everyone around me seems also to think the pastor's behavior is terrible. That's the obvious part. But then there's the more concealed messaging I get from the District Superintendent's lack of response.

I learn:

- My voice is worthless and unbelievable.

- The powerful male pastor can get away with just about anything.

- I'm a problem and I should just shut up like a good girl.

I am sitting in a congregation, the first time in years. There's too much pain to come here often.

The preacher makes a joke about needing to find good men for his daughters.

They all laugh, the entire congregation.

I don't.

I learn:

- Women should be married in order to be valuable, and really, a woman without a man is worthless. We have to find those men for our kids.

- If I'm without a man, I can't do anything.

- Everyone around me thinks this, I'm alone.

I am finished with my doctorate. I am known and respected as an advocate and expert in my field. I worked hard to get here. I sacrificed and suffered. I earned my place.

Then a powerful white man with money tries to force his opinion on the organization where I work. It is wrong. Really wrong. It will harm survivors of violence. There is no doubt in any bone of my body that his view will cause extensive damage for an already traumatized group of people.

I speak up. I can't live with myself if I don't.

It's not good. Not good at all.

But, really, I should have known. I've learned this lesson dozens of times over already. He has the power and the money.

Five days later, I don't have a job or a way to provide for my family.

I learn:

- No matter how hard I work or what I do, I will never be a white, powerful, rich man who gets to make decisions.

- If I ever want to get paid for what I can do in the church setting, I need men to support me. When they don't, I'm left hungry and alone.

- So, I better sit down, shut up, and be a good girl.

I'm in a skirt, nearly 40, with my legs crossed. I'm still beautiful and I look nice.
An older man calls for my attention, I look at him.
He tells me I need to respect myself and be more modest.

I want to cry. It never ends.

So much misogyny. So much pain. So many messages that teach me that my voice does not matter. That my female body is a problem.

I spend my days fighting a war that never ends, a war that takes place on the battlefield of the bodies of women.

The layers are so deep, sometimes I cannot even recognize the misogyny when it happens. I can't see the damaging marks on my own body. I've internalized the messages and I know it.

But I fight. I fight. I fight. I fight.

Because somehow, I still have faith. Somehow, I know deep in my bones that. . . .

- **My body is beautiful just the way it is.**

- **My body is mine.**

- **I am powerful, authentic, and courageous.**

- I can make my own choices and be my own person.

- Because I am a woman, I am a dynamic and compassionate leader.

- My gender, any gender, makes me great.

- My desires, thoughts, words, and actions matter.

- What I want is just as important as what men want.

- Women's body, my body, is literally filled with power. I hold creation potential and can sustain life for months, sometimes years.

- I reflect the divine, in all my feminine intensity and anatomy.

- I am a beautiful embodiment of the divine on earth, loving and caring for others.

I am fighting a war to keep the faith. It is hard and difficult. I want to quit sometimes. Often more days than not.

But I will refuse to give up forever. This is a war worth fighting.

Because I've got a little girl now. And I'll be damned if she ever writes a chapter like this.

Meet the Author

Dr. Christy Gunter Sim offers expert advising, training, and consulting for domestic violence, sexual assault, family violence, secondary trauma prevention, and trauma healing. Her new book "Survivor Care: What Religious Professionals Need to Know about Trauma" will be released spring 2019 by GBHEM's Wesley Foundry Books. Sim graduated August of 2014 with a doctorate in Global Health and Wholeness with her main area of emphasis and research in healing after domestic violence from St. Paul's School of Theology. Sim has over 500 hours of additional training (beyond her formal education) in domestic violence, sexual assault, strangulation, legal and forensic implications of violence, the neurobiology of trauma, trauma-informed care, developing a community's response to violence, and more. Sim currently works with AIMS Training and Consulting, with Police Chief Anthony Williams, through Cedar Valley College, as the Family Violence Subject Matter

Expert. Sim frequently speaks, trains, and consults with nonprofits on trauma and healing. Sim has taught several courses for Friends University (Wichita, KS), including Imagining Healing for Violence & Poverty, an Introduction to Ethics Class, and Philosophy.

You can follow her other work and support her at www.patreon.com/DrChristySim and see more of her work at www.DrChristySim.com.

HOL(E)Y JEANS AND FRAYED KNEES

Christina Smerick

Iknelt at the altar, and I sweat.

My jeans cut into my knees where the holes had frayed, a result of my attempting to bleach them 'cool,' which just resulted in white blotches and unraveled fabric. I knelt there and waited for something to happen, while a part of me — and there is always this part of me — argued, and analyzed, and rolled its eyes. While an even deeper, quieter part of me said, "You're praying for what you already have."

I knelt, and I waited, and I wept (probably). This was the third, or tenth, or twentieth time, after all. My new church cajoled and pleaded with us teen-agers to accept Jesus into our hearts, and I sure as heck was not going to be the only one without Jesus in my heart. Never mind my Catholic upbringing, my passionate engagement with the Catechism (I was weird even then), never mind my deep childhood conviction that when I prayed to God — calling him Jehovah — He would always answer my prayers. That didn't count (according to my new church). That was Catholic. This did. This was Real Jesus.

This new church *loved* me. My youth pastor would say every time he saw me, "Has someone told you they loved you today? I do." And he meant it. These beautiful people took in the jeans, and the hair (which changed color regularly, and was currently ink black and rather . . . spiky), the attitude, the earrings . . . and I really think they did love me. And they didn't judge. Those folks are a rare breed, and are dear to me, even if I never speak to them again on this mortal coil.

But this new church also produced in me an anxiety I had never felt before. Before, I knew *GOD* loved me. Before, I *knew* we were buds. Now, I wasn't so sure.

So back to the altar I went. But it never took. I couldn't tell what I was supposed to be feeling, but it was probably supposed to be more moving than confusion and a sense of failure.

So I tried harder. And then the pressure started — the pressure to look the part.

It was subtle — gentle asides from church ladies about my jeans or my hair; comments about how pretty I was in spite of my appearance. Always done in love, never meant to harm. So slowly, like water wearing away stone, I grew my hair out of its short, black punk style. I got a (I am so ashamed) PERM (it was the 80's — be nice). I stopped wearing my shark-tooth earring and my holey leggings and started to 'cover up' in shapeless t-shirts and baggy jeans. My boyfriend's coat. I thought I was just 'growing up' by putting away my childish things. But something I never thought could erode, did — my sense of self.

I am quite possibly the most stubborn person I know, and that's saying something considering I know my daughters. I had deep insecurities about some things (like whether I *was* indeed pretty, or pretty enough), but I also had a strong sense of 'self' — I knew who I was. At this point in my life, I was angry, but I had a rootedness in my own being. In the midst of making stupid mistakes and being a teenager, I still had a strong self-presence.

It was this that began to erode. Jesus was not coming into my heart. Perhaps my self was too strong for Him. Perhaps if I changed my appearance, stopped trying to be a nonconformist, He would find it easier to penetrate this heart of stubborn stone. I learned that people think you're born again if you look the part. If you volunteer to sing in church, and go to all the youth group events (because the boyfriend was there, but hey!), and keep going to that altar; if you dress modestly, have the right hair, the right clothes; if you look the part, maybe you can fool Jesus. Maybe you can fool yourself.

My conforming infected my choice of college as well. Whereas prior to attending this church, I had planned on going to a local college or university and major in music and English, now I wanted to mirror my youth pastor's life. His wife was a Christian counselor, and so I quickly decided that I, too, would become a Christian counselor, and then marry a youth pastor. To do this, of course, meant to attend the church-owned college that everyone from my church went to. I will say again, one could do a lot worse than imitate the people I was imitating — they were and are kind, loving people, and I owe them a great deal. It wasn't their fault that I glommed onto them as my ticket out of the Hell I'd been told I was heading for.

So off I went, against my father's wishes (he thought these evangelicals were cultish), to a Christian college, where I found a level of body shaming that topped anything I had experienced before, and infects me to this day.

Let's call this place Mt. Nebo. Mt. Nebo was in the Bible belt, which was the first shock to my east coast self. Mt. Nebo had dress codes for women: no tank tops. No shorts before 4:30 pm. Not even culottes. If a woman wanted to work out, she had to wear a skirt over her shorts to walk to the gym. And these skirts needed to reach the knee. My body was now policed in a way I had never experienced, with fines issued if one broke the dress code. A sense of self-consciousness quickly developed in me, with the attendant self-policing. Suddenly, my derriere became a site of scrutiny; my shirts, which were just fine at home, were immodest here. The younger me, the more 'me' me, would have quickly rebelled, amassed a truly glorious number of fines, and would have launched a feminist-punk protest. But this new me, already schooled in the art of appearing as if Jesus was in my heart, feared (rightly) that a lack of conformity would equal, in the eyes of the school, a lack of Jesus.

I spent my first two years of school trying on friend groups like prom dresses, trying to figure out who I was. I dressed like whomever I was hanging with. My body became something external to me, something I hung clothes on as if they were selves, as if they could transform me from the outside in, into the person evangelical Christianity told me I should be. I campaigned for and was elected sophomore-class chaplain, a joke only I got. I went to Bible studies. I attended chapel. I went to church. And Jesus, I felt, still eluded me . . . but if I kept up appearances, that was good enough.

Then I read the philosopher Immanuel Kant, of all things, as a class requirement, and my fragile facade of faith shattered. Kant suggested that God was only a regulative idea in my mind — an organizing principle to make sense of things. God was not necessarily real, but perhaps simply a crutch human beings invented to explain the inexplicable. (Please note that this is *not* what Kant actually wrote. But boy is it what I heard.) Then I read Soren Kierkegaard, and all my fears were confirmed: the leap of faith *was* hard, terrible, scary, *and* all up to me (see above: I was not a careful reader!). The leap of faith was what I had been attempting at the altar — the final decision to truly follow Jesus. But it's a leap without a guarantee, and it's paradoxical: I have to trust God, that God is real, in order to make the leap of faith, which is . . . to trust God and know that He is real. But how could I *know* that I was not just inventing God — would I, or anyone, really risk everything on less than a sure bet? I was sure it was all a mind game. I was sure that faith was simply a mental contortion some people did to feel better.

Crisis hit; I utterly gave up pursuing Jesus. I faked my way through the chaplaincy. I became a philosophy and English major, and I definitely stopped dating youth ministry majors. I cut off my hair and put on some flannel but kept the baggy jeans (it was the grunge era). I quickly gained an (unearned) reputation as a lesbian.

The message, again and again, from this southern evangelical community was that the clothes make the (wo)man, that my identity and even my faith can be demarcated by my clothing. "To seem rather than to be" seemed to be just fine amongst such folks. I watched my preppily-clad classmates treat others with disdain and participate in fraternity hazing and still be treated with love and respect, while my scruffy friends and I were objects of suspicion. I came out the other side of this conformity only by abandoning my search for Jesus. I gave up. I refused to use God as a crutch, and I felt that all my years of trying to make that leap of faith demonstrated my fundamental inability to trust in Him. So I stopped trying to conform to the expectations of evangelical Christians *only when I* stopped trying to pursue God.

What a terrible choice to have to make.

I *am* my body; and I was tired of cloaking it in conventions and external expectations; tired of it being treated as a site of sin and control; and even more tired of it being used as an external sign of my salvation. The clothes came off and my sin of unbelief was exposed.

And for ten years, that was the end of the story. I moved to Chicago, began graduate school, and had sex in monogamous but not marital relationships. I wore what I wanted, still conforming of course to America's standards of hotness (and Chicago's weather). I was ashamed of my provincial education (although academically I was well prepared), ashamed of having to explain what I used to belong to. There may be no lonelier place for a woman than in an academic philosophy graduate program; there may *really* be no lonelier place for an *evangelical* woman. But my body was my own, I thought, as I wore mini-skirts and tights on cold Chicago nights and froze my derriere off for the sake of fashion. My body was my own as I awkwardly tried to make up for what I thought was only *my* sexual inexperience. Give me back my body, I howled at that college. And I thought I was taking it back. But the voices of the body police couldn't be so easily silenced, and most of this activity was in response to them, rather than an act of freedom as I thought it was.

Life continued to happen: I had a child, finished my PhD, went to therapy, and faced a lot of my distorted thinking. And then two small things occurred. One was my therapist mentioning a church in Evanston her best friend attended. The other was a revelation on the road to Damascus (I mean Wisconsin) when out of the blue a light shone and I understood Kierkegaard.

I was so *mad* at him. For years, I was mad at a dead Dane for setting me an impossible task. In my teenage self-obsession, I never saw that he was writing to *himself*. Only when being pregnant and alone had brought me lower than I thought I could go did I finally see that it *wasn't up to me* to make that leap of faith. Or even crawl to that altar. Or garb myself in the royal robes of evangelicalism. No amount of my flailing and conforming would bring me one inch closer to God — because God already had me. I'd been thrashing in a nightmare, fighting my blanket. I'd been running, and running ragged, not hearing the labored breath beside me. The world turned, and I saw the leap as being-carried, not as carrying. As grace, not law. This is not Kierkegaard's fault — he literally says all of this, really clearly. I just wore too many layers to hear him.

Kierkegaard writes, "'Come Here!' Oh, do not stand still and hesitate — consider that each moment you stand still after having heard the invitation you will hear its call more faintly. "Come Here!" However tired and weary you are of the labor, or of the long, long, and yet up until now futile going for help and rescue . . . oh, just one step more and here is rest! "Come Here!" Alas, but if there is someone so wretched that he cannot come, oh, a sigh is enough; that you sigh for him is also to come here."[20] (22)

---

20. Soren Kierkegaard. *Kierkegaard's Writings, XX, Volume 20: Practice in Christianity* trans. and ed. Howard V. Wong and Edna H. Wong (Princeton, NJ: Princeton University Press, 2013) 22.

I am a woman, with a woman's body. The church dresses me. She dresses me up in modesty and middle-class values; she dresses me in business-casual and urges me to cover my shoulders, my knees, my breasts. She reads my faith via what drapes me, what holds me in, and masks me. She tells me how to appear. She is so intimidated by my body — what it represents, what it does, what it produces in itself and in others. She is afraid.

I am a woman, with a woman's body. I undress myself and stand naked before the Lord. Jesus discloses the thoughts of humanity; He discloses me. He dis-clothes me. My body is not a site of erotica or possession — or not only that. My body can be my expression of faith, or joy, or hope, or love. Of righteous anger, of deep sadness. But my body can only be those things freely in Christ. And sweet Mother Church all too often wishes my exuberance, my self-expression, to be muted in proper layers.

If I could go back to that girl in the skintight holey jeans, with the dirty jacket and Converse hi-tops and ink-black hair . . . Well, no. I don't need to go back to her. I brought her with me. Her constant altar visits still happen in the quiet of my own heart; her doubts, her rage, and her fears still percolate within me. She's safe, though, here inside, because the loving gaze of Christ is upon her. Upon me. And she is told, again and again, that she is, yes, beautiful, and she is enough, and never too much. And that her holey jeans are just that — holy. Thanks be to God.

MEET THE AUTHOR

Christina Smerick is the professor of philosophy and chair of the Bastian School of Theology, Philosophy, and Ministry, as well as dean of instruction and accreditation liaison officer for Greenville University. She is also first vice president of the Wesleyan Theological Society and past president of the Wesleyan Philosophical Society. Her latest book, Jean-Luc Nancy and Christian Thought: Deconstructions of the Bodies of Christ, *is available through Lexington Press. In her spare time, she enjoys difficult hikes, knitting, reading way too many fantasy and sci-fi novels, and drinking way too much coffee.*

Eggs and Bodies and The God in Both

A.K. Carroll

I sit on a bright red chair beneath a stretch of slatted sky, protected from the sun by a canopy of fiberglass and a yellow umbrella. Mid-morning on a Tuesday the outdoor cafe space is quiet, even in the center of this Silicon Valley campus where the busiest techies come to whiteboard and code. My laptop is open and I am staring at an image of a man holding hands with a toddler.

I've been a tech employee for exactly six weeks, just long enough for the shock to wear off and the work to set in. Today I'm exploring my benefits page. I already opted in for dental, vision, and preventative care. I set up an HSA and designated my parents as beneficiaries. Then I clicked on a link for "fertility benefits" and came to this photo of a man and a child, both dressed in plaid.

Funny, I think, that there's a man on the front of this PDF pamphlet. I wonder who made that marketing decision. I read about the "bundles" and "cycles" that I'm eligible for, and ponder the prospect of freezing my eggs — those 100-micron seeds of potential that pass each month with only my notice. When I was 25, I had a boyfriend who told me I should capture my fertility and preserve my chances for children before it was too late. I brushed off his comment like a horsefly in summer. Now five years later, I'm reconsidering.

Hormone injections. Fertilization. In vitro. They're procedures I've heard of. Treatments I know. But the step-by-step process of prepping and harvesting parts from a whole seems different when those parts are the substance of life and that whole is the body I live in.

It is a body I have not always been fond of. A body I've hidden and hated, neglected and left. A body I've kept to myself or shared softly in secret. But it is also a body I've fought for and stayed with. A body I've worked in, cared for, and defended against judgement. I believe that this body holds untapped power, but it's taken me a long time to see this as true, and to see my body as something to love and embrace rather than an object to alter or avoid.

Here is a story they told me was true.

In the beginning, God created the heavens and the earth. In the beginning, God made creatures and constellations. In the beginning, the formless found form, and the forms that found it were good.

Until they weren't.

Unfortunately, this story took a turn before my form set foot on the ground.

I was raised in a church that taught the law and the gospel in that particular order. Sin, then redemption, but first start with sin.

Sinful from birth, that's what they told me. Sinful from the day that my mother conceived me. Forget the part of the story where God saw the humans and said they were good. Forget the image of divinity that dwelled in creation or the breath of life that sustained bare-skinned bodies. None of that mattered once Eve ate the apple and shared her discovery with the boy next door and, thereby, broke the bond between God and man.

We debate what the first sin really was. The first act of defiance, if that's how you define it. Some say that it started in the head of the woman; others, the heart. But most take it back to the body.

If it was only a thought, a curious notion; if Eve had dropped the fruit and gone back to naming the lemurs and toads, would she still have been cast into exile?

This is the first story I was taught about humans, and it led me to question what sin really is. Does one need to repent for an action not taken? Or is it only through the body that intention results in conviction?

To be "in but not of" was my youth group mantra. It was based on a verse out of Romans: "Do not conform to the pattern of this world, but be transformed by the renewing of your mind." Plucked out of context and pasted on posters, this small scrap of scripture reinforced an imagined division between holy and unholy, mind and body.

Renewing the mind meant rejecting the body and its immoral inclinations, repenting for the sins that put Christ on the cross, and nailing them there like scraps of white paper. It meant transcending the body for the substance of the soul and avoiding the world as you packed your head full of doctrine and creeds.

From the forensics team to the student council, every school club that I joined or team I was on started practice with prayer and sported t-shirts embellished with verses of scripture. As a sophomore in high school, I was a member of the Blue Angels dance team, who woke up at six to spin and jump and move their bodies to music. Early one morning, the varsity basketball coach passed through the gym during a practice and saw us thrusting our hips to the electric scream of AC/DC's *Thunderstruck*. She took it up with the activities director, who sighed in agreement and told us we wouldn't be allowed to perform the routine. It wasn't appropriate for a group of Christian girls. I'm not sure which was worse, the music or the movement, but we'd somehow crossed the line from performance to impropriety. I still think of this whenever I hear AC/DC. I'm sure it would have been one of our best numbers.

The world was a place I was told that God had created, and yet the world was the hot seat of sin. It was pornography, violence, and R-rated movies; drugs and addictions, and, most of all, lust.

I learned that sex was something you shouldn't have before I even knew what sex was. I learned that about a lot of things.

I learned not to trust my body, but to hide it, just when it started to get interesting. I learned to cover my body with loose-fitting clothing. To cross my legs and conceal my breasts as if the parts that made me a woman were something to be ashamed of. I learned to judge other women who didn't. I learned my body had the power to seduce boys, and then men. I was told that it wasn't their fault. They couldn't help but react to the curve of my hip or the sight of my skin in the sun.

What all of this meant about God and my body, or God in my body, I wasn't quite sure. I wanted to believe in *imago dei*, the image of God woven into the fabric of humans. I wanted to confirm what I'd felt as a child spinning wide wandering circles with my head toward the sky — that something holy was within me and waiting to break through; that it flowed in my veins and lived in my skin. But how could divinity dwell in a body? How could God take up space in my shoulders and feet, when that same territory was something to shame?

"You're such a great girl," my relatives tell me as we stand in the back of the church where my brother has just gotten married. "You'll meet someone," they say. "You're so pretty; so smart."

I will hear this again when my sister is wed, and whenever I visit my parents and we end up at church.

"You're such a catch," they say, as if I need to be reminded that I am valuable. I guess they assume that, still being single, I am likely to believe something is wrong with me. Eventually, I do.

I don't think anyone ever explicitly told me that marriage was an indication of a woman's worth. It isn't the sort of lesson you learn from a book. You pick it up in the foyer while hunting for donuts or take it in with the gossip at an afternoon potluck. It's in the tone that they use when they speak of divorce or the pity that's shown for a woman on her own. You absorb it like language. You don't think to question.

Marriage, I learned, was the place where the body was redeemed, where the fruit of Eve's womb made up for the lust of her eyes. Within the safety of marriage, the hidden could be revealed, the body was seen, and the woman was wanted for being a woman. Marriage was the payoff for protecting your purity, or that's what I gathered from my sex education. The lust you battled as a human with eyes and a libido somehow turned into love through the magic of a wedding.

Within marriage, there were children. Within marriage, there was life. There was the hope of bringing something good into the world.

But what does one do with a woman unwed? With a girl in a body who wants to be free?

Sometimes I wonder why God did not become incarnate as a woman with a womb and the ability to birth more holiness into the world. Why did God not turn the tables in a headscarf and heels or sit among the outcasts because she was one and the same? I suppose because no one would have taken her seriously. She would have been shut out from teaching in the temples or learning to become literate. Maybe God became a man so that men would actually listen.

Or maybe God did not enter the world as a man at all.

What if God first brought fullness to flesh in a teenage girl's ovum? If God was embodied in the organs of an unmarried woman before God as a human had a gender at all?

A woman is born with all of the eggs she will ever have. All of the life she might possibly grow is there from the start, from the day that her story begins. And so the egg that grew into the fetus named Jesus was there with Mary from the moment of her birth — sinful or not.

Mary was born with the capacity to embody God and bring holiness. It wasn't something she studied or trained for, or a reward that she earned. It wasn't even her choice. But when Gabriel came knocking, Mary said yes.

Maybe God is like that — within us from the start. Maybe God is embodied and ready to grow, waiting for us to come back to ourselves and acknowledge as good what was there all along.

Back in California, under sheaths of sun and an awning of yellow, I can't stop looking at the picture on the pamphlet of the man and the child, both dressed in plaid. Something in the image reminds me of redemption. I ponder the possible repercussions of injecting, extracting, and implanting potential into my body, all with the hope of creating a life, of creating a goodness to add to the world.

I think of growing a baby and then raising it up, of sharing my substance by making a person.

But there are so many ways I could move in this world. So many ways that my life might matter. I think wifedom and motherhood don't need to define me. But then I struggle with feeling like maybe they should. I think somewhere, deep down, this is what I want anyway, and my feminist fight is just an act of defiance. But it too feels like something that comes from my core — this need to express what I've seen and survived.

I click out of the pamphlet and close out the tabs of my inbox. I open a new window and create a fresh doc, zoom in the screen, and put fingers to keys. I begin to form life the only way I know how. I enter my body, and my hands start to write.

MEET THE AUTHOR

Raised in the cornfields of Nebraska, and based in the Bay Area by way of England and France, Amanda has been writing for as long as she can remember. From essays and blog posts to profiles and poems, her work is driven by a desire to connect to a fragile and fascinating world. She holds a Bachelor's in writing and rhetoric from Northwestern College in Orange City and an MFA in creative non-fiction from Saint Mary's College of California. Among other things, Amanda has been a youth program director, bakery clerk, ESL instructor, content strategist, and food writer. Like all good writers, she is working on a book, possibly two. Someday she hopes to share more about that. For now, you can find her at akcarroll.com.

THE SPACE TO DANCE

Joanna Leidenhag

I do not know when I stopped dancing, but I'm told that as a four-year-old I would clumsily move down the central aisle of the church waving my arms and falling over playfully. I don't remember anyone telling me to stop but, of course, it is possible that someone did. I never saw anyone else dance in this church (although hands were frequently lifted from amongst the pews). Perhaps, I just became aware that it was "different" to dance in the aisle or beneath the pulpit. Given my lack of memory in all this, I imagine I stopped this dancing before I was seven.

However, I do know when I started (or returned to) dancing in church. I was seventeen, and my life was a turmoil that I did not know how to experience, process, or express. As is common for seventeen-year-old Western teenage girls, a large part of this turmoil was to do with learning to relate to my (female) body. I struggled with conflicting understandings of bodily beauty. I fought issues with control surrounding food. I wrestled with questions of the goodness of female sexuality. I always believed in God. I knew God's love and forgiveness in my life. I felt God speak to me regularly. I lead Bible studies, and I told friends and family about Jesus with boldness and certainty. I sang in choirs and worship bands, and I had been trained to do so with a level of skill. In these things, I had a level of confidence, but with confidence there is a creeping perfectionism, a subtle pride, and a different type of hiding.

I started to dance at the back of the youth group I attended on Friday evenings. Actually, I danced out in the lobby, at the top of the stairwell, rather than in the main room where worship was taking place. This reflects my distorted perceptions at the time — I did not think there was *space* for my body. My body needs space; more space than I wanted it to need and dancing needs more space still. What I had not yet learnt, but what dancing in worship would slowly teach me, is that God's presence always creates space. The space that is necessary for my life, my existence, my faith, my emotions, my freedom, and my body is not created when God retracts; but when God is present. In God's presence, there is space for my large, white, beautiful, uncoordinated, complex, abused, objectified, and powerful body. My body is not in competition with God for space; quite the opposite is true. My body is not only a solid which moves through space; it is itself a space created by God's presence. Thus, we are told that our bodies are the temple of the Holy Spirit, a special place in which we can meet God. When I dance in worship, I enlarge this space, I give thanks to God for it, and I celebrate God's presence as it is experienced in this, my body-space.

My experience of faith has often, but not always, been mediated through dance in worship. Dance is not the whole story, I am also an academic theologian and spend most of my days reading and arguing about doctrinal matters of faith from a purely sitting position. I am also training for ordination and find God in the practice of the sacraments, and in the stories and faces I encounter in pastoral settings. But, in the deepest, secret, and most painful places of my life; God has been met in the movement of my body. It is an expression of who I am as an embodied soul and an experience of God as creator and redeemer. On the one hand, dancing in worship is a counterbalance to the rational and relational cognition where I spend most of my time, and on the other hand dancing counteracts the lies that I could argue or persuade my way into God's love; or that I would ever need to.

I am a natural performer; I perform in social conversation, I perform in intellectual debate, I perform in singing. However, I do not perform in dance. For one, I am simply not a very good dancer! I am not confident in my coordination, flexibility, or elegance. This is not false modesty; there are plenty of other "churchy" and worship activities that I am very good at, both naturally and as I have been trained for. But, it is for this exact reason that dance is such an important part of my faith journey. God does not want my performance; God wants me. This makes dance vulnerable, personal, and private, and it means that I cannot hide before God when I dance (as I can with other "skills").

Above, I noted that my struggles with beauty and food as a teenager were connected to questions of the goodness of female sexuality. Dance, and I would argue worship more widely, is always connected to human sexuality. The desire which drives us and the longings for connection and acceptance which move us towards God are not identical to sexual desires, but neither are they disconnected from them. When I dance for God, I bring my sexuality more explicitly into church; and I find this very difficult. The male-gaze, the objectification of a woman in the eyes of a man as an object to be possessed or enjoyed, is not absent from our churches. I still dance at the back of the church, or to the sides, but now always in the main worship space as part of the worship of the whole people of God. I do not want to be gazed at; I do not want to take the attention away from God. I need my whole person, sexuality included, to be laid down before God and not used as a power in or for the world. I dance before Jesus, and not before men, because Jesus' gaze is not the male-gaze. Jesus, the Lord of the dance, does not see a performance or a power, but a weakness and a hope.

My experience of faith is multifaceted, but movement (perhaps it has been overly generous to call it dance) in times of worship has been a very important element of my faith which is not frequently talked about. I know men that dance in worship too; but it is more often, in my experience, women who experience God in this way. I encourage all women to wiggle a bit, sway a bit more, tap your foot, lift an arm, and jump!; celebrate your body as a place and sacred space that God has created to be with you.

MEET THE AUTHOR

I am a young British woman studying for a PhD in Systematic Theology at the University of Edinburgh and married to another academic theologian. I am also training for ordination in the Scottish Episcopal Church, having grown up in charismatic, evangelical Anglican churches.

REFLECTION

"In my experience, there are lots of ways to feel lost, sometimes without even noticing. For years, I felt things without noticing. I internalized all sorts of ideas and feelings about myself, my place in the world and whether or not it could change. I wove those things into my foundation, learning to lean on false truths that had come from Nothing."

ALYSSA

Right Hand of Mother

By Anonymous

Trigger Warning: Sexual Abuse

On my mother's right hand, the pointer finger has a curious bend at the tip. Very few people notice the anomaly, but once seen, it is not easily forgotten. You find yourself following it with your eyes as she talks, its needled tip the forerunner of every expression — or you project its image when chopping carrots, clipping nails, or riding your bicycle.

The story originated with a bicycle, my mother aged ten. She and my aunt set the wheel of an upturned bike spinning, all the while attempting to hurl nickels and dimes between the spokes. Unsurprisingly, the story ends with my mother palming a sliced bit of finger all the way to a hospital where a doctor eventually sewed it back on like one blood-marbled button. Maybe the doctor had been distracted by the rivulet of red, or maybe the spokes claimed some of the flesh for itself, but when the finger healed it was crooked — permanently slid off-kilter from the straight-lined scar.

Growing up, I watched that finger raise to the fluorescent apses every Sunday, accompanied by the same voice that scolded me most nights before. People shook and danced with holy ghosts, tongues weren't body parts, and women never gripped the music-stand pulpit. I recorded a diary diagnosis at age eleven: "When I look in the mirror I see a demon there."

I also wrote about a recurring dream. Only recently did my mother tell me about a nightmare she kept having at the same age; it was of just a cloud,

189

an ominous and blackening one. After a series of insomniac nights, my grand-parents revealed to her the memory that the nightmare had repressed and re-placed: a twenty-three year old man chasing her into the woods, pinning her down to Midwestern leaves, and pulling, touching. Mine was of my mother biting off the head of a living snake.

The crooked finger wrapped my Christmas present that year: a ring with "purity" etched and dyed on its torso (it had been the only thing on my list). My youth leader had hers melted into a heart that she handed her husband on their teenage wedding night, though he had no emblem to offer in return. She had been molested by her previous boyfriend, but the line was never crossed, her virginity and her metal heart intact. After telling us this, she had all the girls in the room write lists of qualities we wished to find in our future husband, urging a universal number one: "Lead me in my walk with God. Lead me." I stapled it to a new page and began to usher prayers penned only to him.

Later, that one finger would smush and spread "lip spuz" — my mother's own word for what the rest of us call Chapstick — and from coated lips I would be told to stop asking for the male gaze with my clothes and my large breasts, a sentiment like a stone in purity culture's cairn of shame. Or stones: black, splintered by waves and wind, across from the distant white-sand shores where my mother beckoned and sat.

That single finger may likely have been burned by curling irons each year as my mother beautified my sisters and I for our church's "Princess Party," a purity-themed occasion for young girls, planned and put on by the very young woman who later spoke her story into a tape recorder — four years of sexual abuse by the lead pastor's son, an associate pastor and married father of two girls. One year he sat on a stool facing all the princesses and told us we each de-served to be pursued by men. The woman on the other end of the tape recorder mentioned that night, when her own first-time-curled hair and sequined dress had been pulled.

My mother and my church co-authored vague commandments of bodies, so I drank, and I abstained, and I shook off kisses like yellowed leaves. The demon, which a doctor belatedly named depression, made me resent my high school's mirrors.

My mother's uneven hand waved goodbye when I eventually left for the small Evangelical college I had chosen. The first Friday night, my newfound roommate and I wanted to try jumping out of our second-floor dorm window.

She landed fine, but I hung above her from the fourth proximal digit of my left hand — the thick metallic commitment somehow stuck onto the window frame, slicing into the skin below my knuckle. The ring had to be sliced off afterwards, sawed with the ER's huge whirling pizza cutter. I put the broken thing in a Ziploc bag, and never put another back on. (It could have been a tailor-made illustration of my liberation, but instead, it just left me a scar.)

The first class in my major was a survey of British literature, beginning with ancient mystics. We learned about Julian of Norwich, an anchoress of the fourteenth century who is considered the first female author of the English language. Quarantined, she recorded sixteen visions, which she called *Revelations of Divine Love*; she and her contemporaries wrote about sin as behovely, the Holy Ghost as penetration, God holding all of creation as if it were a hazelnut. Her writing so pervaded my conscience that I permanently inked the outline of the latter image onto my forearm. But Julian wrote three words I ceaselessly skipped over: God is mother.

By this point in my life, a cocktail of newfound feminism and Lexapro had begun to infect the demon inside me, but I hadn't understood how surprisingly easy it was to conceptualize Julian's assertion. Most women in my classes were struggling with the concept of God as male, and I played along. After all, we approached the issue from the same pain; pain caused by patriarchal theology and purity culture — all of us playing along and hating the game, and hating ourselves for losing.

I stripped down and swam the in-between waters, every weekend sharing similitude: I stammered about my love for Jesus until inevitably a boy would mirror it back, which allowed my mind to give my body permission to do whatever came next. I always stopped it before what the commandments called sex, but not a single time did I stop the dissociation, and not a single time did I orgasm. When morning came, I would sit in a pew and weep, surrounded by and choking on all the stones.

My junior year, I took a semester to study in Julian's homeland and ended up meeting the man I would later marry. Afterwards, I flew home for minor surgery. Before the operation, my mother overheard which box the nurse ticked after the "are you sexually active?" question. If there had also been a box for layering concealer atop large bruised breasts the day of your sister's wedding, I would have checked it. Or for being locked in a room by the Christian Homecoming King. Or for having a new list for boys who checked off the boxes of that first list all those years ago, each leaving scars rather than rings. But there was only one for each — white and black, virginity and scandal, guarded and lost, whole and splintered, Eve and Mary. And after prayer and study and many respectful conversations, I had done the thing that checked all the former. When we got home, my mother wrapped that finger around a brush, and I watched as she painted the front porch a different shade of brown. Without looking me in the eyes, she told me I was living in sin. She told me she had failed her job as a mother. I looked down at the tattoo that may as well have been a palm holding all creation as if it were a bloody bit of finger.

Then, hours before I was to fly back to Seattle, my mother used that finger of hers to weave my hair into two braids, pulling tighter and tighter as I winced. It tied them up, and pulled out a piece of paper onto which Romans 12:1 was scrawled. "Read it," she said with those wax-pursed lips and quivering nostrils I had become so accustomed to. "Out loud." I repeated the verse from memory, as my God waved her snipped finger in my face, over and over again.

GOD IS A WILD WOMAN

Frances Frames Hubbs

The Maple

Mother Durga stretches her arms down
    and wonders at the little ones
tottering back and forth beneath her,
    and every so often, they reach up,
brush the tips of their meaty hands
    against the thin, leathery stars
she offers, and exhales warm clouds
    that expand up through her lungs
so that she exchanges the taste of life with them.

She pities those who roam without the comfort
Of deep roots to hold them,
Who cannot be rocked to sleep by the storm
Lest it whisk them away.

To her,
Pity
Is a form of love,
No greater or lesser
Than the swaddling of bark.

"Share something I have never felt,"
Said the tree,
So I leaned into you and breathed,
And the tree breathed,
And the sun was warm under your skin,
And air moved through the chlorophyll in our hair,
And we were alone,
Together.

"When I first heard the story of Jesus, I cried."

"Why, Grandma?"

"Well," my grandmother paused to think as she continued to comb my baby-fine curls into a bouquet on my toddler's crown. "Well, because never in my life did I ever feel loved until then. He showed me what it was to be loved, and then I realized that loving me cost Him a lot of pain. He died. I was sad that He died, but so happy to finally feel loved."

My first experiences of faith blossomed just in that instant, like the root of an aspen stretching from my grandma's heart to spring up with sapling strength in my own. As a child not even in school, I didn't, couldn't, fathom the complexity or depth of the story she told me, yet her honesty and careful words changed everything forever. My introduction to matters of spirit: God, Jesus, and religion, were wildly clean of an institution, and because the Christ in this story had made my grandma's life so much more beautiful, I loved Him. I loved him fiercely and with a longing that only children feel, because they don't know how to stop themselves from feeling it. Beyond the bigger puzzles hidden in her story, I wanted to understand Him. I wanted to love Him back and to grow into someone who filled the world with love like He had done for my grandma, and that was where my faith was born.

Understanding the implication of a three-year-old becoming what many Christians today like to call "saved" certainly takes a bit of work, and since there are varying arguments from different doctrines within this belief system concerning the validity of a child's salvation, this is not the place to delve into such a discussion. I will not say if a child that young can make the deliberate choice for redemption from sin. I know only that my clearest memory of holiness is brightly specific. I chose Jesus to save me, not necessarily from sins I didn't comprehend, but from the cold, loveless existence into which I knew my grandma had been born.

Because my parents divorced when I was two, and because my mother and I lived with her parents following the split, I experienced divided lifestyles of faith from a very tender part of my development. My mother's mother, forever a soul sister to me, became a gentle guide to my spirit. I had been to Sunday school a few times with my father's parents, people from a mixed Lutheran-Catholic brand of faith that had more or less devolved into a lazy sort of "wear the uniform and eat the donuts" sort of performance. This is not to say my paternal grandparents weren't genuine Christians; they loved deeply and painfully in humbling practice. I do believe, looking back now, that a corrupt world and a life of hardship had simply left them tired. Either way, Jesus did not whisper to me as I sat behind the pews under the red and blue stained-glass light of their strange church. Instead, Grandma brought me to him.

Being cared for by my grandma as Mom worked long hours led to as untamed and pure a childhood as I could have asked for, and while I craved stories of all genres, it was the stories Grandma told me about her own life that I wanted the most. I have no right to share them here, but suffice it to say that she grew up in a large family wracked with dysfunction and abuse, and her trauma is very real. At that young age, I understood that she had survived terrible things, but I couldn't understand how. I asked many questions, and as always, she gave me her honesty in return, phrased simply and tailored to a child's ears. My grandma taught me well never to underestimate children.

She told me her stories with no lesson or moral intent. No special effort was made to teach me what to believe. Perhaps she knew what Jesus knew, that the right story at the right time can change the world, but I doubt she intended to do anything but share herself with me. Everything I learned about the nature of Grace came from her opening the arms of her experience with no expectation that I would do anything other than listen, but I found myself returning the embrace.

From there, little changed. My early childhood was rich with purity. My days living in my grandma's home were filled to bursting with climbing mossy hills in the woods, breaking up clods of dirt with my toes in the gardens and fields, chasing minnows in the creek. We read library books from heaping stacks and, on lucky weekends, visited the flower shop where I could choose any single stem I wanted.

Later, I gradually learned how unusual my maternal grandparents truly are. As a young couple, they participated in a faith-based commune, like many that existed in the sixties and seventies. My mom's memories of childhood there are fond and innocent, while my aunt, who is older, recalls a darker story. Both truths can exist together, but the corruption of the commune is ultimately what defined much of the rest of my grandparents' lives. The result was a mixture of beliefs that eventually led to me, a child, encountering Christ in what I would call, utter freedom.

We celebrated no religious holidays then, and so I had nothing to justify or villainize my understanding of the roots of my faith. Being taught that Church is a matter of spirit, not structure, meant no preacher was raised to lecture over me, to either idolize or rebel against. Out in the country, I had no dress code, no implication that being a girl meant falling nicely in line. I had only fresh air, trees, and toadstools, rain showers to dance naked in. I had the knowledge that tiny seeds can become big plants hanging with yummy things, and I had love. Wild, pure, unbroken love.

Do I need to tell the story of how the idylls of my childhood faith were corrupted? It's not unfamiliar to many Christians. When my mother remarried, our lives became merged with my stepfamily's culture, that of the standard Bible-church going Protestants who eat plenty of gravy on Sunday as they glance at the portrait on the wall of a humble old man praying over bread in a small, rustic kitchen. I went to church, Sunday school, Bible studies, and camps. I learned to be a "good" Christian young woman (which meant so many conflicting things). Deep inside, I yearned to please a people I admired as pious and good, but it wouldn't be for many years later that I would learn how futile, and toxic, that dream would be.

I could share endlessly experiences I understand to be common among Christian women. I could tell about my conflicting identity as "smart," which was often a boasting point when it came to report cards, and as an "intellectual," which meant I had eaten of the fruit of the tree of knowledge and caused too much trouble. I could hang my head and weep as I told about being taught that God only cares about my heart, but being treated noticeably different for being fat, strong, or not blood kin. I could shake my fist at all the ways my burgeoning sexuality was bludgeoned with shame and unspoken disgust. All in all, I was talented at performing the role of a good Christian young woman, and it broke me.

In my teenage years, I discovered paganism and Wicca, things that appealed to my active imagination and critical mind almost as much as they appealed to my longing for belief in something bright and empowering. These systems of belief seemed, to me, a version of the wild love I knew as a child, so I grabbed them up. Fused with my faith in the Resurrection, I became a chimera of faith, doing everything in my power to be the woman I thought Christ wanted me to be while desperately seeking to fertilize the old roots of my love, to feed that starving aspen tree.

It was a vicious dichotomy, made thorny with shame, and I was completely ensnared. I have only begun to heal after breaking free by realizing that those influences intended to nurture me were not cultivating love, but domestication. Performing Christianity is not the same thing as living it. It is an artifice that enjoys costumes, these for the men and those for the women, and promises safety as long as you stay in your costume long enough to forget who you are. For some, the costume is worn over an identical truth, so the performance is not painful. For me, it chafed.

Paradigm changes so often happen in rolling waves rather than all at once. My shifts of belief came in crashes of revelation and little blades of lightning that sliced at the mortar of my worldview. In tarot, there is a card called The Tower. It's not a pretty card. Pictured on it is a single, once-sturdy stronghold in the process of being battered and razed to its foundation by a raging storm of fire, a fitting emblem of the destruction required for rebuilding, of the death that happens before new life. Embracing the meaning of that card is likely no new concept to many Christians, and it is what had to happen to my faith. The change had many triggers, all of which deserve their own treatment.

Regardless of why or how, the wild, clover-wearing love that ruled me as a child is once again a part of my life, but it is a difficult place to stay in. I have been given shame, and it is a gift that enjoys putting up tall fences and signs that say "Keep Out." Only by reminding myself that I am wild, like the forest God made and walked me through, that I am able to trespass beyond my own inhibitions.

Wildness is the nature of the Spirit, the one with the capital "S." She drives men and women to empathize when empathy seems impossible, and pushes at boundaries when boundaries are most difficult to break. She is unafraid of what "should" and "should not" be, because Her essence is of what IS. Truth is a wild thing. It asks nothing of anyone, cannot apologize. If we, as Christians and as women, are to embrace truth, then we must embrace the ferocity of our own wildness. Love sometimes happens nicely and quietly, but so often is it fierce, messy, and tenacious. Loving requires sacrifice; it demands blood. Love is the wildest of uncontainable ideals, and if we are to be ruled by it, we must open ourselves like my grandmother once did to me as a child. We must take it with all of our imperfections and dance naked in the rain, let it scrape our palms as we haul ourselves into the rough arms of trees, walk through swaths of minnows with no expectation that they will nibble on our ankles. They owe us nothing.

Generations of women have guided one another like grape vines down a tree, so that you cannot discern where one began and the other ended, and my grandmother is part of my story, which will be part of the next. We mother each other, as Christ mothers us, as his Spirit comforts and challenges us in turns. The sharing of truth is a raw thing, but so is every act of true love. Be wild. Hallelujah.

MEET THE AUTHOR

Frances was born a Hoosier and grew up in Terre Haute, Indiana, though much of her youth was spent in surrounding rural areas. After living a few years in Denver, Colorado, she now lives in Bloomington, Indiana with her husband, James. Together they look after the honorable Annie Dog and her feline sibling, Zeus. Frances shares Julia Child's opinions of arugula and cilantro, with a few exceptions. She currently works as a freelance writer and enjoys running, making and eating good food, and generally being outside.

Impermanence, Barbwires, and New Beginnings

Elaine Padilla

I had moved that fall and was just beginning my second semester of teaching there . . . Early in the spring of 2018, our university's gallery of photography put together an exhibit with the title *Snag: Impermanence on the Vast Alberta Prairie* by Wes Bell, a LensCulture Exposure Awards 2017 winner. This exhibit presented us with about a dozen black and white shots of plastic bags caught on the barbwire fence. Not long before the photos were taken, these bags had been floating free. But now they were presented snagged, pulled, and torn by the whim of the winds. The artist explains that when driving on the prairie roads of Alberta, Canada (returning from a trip where he said goodbye to his mother who was dying of cancer), he found himself distracted by how these plastic bags were being whipped by the wind and lacerated by the fences in a "no man's land."

In carefully observing these shots — snagged bags in sixty-eight sites between the spring and winter seasons of 2015 and 2017 — I could not help but to feel a moment's inward queasiness and knotted mass of emotions. My breathing was swallowed thin by the overwhelming sensation of lack of air amidst the strong gusts. Upon being lost in the worldhood of the artist, I became Wes Bell and was grasped by the luminosity of these shredded bags. There, standing among the shrubbery of the Alberta prairies, with my body bleeding at the blows, I felt empathy: the strong winds and fences staked in the middle of nowhere were tearing them apart. With this tone of nostalgia, my sight became faint. I mourned over the 'could haves' of my life, as I was witnessing what (at the moment) could have been the 'possible' of my dreams also being shattered. I felt overwhelmed by the pain of my life's flows, losses running through the crevices of its triumphs. The seeming simplicity of these shots was a cry of an instant's surge of my own life's ironies haunting me. For I too know what it means to be snagged in the turbulence of impermanence.

I wondered what was the most difficult aspect to grasp about the torn existence of these plastic bags. Was it that they were hoping simply to spread themselves, playfully, as if having arms wide open, speedily floating, smiling from cheek to cheek, and having hearts expanded by their adventure? That they encountered paths on the prairies too wildly opening before them? Being blinded by the expansiveness of the land, might they have not foreseen the barbwires? Might they have willed to catch the wind but reaped the whirlwind instead? Perhaps in the face of infinity, there on the horizon of a no man's land, they met not only the limits of their plastic flesh, but also the shredded flesh of this world.

An absolute mind splitting us from our whole selves can sinisterly act like a trickster. For I thought at that moment about how, as a result of decisions made between 2015 and 2017, I had come to reside in the barbwires of the southern borders of our nation. Southern California, one of the territories where we test our limits, is where I have been, in forging my paths, speeding full steam ahead, westward, like a railroad company seemingly with no friends and no companion.

It was nothing like a gold rush, but the weakening blame started to undermine my strengths: too lofty of a dream perhaps, the desire to go after that which has been long dreamed, risking it all at the cost of losing everything yearned for. "The wind has been gathered only to be lost in an instant's snag," blame said within. Still, I affirmed, quite dreamy: there is no comparison to the childlike feeling of the wind on my face as I stretch my arms like an airplane and securely fly resting on the windows of my faith.

No doubt, this is a serious matter. Of course, says the adult and mature voice in me. After all, I have been taught that I can lose my very soul if I go after vainglory. But, I also ask: have I made an idol of my past and of permanence as if I was meant to remain the same through time, invulnerable to the complications of space, unfeeling to the wavelengths and vibrations of time? Did I commit the unpardonable sin of the loss of love?

Wrestling with these past memories felt like fragmented selves battling one another inside me. Winning, losing, at times has mattered little. Who, which one of them, is correct? Would there be a why that can lead me to fully comprehend? Upon leaving behind *everything* familiar, the embracing comfort of quotidian life, is there a home to be found? Yes, with time, after a while, all my belongings were packed and moved across the country. Here I have been with no net to catch me even if I fell; it all came tumbling down. As each step is retaken and each event re-lived, after that which has been lost is searched for once again, in my muttering state, I retold myself the story once again. . . . So there I was in a no man's land as if all alone, facing the snagged bags, holding my suitcases one more time. Agonizingly, impermanence was passing me by . . .

Letting the breezes in the Alberta Prairies thrust me against the barbwires has reminded me of this long journey of self-doubt, and yet, also of my renewed search for self-acceptance, courage and valor, inner strength and love, all possibilities as I also stand before faith.

So what to do when being snagged by these fences that tear my flesh and when being pulled even further by the winds of my many worlds? How to get unsnagged from an existence of eternal inner-punishment for wanting to create a life with the architectonics of dreams? Can I come to hold as truth that this impermanence too can be an unexpected stranger meeting me at the crossroads of Emmaus, a good friend whose resurrection enlivens the most gruesome of deaths?

In faith, I have come to believe that I am a process of my past selves being infused by *the possible* continuously being bathed in the droplets of hope, regardless of the snags of my worlds' seemingly constricting barbwires. Process thought teaches me about such *limits*, for I reside in a space within tangible fences where life is. Nonetheless, space expands me as I interconnect with all others, there, near and far. My body, my senses, my feelings, my hopes, and shattered glories become the very conduits for touching the pulsating heart of life. Even if caught, in the fences of seeming absolute misfortune and endings, the ghosts of no one by my side, in the middle of the darkening of the night of my soul, my solitude could be the connective tissue to a multitude of instances shared with the many hoping, dreaming, trusting, living, enjoying, surviving, leaping also into the unknown.

And time is but a moment, an instant, that as it rises into my consciousness, it is already past. So why live as if my past is determinative of my present?

Faith is the courage to be despite the impossible. To truly live one moment at a time. As the past informs all my past selves, I faintly grasp a vision of the future in the now, in every aspect of my life. Relationally, professionally, personally, and spiritually, newness infuses my very being moment by moment in this time-space. I am not a singular individual but a complexity of selves of past and future unfolding in this very unified present. I share of my very self through a continuum of trust. Such impermanence of myself that *must* not hold on to what has been — even if I wanted to — lets me know that I am only temporarily in this snagging-event!

There seems to be a vastness of eternity ahead of experiencing the fullness of divine exuberance and contentment. But I keep letting that wind that whirls like a storm within me be the murmur and gentle touch of the Spirit guiding me. Faith turns the snagging barbwire that feels as if tearing me apart into that limit that rescues me so that space can become numinous, a portent of good news. Perhaps, as the wind keeps blowing and my life gets unsnagged, might I arrive at a hope-*filled* destination?

Yes and amen. Faith is trust that there, in the open prairies, the most desolate and remote places of my worlds, amidst the whirlwinds that unfurl within and that beyond me blow, the barbed fences seeking to split me into whichever direction, the God of love for life is. Beginnings on the metals of chaos-winds are made possible. There, where no eye sees or hand touches, the fullness of life is being born anew. For there on the prairies, or the mountains of high deserts, the divine life sprouts through the smells of the morning dew lightly caressing the dried grass, the wildflowers blooming in varied colors of yellow, red, and blue, and the sun and moon protectively embracing the vastness of dusty dirt. This divining force breaths in me. And Life within flourishes moment by moment amidst these barbwires as if readying itself to welcome time and again the very pieces of my broken selves.

How to believe? How to hold on to the trust that the divine Spirit is continuously reweaving my worlds, upon my flesh being torn by metal and air, as forces can keep me and pull me? Seeming fragmentation. Amidst my continued prayers, the Wind quietly responds, almost unnoticeably. And all about me is the community of faith that like a pilgrim on a voyage accompanies me and shares its hands of sustenance through words of wisdom and courage. There are the healers who listen intently without judgment and offer tiny bits of insight that like golden pellets help me to pay it forward to the many snagged-others I encounter on the way. Selective friends and intimate family members that like lighthouses brighten forth the path ahead despite my losses and shortcomings tirelessly hold my hands and lighten my burdens. I cannot forget that I run, I play, I dance, I laugh, and climb high mountains, even as fences could be all around me in an open field of dreams. Oh yes, faith is about life being lived abundantly.

What lies ahead will always be unknown, but as far as I can see, I can trust and believe in the now, because God has been there with me. I love again and again. From within that inner being where God resides, I weave my life anew. There, as I contemplated on the exhibit *Snag*, sinews of my torn flesh resiliently threaded by the fibers of my future hopes began to form the fabric of who I am becoming — a flourishing tapestry of all my torn selves.

An artist sees what others cannot. Like photographers who create art, with the right perception, lighting, perfect wind conditions, and a large amount of obstinacy, I can create an award-winning set of me. Like an artwork out of blown bags, I too can recreate myself clothed as black and white.

Faith immodestly runs after the one who is torn, desperately searches for the badly entangled, and wisely teaches the one who has lost it all, that fullness of life is in the *herenow* and remains ahead in the vast prairies. Just look and see, smell and touch, feel with the whole of your being the possible always within! That spark of potentiality that enlivens those areas of dead tissue, a lost love. Even when overwhelmed by the impermanence of life, dreams can regain the intended aim to lead me into an expansiveness of much flourishing. After all, faith is trusting, as the *Manyone* woos me into the divine plenitude.

MEET THE AUTHOR

Elaine Padilla is Associate Professor of Philosophy and Religion, Latinx/Latin American Studies. Padilla constructively interweaves current philosophical discourse with Christianity, Latin American and Latino/a religious thought, mysticism, ecology, gender, and race. She is the author of Divine Enjoyment: A Theology of Passion and Exuberance *published by Fordham University Press (2015), and co-editor of a three-volume project with Peter C. Phan,* Theology and Migration in World Christianity *published by Palgrave Macmillan:* Contemporary Issues of Migration and Theology (2013), Theology of

Migration in the Abrahamic Religions *(2014), and* Christianities in Migration: The Global Perspective *(2015). She has also published numerous articles and chapters, and is currently drafting a manuscript provisionally titled,* The Darkness of Being, *in which she explores views on the soul and interiority with implications for race and gender. She is a member of the American Academy of Religion where she serves in various steering committees, and a member of the Catholic Theological Society of America.*

WILDERNESS

Alyssa Bennett Smith

I have no desire
for wild things
maybe I used to
and too many years
of uprooting
and culling
have dulled my taste for it

or maybe I never did
and all the discovery
and freedom
and uprootedness
were wasted on one
with no appreciation

wilderness
is not comfort
or temptation
or prove that you
can conquer

it is loneliness
and deprivation
and no communion

the wilderness does not
remember
but rather
shreds those
she envelops
with her nothing
entirely full of empty

she will not miss you
when you're gone

When I read stories of exile, I imagine The Nothing. If you've seen The Neverending Story, you'll know what I'm talking about. The Nothing is a dark and not-so-distant force that envelops everything it touches. Not only destroying but removing from existence — a storm fueled by despair and helplessness. I imagine the Israelites wandering in the desert, wondering if they will ever reach the Promised Land. I imagine a sorrow so big it swallows hope. In my experience, there are lots of ways to feel lost, sometimes without even noticing. For years, I felt things without noticing. I internalized all sorts of ideas and feelings about myself, my place in the world and whether or not it could change. I wove those things into my foundation, learning to lean on false truths that had come from Nothing. I thought I understood the wilderness. Having no hometown or other such embedded identity, I built myself out of ideas. If I get married, I'll be a Wife. If I get a degree, I will be Smart, Employed and Secure. If I can settle somewhere, I will have a Home. These things will create me and carve my boundaries into a more desirable shape.

I have learned that the wilderness is everywhere we allow it to be. When disappointment arises, and self-criticism creeps up the back of my neck, I find myself lost in all of the ways I am not enough, or things are not as I thought they would be. On the days when I try as hard as I can, but still fall short — The

Nothing is there. She lays in wait at the back of my mind, watching for an opportune moment to blind me to my joy. Wilderness does not allow for gratitude or silver linings. There is no upside in hopelessness. What happens when you've checked all of the boxes and still aren't where you thought you'd be? What do you do when everything inside you is screaming at the unfairness of it all, and you start to feel as though all of your efforts have been wasted? Graduated, but no job? Employed, but still broke? Marriage not as easy as you were led to believe?

The Nothing is full of unfulfilled promises. I see no hope in meeting empty expectations. I am more than the ideas I thought might shape me into someone different.

This is the beauty of finding identity in Christ: The loveliness of the Gospel is that we are never alone — we survive The Nothing together. In moments where I feel I am not enough, I can sing hymns with my community and realize they are everything I cannot be in any particular moment. When I have run out of options for paying bills despite working multiple jobs, I have people around me to remind me that I am not alone. We are for one another. Without perfection or expectation, we hold one another in grace and love and laughter, even when there is no solution. My failure to meet subconscious expectations fades into the background when I am home in community. We are God's gift to one another, and she is generous.

I see wilderness everywhere. It is to the point that I think the word has lost much of the power I believe the biblical writers intended for it. We cannot escape its presence, only how we choose to engage it. Hopelessness and despair are inevitabilities we all must face, but what a joy it is that we don't have to live and die by The Nothing. We have been given love and grace and joy that surpass our own ability to understand. Behold who you are, become what you receive.

MEET THE AUTHOR

Alyssa Bennett Smith loves poetry, ethics, interpersonal communication, and coffee. She graduated from Central Baptist Theological Seminary in 2015 with a Master of Arts in Theological Studies, focusing on conflict transformation and nonviolent communication.

Since graduation, her interest has been the use of nonviolent communication in online spaces, about which she has written and presented several times at national conferences. She currently lives in Denver, Colorado with her husband and three cats and she works remotely as Digital Marketing Manager for Herald Press. You may enjoy her Instagram @ alybensmi if you also love poetry and cats.

MY GIFT

Jen Fulmer

My gift
my intention that I want to point towards.
is to have
beautiful insights about the presences of god as an experience for discussion.
and my experience, though not confident in arguing or postulating. My
journals, devotional that made me realize how close, I feel to god some
times, how intimately I can experience, him
Without much concrete to support it.
Exactly and experience. Too nebulous? But that's what faith is.
of water or metaphors on religious matter based
and experience of god. And to have a very strong
voice and gods voice sounds the same to me.
I was fortunate at 28 to finally
The first time I travelled alone.
and it was a waterfall into a pool which led to a river. With
conviction that people have knowledge

I cannot wrap up the experience of you in description of experience of similes
Women Experiencing faith. Woman Experiencing faith
Because as I experienced when I went to a being tied down I want to be free to be
I came, a radical act of trust
But when I had a general idea and a list of them that Probably was

Also potentially problematic because
I have seen so many smart, accomplished powerful women defer.
generalizations,,,,, me experiencing faith, I just read some of my old
constellation of thinkers doing new things with these concepts that

The clearest time where I remember experiencing faith was
I do not conceive of myself as an artist.
I am neither apart from my gender nor willing to define myself by any set of
I am quiet and shy and scared of most things. And yet I have travelled by
experiencing faith I have become an single self confident and extremely competent

Women seem to me so much more supportive and willing to flow with
background anxiety and often anxiety attacks.
when it comes to moment and you can move forward without gripping.
real spiritual work can begin" and I knew inherently without doubt or question
within walking distance,
rocks surrounding trees growing and that is what faith feels like that is
existing in faith has made me so much more than any typology can fit me in.
would have them at all. A space where I am totally confident in my thought

But today I was writing how I feel closest to faith when I'm in or near bodies
I woke up I looked up where it was, and my first gift arrived, it was
not knowing being a fertile ground for
so kind and gentle but kept trying to explain
brain and I was resisting the words and the work so hard that I finally painted into
that resistance
I may not be able to lay out a treatise of faith.
looks like to me.   unknowing
the night before I left it hit me. I have no idea what I am
ideas. They seem so much more flexible,
than   I
Really really someone who liked doing the work.   of faith.

MEET THE AUTHOR

Jennifer grew up the daughter of a pastor and has continued a faith centered worldview which has ever been evolving with the life she experiences. She studied theatrical design at UCLA and works as a set decorator in Los Angeles. She is always seeking new ways that we can more deeply connect with ourselves and others and spaces where our messiest most imperfect selves can be known and loved.

MY SPIRITUAL JOURNEY:
CHANGING PERSPECTIVES

Kaye Judge

*Our farm was the place I really knew with all my bones, brain, and breath.
My footprints left their fading marks across hills and valleys. My eyes,
ears, and mouth absorbed each sight and sound amongst the changing
vapours of the seasons.*

'*D*rumheid — my family farm — was my '*Turangi Wai-Wai*' — my sense of home and place according to the Maori people of Aotearoa. This is where I lived for the first twelve years of my childhood in New Zealand's South Island. Sheltered by two rows of pine trees, our white weatherboard cottage was the last house at the end of a long dusty, country road. Two rivers flowed through mountain passes on both sides of our farm. On a clear day, if we climbed to the top of the highest hill, our eyes could track the turquoise-blue ribbons of the Rangitata river as it widened and emptied its muddied waters into the Pacific Ocean about 50 miles away. At the highest point of our farm, the rolling hills merged into the base of a crouching mountain called 'Mount Tenahau'. Old Pete, our only neighbour, could scale the Mountain in an hour! I often wondered how long it would take my young legs. I remember asking my father —

"What's behind the mountain Dad?"

He replied, "Just another mountain!"

"And what's behind that mountain?"

". . . another mountain and another mountain and another mountain," he said.

I knew that one day I would climb my mountain and see for myself. I remember taking great delight as a child climbing higher and higher, up the low rolling hills, before turning to view the valleys and plains below. This was my earliest experiment with perspective. When I held my thumb up to the Mountain, it seemed so small, only as big as my thumb.

Laid out at the base of the Mount Tenahau, a giant patchwork quilt of paddocks shimmered alongside each other under the hot summer sun. Large squares of bright sky-blue linseed shimmered in the breeze alongside fields of translucent pink and white clover buzzing with swarms of honeybees. Luminous green Lucerne, and pale ochre fields of ripening wheat were edged by the grassy laneways where mobs of sheep would bob along ready to spill out into their new pasture. In winter, these fields disappeared below a cover of purest white snow. Only the narrow lines of fencing or the tall rows of pine trees in the shelter belts broke the monotony of white! This beautiful world reflected its richness upon my soul season upon season. There was no dividing line between the sacred and the everyday. On a bright summer's day, I would lie on my back in a field of green grass and watch a line of white fluffy clouds morph into an array of happy animals that would slowly disappear over the mountain ranges as if led by the Great Shepherd in the sky, to pastures way beyond my imagination. There was no dividing line between the heaven I heard about and the world I got to explore.

I was born the second child in a family of six children. It was not until my brother Murray was born, after a trio of girls that the farming future of our family was secured in my father's eyes. By the time I was four-years-old, I was the right-hand helper for my Mother's nursery of infants. There were three little ones younger than myself to care for. It was a very busy life for my Mother as she had the daily chores of a farmer's wife to fit around her constant caring for five young children.

We grew up in a world without boundaries. It seemed like wherever our legs had the will to take us we could go! For hours on end, we climbed the rolling hills and slid down grassy slopes on flax fronds from the palm trees. We hunted for lizards on rocky outcrops or found slippery frogs in swampy ponds. We spent hours building moss bridges over mountain streams and fished for rainbow trout with a stick and a piece of string! On hot summer days, tall wheat fields became a canvas upon which we designed and built pretend houses with many rooms and hallways. Our plantation of trees was a secret place — quiet, dark, and mysterious — where we built houses of pine needles and played hide and seek until the afternoon sun streaked long golden beams low onto the ground.

It was Papa's stories of his adventures as a missionary in the Pacific Islands and our Gran's letters sharing the adventures of her many brothers spreading the gospel story in many parts of the world that developed my curiosity about a world beyond the valley that nurtured and sheltered our lives. Our weeks were quietly brought to a close each Friday evening at sunset (when time was moved into a heavenly agenda) until sunset Sabbath evening. If our grandparents, Papa and Gran, were visiting, Papa always led us into a family circle of giving thanks to God. We would usually open the Sabbath hours by sharing the twenty-third psalm together. We all learned the words as we recited it together.

I don't recall it ever really being explained to us, as to its meaning. The words just grew into us, and around us, as we imagined into being the word pictures that matched the daily realities of being a farmer's child. The pictures in my mind took me on a familiar journey out across the paddocks with my brothers and sisters all clambering to hold the hand of our Papa or Gran. Beside the creek, we would trudge along as we followed the muddy sheep tracks. We may have found the body of a sheep cast on its back, and the shadow of death would imprint upon our souls.

The LORD is my shepherd; I shall not be in want.
He makes me lie down in green pastures,
he leads me beside quiet waters, he restores my soul.
He guides me in paths of righteousness for his name's sake.
Even though I walk through the valley of the shadow of death,
I will fear no evil, for you are with me;
your rod and your staff, they comfort me.
You prepare a table before me in the presence of my enemies.
You anoint my head with oil; my cup overflows.
Surely, goodness and love will follow me all the days of my life,
and I will dwell in the house of the LORD forever.
(Psalm 23, NKJV)

I was also aware that there was someone else. God, our 'Heavenly Shepherd,' was guiding our lives. I was aware at an early age that the journey of life would take us through some dark times. It was a constant blessing to know that there was a Heavenly Shepherd who was always there to provide comfort, restoration, and hope so that one day we would dwell in the 'House of the Lord forever'. This narrative was an anchor for my faith development and its many metaphors continue to enrich my understanding of God's ongoing protection and grace. Our significant childhood experiences of faith blessed us with an ongoing legacy, a strong chord of values and connectedness that bound us to our families and the wider world.

Each night I remember my mother — tired after a long day of work — kneeling beside our beds and reading us a Bible story from a small paper pamphlet. We each had to repeat the memory verse before we said our prayers with her. Sometimes she would nearly drift off to sleep before she kissed us and turned out the light. But in those moments, we knew that she was sharing with us stories that she wanted us to remember for always. Sometimes the words on the page made no sense and I longed for more pictures to fill in the gaps of my understandings about these great heroes of old, and about Jesus, the friend of little children.

Two or three times each year, our mother convinced our father to take us to church in the city which was a two-hour drive away. The girls were dressed up in pink or blue smocked dresses with stiff petticoats made by our Aunty Olive, and my brother wore a little suit jacket just like Dad's. His hair was slicked down with an oily hair cream that nearly made us all carsick on the windy roads into the city. The long drive was a challenge enough.

But then, sitting on cold wooden pews with our stiff petticoats scratching the back of our legs, was slow torture for country kids who were used to running free and staying active. I never could reconcile the ranting of the preacher with the Bible stories told to me by my Mother or Papa. I remember wondering why he seemed to be in such a bad mood about something. Looking back on these church visits, I am thankful now that we were not weekly attendees to these dramatic reminders that all was not well with the world and that somehow it had something to do with us.

My wonderful childhood was interrupted by my transition to high school in the big city (far away from my childhood paradise). It was a culture shock, in many ways, as I went to live with relatives in the city whose routine was to attend church every Sabbath. I don't remember much of the weekly sermons, as I had developed an excellent imagination and could pass the time by visiting far-away places in my mind. My parents sold the family farm and moved closer to our high school so that we could live at home. By the third year of high school, I was already interested in big ideas and deeper learning.

One quiet Sunday afternoon I found the book *Early Writings* by Ellen White, on the bookshelf in our lounge. I still remember pushing other books aside and choosing it. It was a God moment; my invisible 'Shepherd' seemed to guide me. The vision of *a people being led up a steep mountain* seemed to call me to join these battling adventurers and to one day cross the bridge into the 'Kingdom of God' where Jesus would finally welcome me home 'to dwell in the house of the Lord forever' — just like in the Psalm. In that moment, I decided to pursue the Christian life.

While my childhood was constantly nurtured by the love of family and the Christian truth shared through bedtime stories and early church experiences, it wasn't until I read this book that I took ownership of my spiritual journey. I asked for baptism when I was 15 years old and became fascinated with prophetic stories. In my final year at my secular high school, I rose to the challenge of suggesting a debate entitled "Is the Bible relevant to today's world?" My friends thought I would join the opposing side. I surprised them and my history teacher when I went on the defense. Our teacher diplomatically decided that there was no clear winner. Almost half of the class followed me into the corridor wanting to know more about the Bible. It was there, in that corridor, that I gave my first Bible study.

As humans, we often label ourselves with earthly titles. Even so, we are all His witnesses called to give account of the gifts He has blessed our lives with in order that all would know of their freedom and salvation in Jesus. Ephesians 2:10 says, "We have become his poetry, a recreated people that will fulfil the destiny he has given each of us, for we are joined to Jesus, the Anointed One. Even before we were born, God planned in advance our destiny and the good works we would do to fulfil it!" (The Passion Translation) This reality has always informed my life and my career as a teacher.

During my second year of teacher training, I wrote a poem that I titled "I am a Woman." Perhaps this announced my willingness not only to move on from childhood but to announce to my world that being a woman was no passive commitment. I remember two lines: "I am a woman. I will not be squeezed into a mold or labelled — prepare to contend with greater things than your expectations!" I believe this was the first time I had voiced my opinions about the injustice I had observed towards females within the wider constructs of society. Much later now, in part due to the untimely death of my brother and the impact that had on my family structure, I have realised that patriarchal values don't serve either gender in a way that is supportive of lifelong identity, autonomy, and wellbeing. These values distort God's view of how He perceives his male and female children.

Space doesn't permit me to give an account of the ways that my teaching career has developed my Christian understanding of the world, of others, and of the way God works. I have learned to expect the unexpected and to realise that while we are busy planning our lives and our teaching schedules, God will arrive in the unexpected circumstances of our day and fulfill those unspoken prayers. My teaching career has led me from focusing on primary education for six short years to over thirty years of work in the early childhood education sector both in Christian and secular settings. I am now working with beginning teachers as a lecturer in early childhood education, while also fulfilling a long-time goal of earning a PhD in leadership. "The Shepherd" remains a guiding metaphor for my leadership journey.

As I sit here on a Sunday afternoon at a Christian University in America, I am mindful that I am half a world away from my childhood home and my mountain — Mount Tenahau and the beautiful Rangitata River. Those beautiful days are only a memory. My aging father sits in his old leather chair fully knowing that his daughters are equally valued and equally loved, as was his only son. But both he, and those who remain, have lost dear ones that once walked the hills and valleys of our childhood home called "Drumheid."

The Shepherd Psalm remains a comfort as I look to the day when together we will "dwell in the house of the Lord forever." I have climbed many mountains real, and figurative, to achieve my goals, and to fulfil my meaning and purpose in life, both for now and for eternity. When I look back to the perspective I gained as a small child, I realise that the same God who leads me over many mountains and half-way across the world for His purposes, will one day bring me to stand before the Ancient of Days where ten thousand upon ten thousand's will minister to Him. There I will be, standing on tiptoes alongside all those women and children who I have loved along the way. People from every denomination, culture, tongue, tribe, and people will gather for that great day.

MEET THE AUTHOR

I am a Lecturer in Early Childhood Education at Avondale College of Higher Education in New South Wales Australia. My career up until the present day has been focused on primary and early childhood educational contexts where I have served in Christian and state settings as a classroom teacher, headmistress, and early childhood centre director. My current research interests focus on Early Childhood philosophy and educational leadership with a special focus on the arts and wellbeing as a way to enhance and strengthen communities. I have four adult children who are all leaders in their fields and who are a constant inspiration and joy to my life. I am honoured to have been accepted into the PhD Leadership programme led by Andrews University in the USA. I have met inspirational leaders from all over the world through this programme that continues to broaden my horizons for learning, ministry, and service. My faith, my family, and my friends provide a constant source of strength and encouragement to me and I consider myself truly blessed to be part of this wonderful supportive community.

RELATIONSHIPS:
LIVES WOVEN TOGETHER

Raquel Alves Espinhal Pereira

Living the second part of my earthly existence has led me to pursue a simpler way of life. However, simple is not simplistic. Rather than taking a more extensive, wider, and diluted mode, it became deeper and aimed at what is fundamental. In truth, this way of living is not new or innovative, but a turning back to what is essential — that which I cannot live without.

I believe that the bottom line of my existence is undoubtedly God. However, this God I believe is not distant, but One, who being relational in nature, is close and involved with His own creation, enabling relationships not only to the Godhead but among creatures themselves.

Relationships are lives woven together. Nevertheless, instead of being static, they are dynamic and always evolving. Being made in God's image, human beings find their relationships more fulfilling when they are founded on the recognition of God's love, from which commitment, trust, and forgiveness flow.

On that assumption, it is not difficult to understand the importance of the Ten Commandments God gave Israel, which then Jesus summarized for His followers: *"Love the Lord your God with all your heart and with all your soul and with all your strength and with all your mind and, love your neighbor as yourself."* (Luke 10:27, NIV) Love — God's love that is accepted and filling my life — is what characterizes my relationships with God, others, and myself.

WITH GOD

This relationship, which God initiated, is the basis for all other relationships. God's loving nature enables me to live as the beloved daughter of God. I am loved, not only as a doctrine I cherish in my mind, rocked by the infant lullaby, "Yes, Jesus loves me," but loved, in my innermost being. As the Psalmist puts it, "If your heart is broken, you'll find God right there; if you're kicked in the gut, he'll help you catch your breath." (Psalm 34:18, MSG) The assurance of being God's beloved awakens me to the fact that others are also the beloved children of God. Such realization helps me to see my fellow sojourners as equals in the same love.

My little step, enabled by God's grace, towards a positive response to His loving initiative, has brought me to this relationship. Nevertheless, even though it is personal, it is not a private relationship. I am one among God's people, and as such, my relationship with God will probably not get further or deeper than my relationships with others. In other words, my life in God will only flourish when shared in a community. One of the dimensions where this has become real to me is that it is in community where I am faced with my life's "blind spots" that need pruning. Oh, but it is so much easier said than done!

Living in this belovedness of God with others becomes life in mission — the mission of God, that of ". . . reconciling the world to Himself in Christ" (2 Cor. 5:19, NIV). Believing and accepting Jesus' supreme manifestation of godly love — by His life, death, and resurrection — we are not only reconciled but enabled to become reconcilers where we have been planted. This loving walk with God, initiated and enabled by His presence in me through His Spirit, is personal, communal, and missional.

WITH OTHERS

The relationship with others, in the upside-down realm of God's love, is characterized by vulnerability. But this is difficult, particularly for us women — known for being 'the weakest link', emotional or too sensitive, 'acting from the heart'; when we are constantly being invaded by commands and callings to prove ourselves, to excel, to be competitive and strong, even in the community of faith! Our model, Jesus, shows a different way of relating. It is what Henri Nouwen calls ". . . downward mobility. It is going to the bottom, staying behind the sets, and choosing the last place!"[21] Jesus' greatness consists in becoming and living as the lowest, and His life in me will bring forth that same attitude.

Love is certainly vulnerable in its essence. It risks not being understood and accepted. Love rises to its highest when it is at its lowest point. Genuinely loving others is a risky endeavor, as it implies looking first not to fulfill my agenda or interests, but to others and their needs. This is an impossible love to practice on my own, and it indeed requires a re-learning with Jesus how to live that out in my daily life in the midst of my context and circumstances.

Lately, I have been challenged about the ways this loving relationship with others is expressed. Forgiveness is one of them. I have been faced with my own shortcomings in this matter as I have been reading *The Amish Grace* by Donald B. Karybill et al. and *Unconditional?* by Brian Zahnd. Forgiveness, like love, is a decision rather than a feeling; and it is not the same as pardon or reconciliation. This faith expression says more about me than about what others do or fail to do. It does free me from holding on to others' wrongdoing, and creates space within me to experience God's forgiveness for my sins. Nevertheless, sometimes it is so much easier to hold on to familiar grudges than letting them go.

Also, there is the listening — that active attitude of not preparing my "smart" answer but really paying attention to what the other is saying and not saying, verbally and non-verbally. It takes re-learning as well, as I have been accustomed to my need for talking, sometimes just to fill the silence. The proportion in which God created us — double capacity to hear (two ears) than to talk (one mouth), as well as the fact that "listen" and "silent" use the same letters, regularly draws me to confess my need of God's continued work in me and the need for help from others to become a better listener.

Mutual aid is another means of expressing God's love to each other. I probably have blamed our western society's values of individualism and "doing it yourself" more than I should. The truth is that, in most cases, I get to my intended goals more quickly when alone. However, this prevents me from seeing the reality that I could go further when working together with others. Paul challenged Christ's followers: "Carry each other's burdens, and in this way, you will fulfill the law of Christ." (Gal. 6:2, NIV) It is the law of Christ — love — that compels us to live in this togetherness and mutual assistance.

---

21. Nouwen, Henri. "Downward Mobility." Henri Nouwen Society, 28 June 2017, 2 Apr. 2018, http://www.henrinouwen.org/meditation/downward-mobility/.

Loving relationships with others are only possible when one keeps allowing God to love them through us. It is not necessarily a common, popular, or easier way of living. However, going back to the idea of living under the mission (sub-mission), it is love, and not an obligation (burden), that compels us to care for each other, fulfilling the design in which God has made us — relationships. Yes, it implies vulnerability, humility, forgiveness, listening, and mutual assistance, but ultimately it is worthwhile.

WITH SELF

Being a difficult apprentice on this matter, I tremble even more as I write about this. I grew up hearing very often and in varied ways that it is wrong and ungodly to love oneself. Although society has evolved since then, in the 60s-70s, women in my culture were brought up to care, first and foremost, for others: the parents, the husband, the children, the needy in society, the people in the church. There was no place for the care of self, which was considered as selfish and un-Christian.

Even though I still struggle with those concepts sometimes, as they seem to be ingrained in me, I have started to understand that love of self is different from self-love. More than a play on words, it means that I need to un-learn being centered on myself and re-learn how to love myself as God loves me. It is when I start to see and care for myself as God does, that I am enabled to care for others in like manner. The reverse is also true: in loving others as God does, I learn more of what it means to care for myself as God's beloved.

Probably as a result of those misconceptions about the love of self, the way I perceived myself was associated with two dimensions of myself that continue to grow. The first one is distinguishing 'who I am' from being solely dependent on 'what I do' (and then on what I do not do). If I think, speak, and act justly or do them well, I am ok; if not, I am a terrible person. To a certain extent 'who I am' is related to 'what I do', but it cannot be dependent on it. My identity is who I am in God, through what Christ accomplished and His Spirit enables as a child of the Almighty God (2 Cor. 6:18), from whose love nothing can separate me. (Rom. 8:39)

The other dimension that usually distorts the way to loving ourselves as God does is the pleasing of others. Again, it is human to be liked, but when our way of looking and caring for ourselves is solely dependent on that, we live on a roller coaster without an escape. It may seem counterintuitive, but the thought always humbles me that God has started but not finished the work with me. That awareness becomes real when I regularly pray the Litany of Humility: "O Jesus, meek and humble of heart! Hear me. From the desire of being: esteemed, loved, sought after, honored, praised, preferred to others, consulted, approved. Deliver me, Jesus."[22]

NOT YET

My simple way of perceiving life — an interweave of relationships immersed in God's love — may sound too feminine for some. That will not be the first nor the last time I get that reaction. I do believe, though, that this is what Jesus — the most fully human being — evidenced in His life, in words and actions. So, while I journey towards that goal in following Him, I realize I have not yet attained it. In many cases, I am far from it, but using Paul's expression, "I press on toward the goal for the prize of the upward call of God in Christ Jesus." (Phil. 3:14, NASB).

To anyone who may identify with anything I have shared from my experience, I would like to say, using John Wesley's interpretation of King Jehu's phrase (on 2 Kings 10:15) in one of his sermons[23]: "If your heart is like my heart, take my hand" . . . and let us live and keep on learning to live in an ever-growing and deeper loving relationship with God, others, and ourselves.

MEET THE AUTHOR

My name is Raquel (Rachel), and I was born in Lisbon, Portugal. I completed a B.A. in Religion through EuNC/MNU, and an M.A. in Spiritual Formation through NNU. As EuNC Registrar, I work together with different people, mostly from European and CIS countries, towards the ministerial preparation of those who answer positively to God's call

---

22. Rafael Cardinal Merry del. Val, "Litany of Humility." Apple seeds. n.d., April 2, 2018, http://www.appleseeds.org/Lit_Humility.htm.

23. John Wesley, "Catholic Spirit," in *John Wesley's Sermons — An Anthology*, ed. Albert Outler and Richard Heitzenrater (Nashville: Abingdon Press, 1991), 300.

in their lives. I also have the privilege of coordinating the Nazarene literature endeavors in Portugal. It is a special joy to work with a team of translators, editors, proofreaders, and hopefully soon with authors, to make Wesleyan-holiness literature available to Portuguese readers. The sight, aroma, sound, and movement of the ocean bring me calmness and energy. A good book with relaxing music, or a friendly conversation, makes up good moments for me.

SNAPSHOTS OF FAITH

Lori Wilson

If faith is a journey, my experience has been anything but a straightforward one. With more twists, turns, and dead-ends than I could have imagined, even in hindsight it fails to converge into anything resembling a path. That there's been movement, I have no doubt. Progress? I hope so. Rich memories made along the way? Definitely.

I suspect this "not-path" isn't unique to my experience. For some rare mortals, life might follow a clear, linear trajectory from beginning to end; for most of us, though, surprises, detours, and confusion show up regularly along the way. The most sense we get to make is in the form of snapshots — understanding in the moment, perhaps some clarity in the rear-view mirror.

I don't offer a single story about my experience of faith. Instead, I'll lay out a series of sketches, brief reflections on themes that come to mind as I consider what it has meant to me to follow the mysterious, high-stakes adventure of faith.

ART

I'm a word person. I love to read them, listen to them, and speak them. Engaging with faith has, for me, always been a highly verbal process.

Then I gave birth to an artist. I did all I could to foster his creativity, and now he's returning the favor, generously.

He takes me to visit museums and art galleries, where we stand in silence before abstract paintings or acrylic sculptures that defy any sort of verbal articulation. Still, chills wash over me from head to toe. I've learned that vivid insight can penetrate and transform without a single word exchanged. My heart can be changed without my ever knowing what, exactly, happened.

My exclusive allegiance to the art of words crumbles. And my faith finds new and startling expression, beyond the confines of language.

AGENCY

Agency is all the rage in my professional circles. How do we empower and equip persons (and especially women) to effect change? Three elements, especially, promote agency:

- *Agency* itself is the inner confidence or determination that helps me instigate change.

- *Access to resources*, without which no amount of personal agency will move the needle.

- And *structures* that give me space to exercise even a bit of the agency I already possess.

In the corner of the evangelical world where I grew up, personal agency was a real thing. "I can do all things through Christ, who strengthens me," (Philippians 4:13, NKJV) weren't just words on a t-shirt. From a young age, I was taught that I had a great deal of control over my attitudes and behaviors; not only was I *able* to make the right choices, but I was accountable to the God of the universe for getting them right.

Heaven help us all when a child endowed with a sense of *agency* grows into a woman who discovers she's been barred from *access to resources* and empowering *structures*. [See *Leadership*, below.]

BIBLE

For a time in my 20s, I stopped reading the Bible. We'd spent decades together, but the text had gradually grown opaque to me; nothing new or compelling had surfaced for ages.

Then I found Kathleen Norris' *Amazing Grace: A Vocabulary of Faith*, and woke to the wonder of living words. The language of our Scriptures needn't be static; instead, it can become a potent force that opens our eyes to ever-new ways of seeing and being.

In all its vivid insight, the Bible now comes most alive to me through the voices of others. Reflections from saints long-gone invite me into the text's remarkable historic breadth and adaptability. Shared practices like *lectio divina* or *Midrash* foster imaginative reflection and reveal astonishing relevance for all walks of life.

Perhaps most significantly, during this season of my life, I'm privileged to hear Scripture read and interpreted by persons whose experience has been silenced for so long: women, persons of color, and my LGBTQ+ sisters and brothers. Their allegiance to texts that have historically been used as exclusionary tools speaks volumes to me. And their ingenious interpretations tease out significance I could never have found on my own.

In the give-and-take of Christian community, I've grown into a new discovery of the marvelous, chaotic, complexity of the Bible, and opening its pages once again feels like a bit of a hair-raising adventure.

CLOUD OF WITNESSES

Being a bookwormish sort of woman who asks uncomfortable questions, especially about faith, and especially in the wrong places, can be a straightforward path to loneliness. Over the years, though, I've found good company in what the writer to the Hebrews describes as the "great cloud of witnesses" (Hebrews 12:1, NIV).

One "cloud" holds the faithful ones who, over our long shared history, have charted their own unpredictable and sometimes subversive journeys. Theresa of Avila has been an outstanding companion: an intelligent, motivated woman of immense capacity who also found herself quite alone in the church of her day. Florence Nightingale, who captured my childhood imagination, continues to inspire me with her piercing questions about faith and vocation. And then there is Diet Eman, less well known, perhaps, but a clever, defiant woman whose faith drove her fierce energy into defying the Nazis in the Netherlands. In these women — and so many men and women like them — I have found the comfort of kindred spirits.

Another "cloud" is a much more recent invention, that human platform known as the World Wide Web. I won't challenge the significant (and growing) concerns about the impact the internet has on us as individuals and societies. I'm quite sure we've still got a lot to learn about this medium, and that at least some of it we'll have to learn the hard way. What I do have to say, however, is that I will be forever grateful for the way the internet has connected me to other Christians who identify with the unpredictable path on which I've found myself. It's given me a space to ask my uncomfortable questions, and face into ones I'd never have dreamt up on my own. This "cloud" has opened the door to new friendships and collaborations, to challenges and encouragements I could never have found anywhere else.

DAYENU

My daughter's first tattoo is a beautiful Hebrew word that means, "It would have been enough." It's a beautiful rendering of the refrain chanted during the Passover *seder*, reminding us of all the ways that God provided for the Israelites as they made their hasty escape from Egypt.

Dayenu tells a story: at the heart of our histories, we can find overwhelming generosity, if we choose to look for it. *Dayenu* teases out the narrative of grace, reminding us to watch for this thread in our own stories, and to celebrate when we find it. *Dayenu* is a revolutionary way of being in the world: a claim that our lives are grounded in abundance, and that gratitude is the only right response.

HOSPITALITY

I know, I know. You're thinking teacups and doilies.

But if you know me at all, you've heard me explain (probably with some degree of impatience) that this practice is about so much more than meals. Really. It's huge.

In the words of Christine Pohl, hospitality is about *making room*. And in my interpretation of her work, it's not just about making up the guest bed or setting another place it at the table, but about *making room* anywhere, any time.

How do I *make room* for someone else? Maybe I ask a question when I'd rather speak. Or listen to your perspective when I seriously disagree. Maybe I invite a person of color to participate in what was shaping up to be yet another all-white panel. Or simply sit down in the pew next to a stranger.

Christians have been known for their hospitality for millennia. Hospitality so radical, in fact, that some early Christians were criticized for their lack of standards, accused of accepting all comers. If the practice of hospitality will land me a place in line with this rich tradition, I'm in!

LEADERSHIP

I'm not great at math, but the basic equation for women of my generation and background goes something like this:

$$(\text{leadership ability} + \text{high degree of personal agency})$$
$$-$$
$$(\text{access to resources} + \text{empowering structures})$$
$$=$$
$$\text{something much} > \text{frustration}$$

Trusting that my fellow contributors have covered the question of women in leadership extensively, there's really no more for me to add.

RELATIONSHIPS

When my daughter was in middle school, I was trying to explain to her the "Billy Graham rule." The assumption, I explained, was that it was impossible for a man and woman to be in a relationship without experiencing sexual temptation and, eventually, caving to it.

I also explained how her dad and I weren't sure this was right, that sexualizing every friendship seemed to us fear-based and likely, in fact, to feed into the very problem it was supposed to solve. Also, frankly, it hadn't lined up at all with our lived experience. I had friends who were men and was trusting that I'd be able to keep it at just that — friendships.

"Of course," I added, "maybe women and men *can't* be just friends. It could turn out that I'm wrong on this."

"Um, Mom? I don't think so. Don't take this wrong, but I'm pretty sure you don't have what it takes to turn every one of your friendships into an affair."

RESTROOMS

Picture a Venn diagram: Christians who trained as scientists, and Christians who studied as theologians. Now imagine a conference that invites only those in the small overlap space between the two. You'll understand why, in all the years I did that kind of work, I never had to wait in a queue for the restroom.

MEET THE AUTHOR

The child of missionary parents, Lori grew up in northwestern Argentina. As an adult, she's made her home in Denver, Grand Rapids, and London. She offers writing, research, and facilitation services for non-profits, with a particular interest in conflict transformation. She and her husband enjoy reading, hiking, and traveling with their two adult children. Lori also makes a great piecrust.

BEING FEMALE

"*Patricia Yancey Martin is a professor of sociology who has studied gender and organisations for many years. She talks about the importance of 'catching the sayings and doings of gender', of identifying and talking about the ways that women and men relate to each other in practice, particularly in our instinctive reactions and unguarded moments. It's not enough to believe in or talk about the equality of women and men; we need to look at what we do and how we interact with each other. Are we really putting that equality into practice?*"

JENNY

CALL THE MIDWIFE

Sarah Winfrey

I may be the only person on the planet whose feminist awakening, or whatever you want to call it, started by reading "Call the Midwife." I'm okay with that.

I'm a reader. I always have been. Books have this way of getting inside of me, of showing me myself in a way that opens me to new possibilities. This one wasn't any different. I started watching the television show but, like any good reader, I figured the book would be better. I was right.

To grasp fully how this book opened up a whole new world for me, you have to understand the environment in which I grew up. I grew up "in the church," and the particular church my parents chose was mostly more conservative than we were. There was no requirement that women wear skirts all the time or keep their hair long, but some did. Some wore head coverings, many homeschooled their children out of fear of what public schools would teach them, and most of the women stayed home. If they couldn't stay home because of financial necessities, they longed to.

I don't want you to think that women weren't valued, because they were. Most had husbands who legitimately loved and cherished them. Some of their husbands would even laud them in front of the church, saying, "My wife thought of this . . ." or "Here's what my wife did this week."

They were loved, but they didn't have a voice. Women couldn't preach or teach, even if they were on stage with their husband speaking to teenagers. They couldn't even get up during the worship part of the service, where individuals stood and shared what God had taught them that week on a predetermined topic. Their husbands could share their wives' thoughts, but the women couldn't speak for themselves.

In that space, feminism didn't exist. It was pooh-poohed as a social movement that really didn't need to happen. Instead, the church taught that, if women only knew how much God loved them, they would be happy with the roles they were given in life. Feminism was only necessary outside of the church because those people didn't know how much they were loved.

I did my best to fit into this space until I became a mother. Even though I did well in school, I never chose a career because I assumed that I would be a mother and, as such, I would want to stay home with my kids. I assumed that I would feel fulfilled keeping house and home and little people together, being mom and wife with everything that entails.

Instead of being something that ordered and settled my life, though, motherhood came in like a whirlwind. It started in the hospital: they put that beautiful baby girl on my stomach and, instead of love, I felt a dull panic. I didn't know the first thing about babies! How could they give her to me, how could they expect me to keep something so small and helpless alive?

I know many parents go through that panic, but mine was different. It became a deep-seated terror that I was doing It. All. Wrong. I was afraid all the time. I slept, but only because I fell into bed exhausted every night. I'd wake in middle-of-the-night panics, sure that the baby was dead or that we'd lost her. My particular terror was that she wasn't eating enough, that she wouldn't grow and they'd take her away from me because I was clearly incapable of caring for an infant.

There's a lot to be said about that time. I wasn't depressed, but my significant postpartum anxiety was missed entirely by the half-assed questionnaires they gave me at my follow-up appointments. (Seriously, who tries to diagnose mental illness in people who just had a baby by asking, "Have your sleep habits changed recently?".)

I also don't have the personality that is best compatible with motherhood. I'm an introvert, and I like my alone time. More than that, I need it. When I don't get it, I crave it, and I start to check out, even when I'm around the people I love, because I just can't connect anymore. Also, I'm extra sensitive to things like bad smells, loud noises, lack of sleep, being interrupted and . . . well, you get the picture. None of these are bad things about me, but they definitely made motherhood harder.

So, I struggled through my first years of motherhood. We had a second child, and things got a little better, but that was mostly because I kept myself on a strict diet and exercise regime that kept the anxiety down to (mostly) a dull roar. I could function, but I wasn't happy.

Enter "Call the Midwife." I didn't expect to find myself in the book. Instead, I found a story that closely resembled my own.

For those not familiar with the story, "Call the Midwife" is about a group of student midwives who studied with nun-midwives in a poor area of London in the late 1950's. The book tells how a doctor trained the nuns because, otherwise, these impoverished women weren't getting any medical care. The area was largely Catholic, so most women literally had babies from the time they got married until they passed through menopause. The book tells of women who had 10, 12, even 15 or more children!

For years, women's health was largely ignored; what drew my eye and my heart was the book's description of the process of getting medical care for these women. Doctors were male, and they focused on health issues that were important to men. Even in wealthy families, women were allowed to die of easily treated conditions simply because those conditions were "women's issues."

Pregnancy, childbirth, and even infants were all considered women's issues. Think about it for a moment: men let their beloved wives and infants die simply because healthcare for women wasn't a value. Men died without heirs, wept through the night, and mourned over graves because they couldn't be bothered enough to invest in some basic health care for the women they loved and the babies they'd helped create. Many women — who died during pregnancy or childbirth — died of conditions that would be easy to detect and treat (that ARE, now, easy to detect and treat) simply because they were women.

On an unconscious level, I saw parallels to my situation. My own postpartum anxiety went undiagnosed because no one bothered to assess me fully. They didn't try to ask the right questions to make sure that I was doing okay and to figure out if there was anything else that I needed.

Did this happen because I'm a woman? I don't know, but I have my suspicions. I was always given the questionnaires with an attitude of, "We have to give these out. You're probably fine. Just fill it out so we can cover our asses." No one ever invited me to talk about how I felt. They never asked how I was doing or if there was anything else. 'Postpartum depression' had become something that they had to screen for, so they did it, but they did it perfunctorily and without a lot of actual care.

I can't prove this, but if the same percentage of men were struggling with something as women do with PPD/A, I'm sure there would be more than a basic questionnaire at their follow-up visits. There would be studies and sit-downs and all sorts of things.

Instead, I diagnosed myself and did my best to take care of myself. I also read, "Call the Midwife." I read the book, and I felt like my eyes opened. All of a sudden, I could see things that I'd never seen before. Feminism wasn't a non-issue, it was a huge issue. It wasn't, as I'd always been taught, a bunch of women who wanted to be exactly like men. It was women who wanted to be treated as equals to men, who wanted their health and education and comfort to be just as important to society as that of the men around them.

Women wanted to be heard.

Once I saw that, I couldn't look past the enforced silence of the women I'd grown up with. I believe they were loved, but I also believe that love was lacking. Even children want to be heard; they often find comfort by simply being able to say the things they see and experience. They want to tell their side of the story and have someone listen, even if they ultimately don't get what they want.

To deny women a voice is to deny them love. To say, "You can't speak," is to say, "You don't matter," or maybe, "You don't matter as much as I do." Moreover, to say that a loving God would deny women — all women, everywhere, no matter what — the chance to speak, to preach and teach, to share themselves publicly, is to say that God isn't as loving as he could be.

I haven't made sense of it all yet. I still process, on a daily basis, the things that I was taught, the things that are ingrained so deeply inside of me, and the things I now believe to be true. I still wonder if I'm wrong. I still feel guilty and ashamed and like I'm getting too big for my britches. But I now know this: I can't believe in a God who doesn't want to hear what I have to say, and who hasn't given me these things to say not only for myself and my family, but for whoever happens to hear them. I tried that, and I can't do it anymore.

MEET THE AUTHOR

Sarah Winfrey is a freelance blogger, life coach, and mala maker. She lives with her family in the shadow of the Rocky Mountains and spends as much time outside as possible. She tries to write a few words for herself every day, and sometimes she shares them with others.

Space for We

Crimson Sparrow

Trigger Warning: Marital Rape

When presented with the opportunity to share something even remotely personal, does anyone else feel the need to run wildly through a gamut of emotions with her arms flailing like she's being chased by bees?

"I want to contribute!" Enthusiasm cheers.

But no sooner than she does, Inadequacy quails, "I have nothing worthwhile to say."

"What difference will my story make anyway?" adds Discouragement discouragingly.

"But this is important!" Determination grumps.

Then Avoidance calls, and the next thing I know I've forgotten what I was even talking about . . .

What was I talking about?

Oh, yes — maybe it is just me, but if God didn't find ways to put my feet to the fire on a regular basis, I surely would not do anything even moderately vulnerable in my life. Ever.

For example, I do not want to share my story as a woman of faith. I do not want to write because my story seems somehow unacceptable — at least to what my friends call the "churchy church." I do not really want to describe the neglect, the abuse, the objectification, the mixed messages, the impossible standards, or the other insane things that were and still are being created, sanctioned, or enabled by my church community and its posture in the world. I do not want to talk about it because it seems that the men in power — and by sheer numbers alone, it *is* men who are in control in our churches and our world — do not seem to want to hear it. To be candid, there are plenty of women who do not seem to want to hear it either. And I am a coward; I do not fancy telling people things I imagine they do not want to hear. That is the Jonah in me.

And yet.

And yet there is a little girl in me who just wants to prattle on in a little-girl way about her childlike experience of God.

I wonder, do we have space in the church, in the Christian faith, for *all* of what it means to be a woman? Is there space for the gamut of emotions? Is there room for our childlike-but-not-ladylike enthusiasm, freedom, wonder, and imagination? What about the Jonah-like struggles or the Deborah-like prophetic leadership; is there a place for these? Are we allowed to have classically masculine as well as overtly feminine thoughts, parts, experiences, gifts, and graces? What about the trauma and recovery parts of our stories?

Because I know I have it all. I think we all do.

I grew up an eclectic tomboy. I did not like dolls or playing house. I did not have dreams of getting married and having babies. I dreamed of being an architect. I built forts out of whatever materials I could find, usually spare cinder blocks, random pieces of 2x4, and mud. I liked climbing on the swing set as if it were a jungle gym. I was particularly interested in inspecting dead animals to see what their bones looked like. I also loved to wear dresses; I consistently got my skirt hem caught in the chain of my dirt bike as I rode in the open fields surrounding our neighborhood.

When I didn't want to be an architect, I wanted to be a singer, an actress, an attorney, and eventually a writer. Interestingly, no one ever asked me what I wanted to be when I grew up. If anyone had asked, they might have found that the only thing I was truly and deeply and consistently passionate about, the one thing that drove and shaped my interest in anything and everything else was God. From the time I was about four years old all I wanted to do was learn about, love, and serve the God who loved me enough to die for me.

In my church, I was taught that a woman's place was in submission to men. There were no women in pastoral leadership. Women were the secretaries or receptionists at church. They were allowed to teach children, to facilitate women's ministries, and to sing on stage during worship services. I even got to sing a special or two myself when I was a child — though I was never invited to do so again after singing a rap song one Sunday morning.

Note to self: There is apparently not a lot of space for rap music in a white Christian worship service. Not even worshipful rap music.

So I started playing guitar.

Men are the Head, or so I was taught. And while it was never explicitly spelled out that woman was created for man — well, not until I was 33 years old and single, anyway — I got the message loud and clear: My purpose as a woman was completely based on and for men, namely, being 'helpful' and 'submissive' to them. It was also clear that my helpfulness correlated somehow to both servitude and sexual desirability. (Ick!) Submissiveness, on the other hand, seemed to have something to do with constant selflessness, perpetual sacrifice, and the spiritual discipline of avoiding any appearance of having a personal opinion. It also seemed to entail saying "no" to a man's sexual advances before marriage (because men can't control themselves) and refraining from saying "no" to my husband for happily ever after.

In all actuality, what I was taught was that my real value as a woman was about sex. First, it was about my being desirable for, but not actually having, sex. My virginity was The Pearl of Great Price. It was my gift to my husband — my only gift, my most valuable gift. When I gave it away, I gave my body away; it was no longer my own but my husband's. And if I tampered with it before then, I would lose any value that I had.

This meant, secondarily, that I had to work for any worth beyond virginity. Instructions to accomplish this included "keeping myself up" or otherwise marketing myself to my husband. It was also necessary to participate in sex as much as possible, whenever the husband so desired, however the husband so desired.

I was a glorified, interactive blow-up doll.

But it was worse than that: My spirituality as a woman — my fundamental ability to *be Christian*, to love and serve Christ — was based entirely on loving and serving men and/or one man in particular.

This milieu is one of those things that I do not want to share about my faith journey. As I remember it, I grow angry — not angry at any one man or even at men in general (though I have been guilty of both). I am angry because I feel the great weight of objectification on my wild-horse, little-girl soul. I am not a doll, an object, or a tool. Any story in which I am cast as such feels like . . . well, like hell. It feels like suffocation. It feels like death. And any part of me that has the power to push up and gasp for air does so — kicking, screaming, crying, calling, begging for rescue and worth.

I grow angry now, but I was taught back then that anger was a sin — particularly in women. An angry woman was a woman who was not submitting to authority. An angry woman was a rebellious woman, a woman who was not honoring God. Because I loved and wanted to honor God in and above all things, I did not grow angry as a young person. I turned and let the waters of fundamentalist theology and dehumanized sexuality swallow up my identity and my soul. As they swirled over my head and crushed the breath from my chest, I simply closed my eyes and *died*.

That is what a good Christian is supposed to do, right? Take up your cross?[24] Die to self? Doesn't the Bible say, "Whoever loses their life for me will find it"?[25]

But the Bible also says that the wages of *sin* is death,[26] and this is not the compensation package Jesus was encouraging us to take. It is the one from which he came to save us! In fact, the Spirit of God warns us, in many vibrant metaphors, about those things that cultivate and bear the fruit of death.[27]

Death fruit: Imagine the Evil Queen's poisoned apple — only worse. Imagine something tainted, something rotting. Imagine something meant to penetrate your soul and rot you from the inside out. Can you imagine what that *tastes like*?

I can. It tastes like the quiet tears of a little girl who has been told that she is a blow-up doll, created for a man somewhere, encouraged to submit to his use as her offering to God. Honestly, it tastes like vomit. And it made me *want* to die.

---

24. Matt 10:38, 16:24, Mark 8:34, Luke 9:23 (NIV).

25. Matt 10:39, 16:25 Mark 8:35, Luke 9:24, 17:33, John 12:25.

26. Romans 6:23

27. Romans 7:5, James 1:14-15

I heard my first story about human sex trafficking at age 35 or so. If you have not seen the documentary *Nefarious: Merchant of Souls*, it exposes the epidemic of sex trafficking around the world as well as in the United States. Disclaimer: It is graphic. And it is *disturbing*. What was most disturbing to me was the way it felt like *my life as a Christian woman*. I felt like they were somehow telling *my* story. I had been sold into the slavery of objectification, packaged, and marketed by the church.

I was married at 18. I don't know how to say this gently except to say that my then-husband was not often concerned about gaining my consent before sex. He did not even care whether I was conscious at the time. I didn't know that a husband could rape his wife; her body belonged to him. But it *felt* like rape.

Conveniently, modernity and the church happily agreed at the time that feelings were suspect and simply not to be trusted. The consensus between these two groups was that emotion was both illogical and irrational — and thereby wholly worthless. It didn't matter what one *felt*. What mattered were the facts.

And the facts were that we were active in our church. I got my wish to be a singer as I played guitar and sang in the worship band (no more rap for me). My husband worked at the sound booth for worship services. We both had successful careers outside of the church. We had a cute little house and nice, new cars. We had a big-screen TV and a hot tub in the backyard, and we always tithed our 10+ percent. We looked holy and happy. And my husband was addicted to pornography, and I wanted to die.

I had been granted my wish to be an actress: I had been cast in a perpetual porn flick that I could not stop and from which I could not escape. Some days I tried to be a good little porn star. Other days, death had eaten away too much of my soul. It was on one of the latter days that I finally prayed a prayer to God, overdosed on prescription medication, and slipped into a coma.

Death fruit.

Produced not just by my church.

This level of objectification has been woven into the very fabric of western language and culture. Parker J. Palmer writes:

The Latin root of "objective" means "to put against, to oppose." In German, its literal translation is "standing-over-against-ness." This image uncovers . . . a quality of modern knowledge: it puts us in an adversary relationship with each other and our world . . . We value knowledge that enables us to coerce the world into meeting our needs — no matter how much violence we must do . . . The root of "reality" is the Latin *res,* meaning a property, a possession, a thing — a meaning most clearly seen in our term "real estate." This image suggests another quality of modern knowledge: we seek to know reality in order to lay claim to things, to own and control them . . . Of course, ownership and control are possible only in relation to objects or things. One cannot own a living being until, by a twist of mind, one turns it into a piece of property, a slave, thus gaining the dominance modern knowing strives for. Knowledge that gives us real estate must turn all its subjects — including nature and human beings — into objective things.[28]

My life is a flesh-and-blood parable to his point: When we objectify ourselves, each other, and the world, we bear the fruit of death.

I say "we" intentionally. Men are victims as well as perpetrators in this scenario. Men, too, have had their personhood villainized and shamed, their hearts and emotions neglected and condemned. My ex-husband was at the mercy of his addiction; he was a tool in the hands of a sex god who was not interested in his humanity, his values, or his life. He now serves that god in prison, a physical representation of his spiritual and emotional bondage.

And it gets worse. Palmer suggests that when we objectify our world, we are fundamentally incapable of learning how to love. When I examine my own story, I see it. Somewhere, at some point, human sexuality was reduced to nothing more than the sex act, and we were all diminished in the process. James K. A. Smith argues that we have falsely dichotomized *eros,* or desire, and *agape,* a selfless or Christian love. A better understanding of *agape* is rightly ordered *eros.*[29] However, the result of this dichotomy is the objectification of an aspect of the love of God. *Eros* has been transformed into a thing, an object, to be boxed up and placed on a shelf when unwanted, then pulled out and blown-up at will.

When sexuality is only about sex, instead of being a part of our personhood, its voice is silenced; it can no longer whisper to us of our unique identity or call to us to participate in something larger than self — in creation,

---

28. Parker J. Palmer, *To Know As We Are Known* (New York, NY: Harper One, 1993), 23-24.
29. James K. A. Smith, *You Are What You Love* (Grand Rapids, MI: Brazos Press, 2016), 9.

relationship, mutuality, and the mystery of God. Sex becomes an idol, a burden, a vie for power, an addiction, a performance, and a right. It bears the fruit of death. No wonder so many Christian young people pray, asking God to take their sexuality away — the way I asked God to take away my life.

Thankfully, God does not seem interested in merely granting us our requests like a genie in a bottle, another object we pull off the shelf to use as we see fit. God seems more interested in responding to our hearts — like a lover, like a *person* who *loves*. At least, that is how God showed up with me. There, in the midst of a distorted theology, God met me; the idol erected by my church could not stand. The god of man, modernity, and objectification could not stop the real God, the God of Sarah, Hagar, and Mary as well as Abraham, Isaac, and Jacob.

God met me, and God saved me. God did not just wake me from my coma but proceeded to deliver me from an abusive marriage and an abusive church culture. Like the Hebrews were delivered from Egypt, God led me safely and miraculously into a para-church ministry based on the 12 Step Tradition. There I met, for the first time, people who were *real*, people who listened and shared, people who sought to humanize and love. They practiced confession. They practiced repentance. They practiced admitting when they were wrong! They practiced, in specific, tangible ways: daily surrender to, connecting with, and honoring God by honoring self and others.

God saved me from a distorted view of God. And God saved me from a distorted view of self. Through this church for recovering humans, God taught me how to be a whole person, wholly known and wholly loved.

"As precious as the blood of Christ is," God whispered to me, "that is how precious *you are*."

I was created for God.

I must practice cherishing myself as an act of worship. I must practice cherishing myself as a part of my covenant of life. I must practice cherishing myself as a practice of cherishing God.

And it is a *practice*; I will never be accomplished or done. I practice it daily by practicing the 12 Steps: The steps God used to deliver me from abuse, the steps God used to send me back to school, and the steps God used to articulate a call on my life to ministry. I practice these steps with my new church community. I practice these steps in my home. I practice these steps at my job even when it requires me to resign. I cannot again bear death fruit. I cannot again serve other gods.

In fact, Step 12 compels me to share my story with others that has compelled me to share my story with you.

Because the truth is, there probably isn't space sometimes in our churches for us — not for women, not for people, not for God. Sometimes we find ourselves in a faith without space, a relationship without space, a job without space, and we bear the fruit of death. We may give up on God, on ourselves, on the church. But Christianity is not *Christian* without *us*.

As precious as the blood of Christ is, that is how precious we are.

We are needed in the church. We are needed in ministry. We are needed in the conversation about sexuality if we are ever to participate with God in restoring it to wholeness and relationship and life. Our hearts are needed if we are to know the fullness of God and the fullness of God's redemption. So where there are those who do not want to listen, let them turn away. And where idols steal our space, may God establish the church for recovering humanity, the church for recovering the world.

MEET THE AUTHOR

Crimson Sparrow *spent 15 years in business, finance, and human resources and 2 years on a Master's in Counseling before responding to a call to ministry, graduating with an MA in Spiritual Formation and Discipleship instead. She now offers counseling, spiritual direction, consultation, and retreat services for those who desire a deeper connection with and experience of God. "Though I may be the 'least of these' in this life, a sparrow, I am of great value to my Father (Matt 10:29-31). The evidence of that value is the blood that was shed for me, that covers me and that ushered me into a relationship with God (Eph 2:13). As precious as that sacrifice was, that is how precious I am. And so the Crimson Sparrow is a symbol of my humility, God's love, my value, Christ's blood, and our Covenant of Life." She still plays guitar and has been known to rap upon occasion. Maybe someday she will be a writer: www. confessionsofachurchgirl.blogspot.com*

MODESTY CULTURE AND WOMEN IN MINISTRY: A POSTMODERN RESPONSE

Melissa Wass

Originally presented at WTS on March 2, 2017

"Modest," they say, "is hottest." And just who are they, you may ask? Well, they are a cadre of individuals from Christian musician Rebecca St. James in her devotional book *Pure,* to popular speaker and author Nancy DeMoss in her series "Modesty: Does God Really Care What I Wear?," to John Piper, who addresses the topic again and again in his blog "Desiring God," to just about any folks engaged in a discussion on biblical womanhood. The phrase and the modesty culture that spawned it have become ubiquitous in church circles. Church leaders can read books on how to create a culture of modesty in their youth groups (or in the greater church), and ladies' groups can learn how to proselytize the mindset of modesty culture. For all the discussion of skirt length, tank tops, and cleavage, the very real problem this creates for women in ministry is ignored. Female ministers find themselves caught between very arbitrary rules on what is appropriate dress with its attending theology and the necessity of standing on a raised platform every Sunday to proclaim the word of God.

What exactly is the theology that attends modesty culture and why is it so problematic for women in ministry? Firstly, modesty culture teaches that women must dress in accord with a somewhat arbitrary dress code to avoid being a sexual temptation to men. And arbitrary is the best term, as what is considered provocative dress varies greatly. In some churches, sleeveless tops or trousers are deemed inappropriate. Skirt length is another issue on which there is much variation. And heaven forbid a busty woman attempt to preach the gospel, as such, curves must be kept firmly under wraps so as not to be a distraction to churchmen. Revealing clothing, women are told, can cause men to fall into the sin of lust. For women in ministry, this is a deeply disturbing teaching, as the goal of the ministry, especially in holiness churches, is to help church members learn to live above sin, not to cause more of it.

Secondly, inherent in the idea that a woman must cover her body properly to avoid tempting men is the further idea that a woman's body is in itself a temptation. When Tertullian wrote "On the Apparel of Women," he began by placing the onus of the Fall firmly on women and he called women the devil's gateway. "And do you not know that you are Eve? God's sentence hangs still over all your sex and His punishment weighs down upon you. You are the devil's gateway; you are she who first violated the forbidden tree and broke the law of God. It was you who coaxed your way around him whom the devil had not the force to attack."[30]

For Tertullian, women have destroyed men by coaxing them into sin. Augustine says, "What is the difference whether it is in a wife or a mother, it is still Eve the temptress that we must beware of in any woman. . . ." [31] While this may sound over the top to modern ears, how is it different from what the Duggar girls, steeped in modesty culture, have said: "We realize that our body is a special gift from God and that He intends for it to be shared only with our future husband . . . We avoid low-cut, cleavage-showing, gaping, or bare-shouldered tops; and when needed, we wear an undershirt. We try to make it a habit to always cover the top of our shirt with our hand when we bend over."[32]

This statement is, in fact, the same in that women's bodies are viewed as the temptation. Effectively, the female form becomes sinful in its ability to lead men into lust, just as Eve the temptress did in the garden. A Tertullian believes that women are the devil's gateway for men, John Piper confirms,

---

30. Tertullian, *On the Apparel of Women*, Chapter 1, Kindle Book.

31. Saint Augustine, *De Genesi contra Manichaeos, De genesi ad litteram liber imperfectus*, trans. Gilles Pelland (Palermo: Edizioni Augustinus, 1992) Vol. 9, pp 5-9.

32. Alex Rees "Duggar Ladies Have Code Words For "Immodest Women," So Their Menfolk Can Avoid Sinful Temptation," Cosmopolitan, January 06, 2017, Accessed February 21, 2017. http://www.cosmopolitan.com/entertainment/news/a21626/duggar-girls-book-quotes/

"Clothes must be chosen, not merely on the basis of whether other women will find an outfit "cute," but whether the message the clothing sends to men is sexually restrained. None of this is easy or convenient, but obedience to God is never easy or convenient."[33] All of this reinforces modesty culture's teaching that a Christian woman's clothing must cover her sinfully tempting body adequately or she will cause men to stumble. If her clothing fails the test, she is not being obedient to God. She is leading men into sin, and, for a woman in ministry, she has become an impediment to the spiritual growth of men in her congregation.

If we examine the situation created by modesty culture for women in ministry, we see some convergence with Jean-Luc Marion's discussion of the idol. To understand the idol, however, we will also have to examine the icon. The two, Marion says, "can be approached only in the antagonism that . . . unites" them.[34] Marion describes the idol as something that cannot help but be seen, as the woman in ministry is seen when she presents the word of God from the platform on Sunday mornings.[35] "The idol," he says, "presents itself to man's gaze in order that representation, and hence knowledge, can seize hold of it."[36] This gaze is what characterizes the idol, the gaze that "forms a stage in the spectacle" by whatever the idol may be ". . . thing, man, woman, or god."[37][38] "The idol thus acts as a mirror, not as a portrait: a mirror that reflects the gaze's scope."[39] The idol, Marion suggests, is idolatrous inasmuch as the man gazing upon it measures divinity and idolatry.[40]

Contrasting with the idol is the icon, which "does not result from a vision, but provokes one."[41] Marion says, "whereas the idol results from the gaze that aims at it, the icon summons sight in letting the visible . . . be saturated little

---

33. John Piper, "Is Feminine Modesty about Sex and Lust?," Desiring God blog, July 5, 2014, accessed Feb. 2017. http://www.desiringgod.org/articles/is-feminine-modesty-about-sex.

34. Jean-Luc Marion, God without Being: Hors-Texte, Second Edition, ed. David Tracy, trans. Thomas A. Carlson (Chicago: University of Chicago Press, 1991), 7.

35. Marion, God without Being, 9.

36. Marion, God without Being, 10.

37. Marion, God without Being, 11.

38. Marion, God without Being, 12.

39. Marion, God without Being, 12-14.

40. Marion, God without Being, 14.

41. Marion, God without Being, 17.

by little with the invisible."[42] The icon is the image of the invisible God, the Imago Dei, that a female minister represents when she, in her humanity, stands before her congregation, but it is the Imago Dei as understood by the viewer. It is not necessarily a true representation of the Imago Dei in her, but is the version of it projected by the one who sees her. Also, ". . . the icon and the idol are not at all determined as beings against other beings, since the same beings (statues, names, etc.) can pass from one rank to the other. The icon and the idol determine two manners of being for beings, not two classes of beings."[43] That is to say, that it is possible for the same woman to be viewed by one man as an idol and by another as an icon, depending solely upon the perspective of the man. If he views her as an icon, he views her as an object, but one that sheds the divine light of the Image of God into his perception, as he understands it. She will only be able to show him as much of the Imago Dei as he is willing to see because the focus of the entire operation is based on him and his gaze.

Even if she becomes the mystic vehicle by which he views the light of the divine, she is still an object, serving the purpose of worship to the extent he decides she serves that purpose. Worse yet, does he view women as Eve the temptress, as sinful bodies requiring covering to keep him from sin? Then he sees the idol before him and measures the Imago Dei represented in her as no greater than the sin he believes she embodies. She is defined by his gaze and how he uses it upon her, having no agency of her own. Her humanity and the Imago Dei she possesses are entirely defined by the male gaze.

But this is not how it was in the beginning. When Eve was presented to Adam by God, Adam first saw her and then exclaimed, "Bone of my bones and flesh of my flesh."[44] The similarity to "the face to face encounter with the other" that Emmanuel Levinas describes provides a basis for discussion in the context of women in ministry.[45] "In the beginning," Levinas says, "was the human relationship." For Levinas, the other person, just by appearing in view, calls to the viewer, addresses the viewer, even without saying anything. But Levinas takes into account not only the gaze of the viewer but also of the other. In the situation of a woman preaching on the platform, she calls the congregation's

42. Marion, God without Being, 17.

43. Marion, *God without Being*, 8.

44. Genesis 2:23 [NRSV]

45. Bettina Bergo, "Emmanuel Levinas," Stanford Encyclopedia of Philosophy, July 23, 2006, https://plato.stanford.edu/entries/levinas/

attention to her by presenting herself to their view and, even as they respond by looking towards her, she gazes at them in the first moments of the face-to-face encounter — interrogating and imploring them to, according to Levinas, not kill her. "This command and supplication occurs because human faces impact us as affective moments or, what Levinas calls interruptions."[46] This is exactly what happened in the Genesis encounter: Adam is presented with Eve, views her, even as she views him, and even as he realizes she is other and not him, also recognizes that she is in some way like him — flesh of my flesh and bone of my bone. The other impacts with a force, Levinas says, and I can see that the other is a human being like me, or as the author of Genesis says "flesh of my flesh and bone of my bone."[47] Recognizing the humanity in the other as he does, Adam indicates his acceptance of Eve and, even as he recognizes her otherness, chooses to accept her, not kill her.

Metaphorically, the request of 'do not kill me' for the female preacher on the platform requires the congregation to acknowledge the Imago Dei represented in her humanity. Refusal to recognize the Imago Dei within her effectively murders her humanity, making her an object and forcing her to be viewed as either Marion's idol or his icon. While the icon can have a positive effect on a congregation in some way, the idol cannot, but both are still objects. Those viewing her have removed her humanity. Oh, she still has it, but they refuse to acknowledge it. She loses her ability to define herself and instead is defined by their gaze, their perspective, and, in modesty culture, by their assessment of her perceived modesty. By refusing to acknowledge the humanity of the other, they effectively murder her.

In contrast, recognition and acceptance of the other, as Adam recognized and accepted Eve, begins the relationship between pastor and congregation and bases it in the perceived similarities between the two. "I can see that another human being is 'like me,' acts like me, appears to be the mast of her conscious life."[48] The demand for this recognition "is part of the intrinsic relationality. With the response comes the beginning of language as dialogue."[49] This allows the minister to begin the proclamation of the Word of God in the sermon on an equal relational footing with the congregation. She is not Eve the Temptress.

46. Bettina Bergo, "Emmanuel Levinas"
47. Bettina Bergo, "Emmanuel Levinas"
48. Bettina Bergo, "Emmanuel Levinas"
49. Bettina Bergo, "Emmanuel Levinas"

She is not the object of the icon. She is the created with equality in the Image of God. Moreover, she is in relationship to the congregation — the body of Christ.

Modesty culture would reduce the female minister to the role of idol — reflecting whatever wants and desires that her congregation projects upon her. At best, it makes her an icon — reflecting the Image of God as much as her congregation recognizes it. At very best, the congregation moves from the stilted views of modesty culture into a model of biblical relationship. When they encounter the pastor face to face on Sunday morning, they recognize and affirm her humanity and the Image of God in which she was created, realizing that she is like them and beginning the dialogue of the sermon on equal footing.

MEET THE AUTHOR

Currently, I am working towards a PhD in Theology at the University of Dayton while also fulfilling the roles of wife, mother, and grandmother. Formerly, I was a children's pastor in the Church of the Nazarene. To manage the stress of school and family, I enjoy knitting, gardening, keeping a bullet journal, and am learning the skill of sketch note taking. This article was my first piece for an academic conference, presented in 2017 at the Wesley Theological Society Meeting at Asbury Theological Seminary.

Preaching, Teaching, and Sharing Home

Bethany Sollereder

I begin with a healthy dose of scepticism about how helpful my viewpoint might be. For one thing, my experience only constitutes my own singular and unrepeatable viewpoint. I don't represent my entire sex or gender, and my experiences as a comparatively wealthy (when compared globally, at least!) Western, white Christian person might overwhelm the effect of gender. Second, I don't have anything to compare my experiences with: there is no control group to measure how my experiences would have been different if I had not been born a woman. I can guess at other people's experiences from what they relate, but that is only the empathic work of the imagination. Finally, figuring out the real cause of things is complex. If someone treated me in a way I found demeaning or empowering, can I tell if it happened to me because I am a woman, because I am young, because I am assertive ("Bethany is not bossy; she has good leadership qualities" our family friend used to say from about the time I was 3 years old), or simply because of some particular experience the other person was having that day?

With all those caveats in place, let me say unambiguously that the vast majority of where faith and gender intersect has, for me, been positive. I grew up hating traditional gender roles. Not because they were strictly enforced in my family, but because I had three brothers (two older and one younger) and competition was the main pastime. Quite naturally, my brothers would take opportunities to point out the differences in dress, size, and strength between themselves and me, and I resented those differences, especially when it came to sports. Male attire at parties allowed one to join an impromptu game of soccer at a family gathering. Pretty dresses and fancy shoes did not, so I refused to wear them, in favour of trousers and trainers. I was also utterly uninterested in children, cooking, or fashion. I did martial arts and weightlifting. And I read books. Lots of books!

I became a Christian in my teens under the influence of charismatic evangelicals for whom the imperative of obedience to the call of God overrode any constrictions of traditional gender roles. If you were called to preach, pray, pastor, or lead a church, then to disobey God was worse than to offend "human tradition." While I often felt that being a woman brought significant disadvantages in the general culture, the church was always a place I felt empowered. I started preaching when I was 16, and have never stopped.

Due to my circumstances and dispositions, gendered teaching in churches that others found restrictive had little effect on me. As a devoted tomboy, verses like 1 Timothy 2:9 (NIV) "I also want the women to dress modestly, with decency and propriety, adorning themselves, not with elaborate hairstyles or gold or pearls or expensive clothes but with good deeds" — suited me just fine as long as propriety did not exclude jeans and a hoodie. (I am probably still, at heart, this way and Oxford's fabulous cultural bubble where everyone naturally obeys Thumper's mother's rule in regard to clothing: "If you don't have anything nice to say, don't say anything at all" is perfect.)

As a single woman, I equally skipped past many of the other negative cultural impacts that evangelical Christianity can have on women. I had no husband to submit to, and since my family did not go to church, there was no one to take the place of authority. In church, I typically had all the freedom I wanted and all the opportunities for leadership and teaching that I desired. (The only thing I have never yet managed to get going is my dream of having a women's group called "Babes, Bibles, and Broadswords": a mix of Scriptural study and fencing with German longswords. This mostly hasn't happened because the equipment for swordplay is expensive, but if anyone ever feels a call to support a cutting-edge ministry . . .)

The one place of friction I vividly remember was that I wanted to be a professor — and a professor of theology at that! The problem was not that there were formal restrictions on this, but that there were no role models. The peculiarity of my educational path meant that in elementary school all my teachers were women with only one exception. Then in Junior High, it was an even mix of men and women. In High School, the teachers were predominantly men. At the small Bible College, I attended there was not one female professor — only one programme assistant who had not yet finished her master's degree, who was brought in explicitly because of her gender. I tacitly absorbed the lesson: women are never as good at teaching as men — at least, not when it comes to higher education.

It was not until I took my Master's degree that I saw powerful examples of women teaching. At Regent College in Vancouver, women like Maxine Hancock, Sarah Williams, and Diane Stinton, demonstrated incisive scholarship, inspirational teaching, and pastoral care that were confidently feminine without being matronly or stridently angry. I finally had the role models I needed that helped me come to peace entirely with being a woman — my sex did not restrict this dream of being a great teacher. I've never looked back.

There have been some demeaning experiences in the Christian academy: the man at the conference dinner who told a whole table of men and me that, "the problem is, you just can't get women to see sense!" Or the comment I received after a small discussion group at a Christian conference on theology in which I was the only person with any theological training, and therefore had spoken up: "I'd forgotten how forthright North American women are!" However, I always assumed that this only showed that these particular men were offensive, and never extended it to structural biases against me. The amount of encouragement, mentorship, and friendship I have received from men has always far outweighed the very occasional bad experiences.

Far more frustrating than my own encounters, are the times I have watched others run up against brick walls in faith communities. I remember going to a lunchtime seminar with a friend run by a conservative Anglican group. My friend had a call to ordained ministry, and they simply shut her down. We left and sat on a couch and cried together. I remember the shared sense of absolute powerlessness and the confusion of the call of God running up against imposed restrictions. Recently, I met with a brilliant young woman, a top-notch biologist, who for both gender and professional reasons is seen as suspect at her conservative evangelical church. I've seen the uphill battles she will have to fight if she stays, yet deeply respect the pull of loyalty that keeps her from quietly going to another church. I pray for her in light of having no good counsel to offer.

Also, as a no-longer-youth-group-aged single woman, fitting into the church can

be difficult. Friends my age are married and involved in child rearing while I am busy scribbling away at the latest publication (as usual, behind schedule and under words . . .). But, I have also found deep friendships in the community of faith that transcend demographics — older friends, younger friends, married friends, and single friends.

Especially precious have been the families with porous boundaries who have allowed me to join them during my sojourns in various cities as I follow academic positions around the world. Not having children is sometimes a deep grief (I changed my longstanding views about not liking children after living with a family with a two-year-old). In several circumstances, the extra time that comes from not having family commitments has allowed me to be part of other people's families in small ways, giving and receiving care and creating a sense of home. I babysit, do magic tricks, listen to long stories about the latest in Minecraft, stay up-to-date on Octonauts and Moana lyrics, join dinner, write stories, make a meal, lead field trips, and share in the joys and hardships of parenthood to just a small degree. It is within the hospitality of the church and the hospitality of brothers and sisters in Christ that the ache for a family of my own has been eased. I think the ease with which I have been able to join alongside families in this way has been greatly facilitated by being a woman: I think it would be difficult to do this as a single man.

Theologically, one thing that has never bothered me has been gendered language about God or traditional gendered language in creeds or biblical passages. If Jesus came down "for us men and for our salvation" and was "made man", I don't have any problem including myself in the inclusive sense of Man. If men can be the Bride of Christ, I can be a "true son" of God when singing "Be Thou My Vision" (originally translated by a woman anyway). In academic writing, God is never He. However, in devotional practice, the use of He and Him adds a more personal element that I treasure. If needed, I can always supplement with Julian of Norwich and the motherly Christ. I do sometimes wonder if, in the push to move to gender neutral language in all these areas, if we miss a sense of being drawn into a whole ecclesial community that is bigger than our distinctions.

MEET THE AUTHOR

Bethany Sollereder is a postdoctoral fellow in Science and Religion at the University of Oxford. She was born and raised in Edmonton, Canada. She moved to England to pursue doctoral studies and has remained there. Her study is primarily on evolution and the problem of evil, but speaks on a wide range of theological and biblical questions. She has written numerous popular pieces on the BioLogos website and in The Christian Century. She was also written numerous academic pieces in journals including Theology and Science, Perspectives on Science and Christian Faith, and The Expository Times.

IS THAT WHAT GOD REALLY THINKS?

Bobbie Jo Morrell

(Names have been changed to protect privacy)

Nine days after Al "prayed the prayer" over me — though my own internal prayer sounded more like, "OK, Jesus, I'll try this thing and see what happens" — I went to a Laborer's Conference put on by a national campus ministry organization. It was 1983, and I was a junior in college. Christine and I jumped in my Pinto and drove to St. Joseph, Missouri for the weekend.

The conference was great in many ways, but on the drive back home to Iowa, I ran into a major obstacle to this following Jesus thing.

Driving across Iowa isn't, perhaps, the most exciting thing to do in March, and about halfway home the two women in the car behind us in our little caravan of Christian students buzzed by, flashing a handwritten sign that said, "Tag! You're it!"

This sparked a vigorous game of highway leapfrog among the three cars of women, with the passengers writing new signs for each pass.

So far, I thought, this Christian thing was fun! So I looked ahead to the fourth car, which had led the way the whole trip, and thought it was a shame that they were missing out on the fun. "OK, let's catch the guys!" I said, punching up the Pinto's accelerator.

Christine's response came like a slap in the face. "No. Let the men lead."

I remember staring at her open-mouthed for a very long time, though it couldn't have been too long since I did not drive off the road.

"What? What?"

My friend Christine was an extroverted, brilliant, natural leader (and a former shot putter to boot), but now she looked uncomfortable and uncertain.

The game of tag forgotten, my friend tried to explain the teaching on men leading and women submitting. She clearly didn't like it herself, but she cast herself as "not being good at submission" and spoke of how she needed to work on it.

I, a severe introvert and natural back-of-the-room wallflower, was gobsmacked. And very confused.

Not long after this, the whole group pulled off to fuel up, and a few sprinkles of rain reminded me how badly I needed new windshield wipers. Now, my Dad taught me to maintain my own car. I changed my own oil, my own spark plugs, my own distributor cap, and of course, my own wiper blades. Just takes a minute.

So I was caught by surprise when, at my announcement about the wipers, all four of the young men in the lead car surrounded my Pinto and began to remove my wiper blades. They didn't speak to me; indeed, they seemed to ignore me completely when I tried to intervene as they were making hash out of a simple process.

Christine could see me fuming. "They are just trying to be helpful," she said.

I did her the favor of not responding to this, and for friendship's sake, refrained from using my martial arts skills on the boys to get them away from my car, though I was vibrating from the effort.

The rest of the trip to Ames was subdued, but once I got into my room and closed the door, I gave God an earful.

"Is that what you think about women, God?!" I shouted. "That we are weak and helpless and should submit to being looked down on and ignored?! That we are second-class citizens?! Is that really what you think?! Because if it is, I am outta here!"

I went on in that vein for some time until exhausted I subsided into disgruntled silence. And in that silence, I felt a Presence; a calm, loving, and rather amused Presence. The words I felt with it were, "Wait and see. I am here."

"OK," I replied, still a little grim, "we'll see."

A little background here. I didn't grow up in a conservative Christian/ Evangelical context, but with a simple rural morality combined with "poor farmer egalitarianism." Our little farm barely paid for itself, and my Mom, who took shop instead of home economics in high school in 1949, was as busy with baling hay and hauling feed as my Dad. My earliest memories are of "driving the tractor" on Dad's lap, helping split firewood with a hatchet while camping in the Colorado Rockies, running all over the farmyard, bounding through wheat and beet fields, and chasing horses in the pastures.

So nature was my first spiritual guide, with little distinction for gender. Then in junior high, I encountered my first "theology instructor" without quite knowing it: J.R.R. Tolkien, through *The Hobbit*, *The Lord of the Rings*, and *The Silmarillion*. Tolkien clearly understood the spirituality of nature. His stories awoke so many longings in my soul! I marveled at the richness and beauty of Middle Earth. Evil I saw there too, recognizing it from where I had already met it here in the real world. I learned about honor, courage, loyalty, and fortitude. I desperately wished that I could go there, to be a part of a great quest.

So then, that one day after microbiology class, Christine asked me what I thought about God. I found myself quoting Tolkien. At length.

Then I began reading the Bible, just as I had read *The Silmarillion*, from the beginning. Here was a universe created in a glorious symphony of words; the earth flooded, then saved; the Red Sea parted and a pillar of fire that led the people through. It was the same kind of world as Tolkien wrought: full of beauty and darkness, resisting evil and giving in to it, and turning again. Messy and glorious and real.

I found the same thing in the Gospels: prophecies fulfilled, prophecies spoken; fish and bread multiplied profusely, mysteriously; people of all kinds healed; this Jesus guy walking on the boisterous sea as though it were the smoothest highway. I recognized what kind of story it was: a bold rescue mission deep in enemy territory. Real danger — torture and death — was necessary to forge the passage out of prison for those trapped. I was one of the prisoners that Jesus had gone to such lengths to set free so that I could journey with him.

Jesus wasn't just offering me eternal bliss in some afterlife, but inviting me to join a great and dangerous quest. Jesus stood before me, offering his hand. He wanted me on his team, and all my shame and darkness was not enough to keep me from him.

So why on earth would Jesus take me on his team just to tell me to sit on the bench and shut up?

As I looked around in that time and place, I saw no churches in which women spoke, taught, or preached. Our ministry organization wouldn't let Becky, the women's ministry head, teach, or speak before mixed groups. (I told her that the ones who were missing out the most were the young men who never heard her wisdom). I remember what a huge deal it was when Cheryl, a staff intern, was allowed to introduce speakers at a mixed gathering.

Then as I re-read the gospels, paying close attention to the women in the stories and how Jesus related to them, a very different picture emerged. Jesus treated women as equals in the midst of a culture that valued them on par with livestock, a radically counter-cultural attitude.

Jewish men were considered ritually unclean if they touched menstruating women, but Jesus not only healed the woman with the flow of blood (Luke 8, Matthew 9) but stopped in front of the crowd of people to loudly point out that she had touched him and been healed. Then Jesus proceeded immediately into the house of a synagogue official to touch and heal his daughter.

At dinner at a Pharisee's house, a woman widely known and ostracized in the town as a "sinner" came to Jesus to weep at his feet, wipe them with her hair, and pour perfume on them (Luke 7). Jesus not only welcomed and returned her love; he flaunted her actions as a rebuke to the lack of love of the Pharisee.

Jesus was counter-cultural in a variety of ways when he discussed theology at a well in the middle of the day with a Samaritan woman (John 4). When the disciples returned, they were most alarmed to find that he was not following the "Billy Graham rule."

Jesus didn't care. He taught women, touched women, healed women, and loved women. Over and over again, he rebuked the religious leaders and his disciples for devaluing women. Women loved and followed and listened to Jesus, and provided most of the funding for his ministry. Women were the last to stand by Jesus at the crucifixion and the first to seek for him at the resurrection.

As I read these things, I heard the Presence whisper, "How about that?"

"Wow, God. That's really different."

Yes, that's the Jesus who called me to be on his team, who I still want to follow, even into darkness and danger. I trust that God, and not the fragile-ego facsimile that gets uptight if women say something out loud or know how to fix their own car.

I was (still am!) incredibly confused at how people who take Jesus and the Bible so seriously could come to those hierarchical conclusions. Even so, I continued to hang out with my friends. They were my community. I rolled my eyes a lot and gained a reputation for being somewhat rebellious. (For example, I refused to share "the Bridge" illustration with complete strangers.) But my friends were on Jesus' team too, and God would help me in the midst of all our human shortsightedness, right?

In the years since then, I have journeyed far (it has been epic!), but whenever my confusion, rage, depression, fear, stubbornness, and past hurts collide with other people — especially Christians who are confused, scared, abusive, angry, narcissistic, and just plain mean — I always come back to this: God is bigger than me, my past, other people, whole cultures, worlds, or the universe. What appears as an insurmountable obstacle to me is a tiny crack in the sidewalk to God. And Jesus picked me for his team anyway.

MEET THE AUTHOR

Born an Ozark hillbilly, Bobbie Jo discovered the Colorado Rockies at an early age. After sojourning across the high plains through childhood, college, and an early career in agronomy, she returned to the mountains to earn her MA in counseling and become, over time, a spiritual director. She leads hiking groups, spends time solo backpacking the Colorado Trail, and is starting up an organization to lead contemplative retreats in nature (more information at ShadowHorse.org). Bobbie is also a writer, and working on memoirs of her adventures in following Jesus through the Evangelical church.

Stop Making the Tea

Jenny Baker

My husband, Jonny, started making sourdough bread three years ago when our granddaughter Flo was still in the womb. He named his sourdough starter 'Baby Baker Bump' in her honour and on Sunday, he took her a loaf of his bread when we went to visit. The next morning, her mum cut her a slice for breakfast, and Flo said, "Grandad made that! It was so kind of him!" My heart melts at her sweetness, but I am also fiercely proud that she has men in her life who are baking for her and that it is her normal. Our family loves food and takes any excuse to gather around the table. During her life, she will feast on dishes prepared by her dad, her Grandad, her uncle and great uncles, as well as by the women in the family.

I grew up in a very different context as part of the Brethren Church, a denomination which prescribed very distinct roles for men and women based on their understanding of the Bible. It was a world where men made decisions while women made the tea. The ideal woman was submissive and silent, a devoted mother and housewife, looking after the children and the domestic details, so her husband was free to follow his calling. As a teenager, and then a student, I discovered feminism, and found myself swinging like a pendulum between two very different feelings about my Christian faith. Some days I thought that if that narrow world was what God wanted, then I would knuckle down and suppress my yearnings to lead; other days I thought that if that was what God wanted, and then I wanted nothing to do with God.

267

Fortunately, the church I attended helped me discover a very different, egalitarian reading of the biblical texts. I discovered that there were women in the Bible who were leaders and prophets, who had agency and courage, who disrupted the status quo and caused holy trouble. When I got married, my husband and I committed to sharing work, domestic duties, and parenting equally. We job-shared when our boys were young so we each got to spend days at home with them when they were small, and for the last 30 years have split things evenly between us which has allowed us all to thrive. This has also enabled me to hold onto my faith.

Whether gender is shaped by nature or nurture is a debate that continues to this day. Personally, I think it's a complex mix of the two. But there is no doubt that most aspects of gender are constructed by the way we are socialised and the role models we experience as we are growing up in our families, from the media, from schools, churches, and life around us. There are many different ways of being a woman or a man; no one size fits all, no 'real' masculinity or femininity that trumps everything else. I've done a lot of thinking and reading over the years about women, men, and faith; but the pattern of gender roles that I experienced during my formative years has been surprisingly hard to shake off. Several years ago, I read the story of Bluebeard and was completely poleaxed by my reaction to it.

In summary, Bluebeard is a man who is outwardly charming, but his blue beard suggests that something is not quite right. He seduces a young woman and takes her to be his wife. One day he goes out hunting and gives her the keys to his castle. He tells her she can go into any room except for the one that is opened by the smallest key. The woman and her sisters set off to explore, and eventually, they come to the last door in the castle. They open it with the smallest key, and inside they find the corpses of Bluebeard's former wives. They slam the door shut and lock it again in fear of Bluebeard's return, but the key starts weeping blood, threatening to give them away. The young woman scrubs the key to try and get rid of the blood, but to no avail, and so she hides it in her wardrobe where the blood slowly seeps into all her clothes. Bluebeard comes home, discovers what she has done, and declares that it is her turn to be killed.

It's a menacing story, and I was shocked when I realised that my gut reaction to it was, "She should have done what she was told." Effectively, I was saying that the woman should have ignored her instinct to investigate and explore, and she should have obeyed her abusive husband even though that put her life at risk. I thought I was enlightened and educated; my reaction took me entirely by surprise. Why was there such a disconnect between my thinking and my instinctive response? What was going on?

Patricia Yancey Martin is a professor of sociology who has studied gender and organisations for many years. She talks about the importance of 'catching the sayings and doings of gender', of identifying and talking about the ways that women and men relate to each other in practice, particularly in our instinctive reactions and unguarded moments. It's not enough to believe in or talk about the equality of women and men; we need to look at what we do and how we interact with each other. Are we really putting that equality into practice? Catching my response to the Bluebeard story made me realise how deep the gender indoctrination of my childhood had gone.

It's easy to think of gender as a personal attribute, something that belongs to an individual that they carry with them when they enter an organisation or institution like a church, business, or workplace. But churches, workplaces, and businesses are not gender-neutral. In every institution, there are expectations and assumptions about what men do here, how they behave, and how they are treated; and there are different expectations and assumptions for how women ought to behave and how they fit in.

Institutions such as churches and workplaces are gendered places that in turn help to construct gender; they give us patterns for norms of how women and men should behave, which then impact how we live. We practice gender in these institutions in the way that we live out our beliefs about men and women in our actions and words, the 'literal sayings and doings of gender in real time and place'. So, for example:

- Men who refer to adult women at church as 'girls' are practising gender, by infantilizing women in the language they choose.

- Women who work better for a male manager, and resist being managed by another woman, are practising gender by favouring the leadership of men.

- Men who only mentor or network with other men at work or church are practising gender by acting on the belief that having that type of working relationship with a woman is risky.

- Women who always clear up after other people at work or church are practicing gender by playing a role that traditionally mothers do for their families.

In all these examples, people are enacting their beliefs about women and men in their words and behaviour. Work and church are not neutral places that men and women enter and leave without it having any impact on their experience of being men and women. The practising of gender at work and church helps to shape who we are and how we feel about ourselves as women and men.

Learning to catch the sayings and doings of gender in contexts like church, to reflect on how we behave as women and how we interact with men and with other women, is important because it shows us whether we are genuinely living out the equality that God wants for us, or whether we're sabotaging ourselves by continuing patterns of behaviour that keep us locked in gender stereotypes and fulfilling other people's expectations of how we should behave as women.

Let me give you one example. When I was growing up, I saw the women at church cleaning and tidying, making coffee and tea, organising the catering, and looking after the children. That's my natural instinct too when I'm in a context where that kind of work needs to be done. I'm good at it, and I believe that if everyone contributes to that kind of domestic work then the load is shared, and it gets done more quickly. The trouble is that not everyone contributes; look around most churches and it's the women who are the tidiers, the cleaners, the bakers, and the coffee makers. And so I've decided that I'm no longer going to play that game.

The trouble is that all of those activities are gendered in that, on the whole, it is women who do them most readily and most often. When they are performed by women at church or at work, they trigger associations in other people of the times and places when they have experienced women doing those same things — and that's usually in a home context where women are carers, mothers, or nurturers. When women perform those activities at work or church, at some level, they can draw us out of the context we're in and make us feel like we are playing the roles of carer, mother, or nurturer instead of the work or ministry roles that we are there to do.

My advice to women who want to learn to lead or to be taken seriously as leaders in the church or at work is to stop making the tea, stop tidying up after everyone, stop baking cakes, and stop smoothing things over for everyone else, at least for a season. You will feel guilty for a time, but you will learn to see yourself and your contribution in a different light.

My friend is Director of HR for a Christian NGO which highly values strong working relationships. The executive team meets together for an evening meal from time to time, to enable those relationships to develop with each other. It is usually the women on the team who are asked to host the meal and cook for everyone, so rather than being fully engaged in the evening; they are engineering the meal, clearing the table, serving the food, and looking after everyone else. On the rare occasions when the men on the team have hosted, their wives have cooked the meal while the men engage fully in the conversation. My friend has decided that she will no longer host those meals, nor make cakes for their team meetings, because of the gendered assumptions it produces in her colleagues and in herself.

Another friend is a vicar who had an appraisal a few months ago. The archdeacon and area dean, both men, were going to do her appraisal at her house and so she invited them to lunch beforehand, as an instinctive gesture of hospitality. She realised afterwards how much that pushed her into a caring mode, making sure their needs were met, a feeling which ran on into the appraisal itself. The act of caring for them made her feel primarily like a carer. Instead of going into the meeting first and foremost as a competent leader, she felt wrong-footed because of how providing the meal made her feel and how she sensed it changed their perception of her.

We need a good level of self-awareness in contexts like this, to ask what's really going on, and to be aware of the dynamics of the situation. But until everyone shares in the domestic work that makes life comfortable, some of us need to stop making the tea at work, stop clearing up after other people, stop organising lunches for the team and baking cakes — so that we can engage at work or church as leaders and ministers — without a whole load of baggage getting in the way.

MEET THE AUTHOR

Jenny Baker is Chief Operating Officer for Redthread, a charity enabling young people to lead healthy, safe, and happy lives. She is the author of Equals — Exploring Gender Equality in All Areas of Life *published by SPCK and* Run for Your Life *published by Pitch Publishing. She has Master's Degree in Gender Studies and Voluntary Sector Management and is a member of Grace, an alternative worship community in London. Jenny is a keen runner, cyclist, and swimmer and has run six marathons. She blogs at www. jennybaker.org.uk, and you can find her on Twitter @runningjenbaker.*

IGNORING OUR VOICES

Bridget Blinn-Spears

I was twelve when we joined a Vineyard church in Arlington, Texas. By then, I had occasionally noticed boys noticing me. They noticed the newly (very) curvy lines of my body, especially when I wore a turtleneck and jeans. Noticing being noticed gave me thrilling feelings of both excitement and fear, so most of the time I wore baggy t-shirts that didn't draw attention.

My parents were always far more aware of my well-developed body than I was. They were also well aware that the youth group at our new church included an astonishing number of attractive and talented high school boys. My interactions with those boys consisted of little more than spirited discussions about politics, pop culture, or sometimes Jesus. Still, when I was included in a trip to the Vineyard mothership in Anaheim as a homeschooled high school freshman, my dad made sure to come along as a chaperone.

I don't remember discussing the details of the trip, but I do remember intuiting that my parents felt like I needed extra supervision because the older boys would also be on this trip. My parents would have said that it was not that they didn't trust me. Rather, they didn't trust the boys. My parents need not have worried — none of the boys seemed remotely interested in me romantically or otherwise.

My first experiences in prayer ministry came during that trip when I prayed for the other girls in my hotel room late into the night. The theme of the conference was "Doin' the Stuff" (because it was the nineties and abbreviated words were in vogue). The "Stuff" was following the way of Jesus in ministry.

There was no gender distinction around who had the power to pray for healing or wholeness. Each night when we got back to our hotel room, we laid hands on each other's heads, shoulders, and backs and prayed fervently for the healing of relationship wounds. Relationships with parents, with boyfriends, with best friends; each of us had something broken that was touched and healed on that trip. So, apart from some parental overprotection and relatively minor inculcation with modesty culture, my gender mattered very little in my church experience throughout my high school and young adult years.

I went away to college and later attended law school. Unexpectedly, after several adventures with Youth With A Mission (YWAM), my sister became a pastor in our church. I don't think she was the first woman I saw preach in that pulpit, but I know she is the first one I remember. She wasn't the lead pastor — her pastoral role focused primarily on young adults — but she was a respected voice in our little community.

The Vineyard officially released a white paper on women in leadership in 2006. By then I had seen women included at all levels of leadership. Although the three lead pastors of my congregation were all male, the elders of the church included both men and women (Although I think only married couples were included during my younger years). Women from the pulpit. Women led worship, in the drums-and-electric-guitar style characteristic of Vineyard music. Women taught classes. Women spoke out the words they received from the Spirit, laid hands on the sick, sad, and lonely, led ministries, and were mostly viewed as equals. (At least the married, cisgender, straight women were considered equals.) Our loving community viewed single women as missing something and they constantly encouraged us toward marriage.

Finally, to the great delight of our church family, I married in 2011. I left singlehood behind at the ripe old age of 33. My marriage was a bit of a modern fairy tale: I reconnected with my very first elementary school crush on Facebook. He came as a package deal that included an amazing, adorable (and complicated) little boy. My husband's shared custody of my stepson meant we had to move to North Carolina.

After a few bumps in the road, we found a Vineyard church that met on both Saturday nights and Sunday mornings. This helped us maximize attendance when my husband wasn't working, and when we had time with our little boy. On Sunday mornings, our tiny new church rarely had more than 50 adults in attendance. When we began attending regularly, the lead pastor was bi-vocational; spending his weekdays in an IT job and his weekends at church. When we met with him to learn about the history of the church, he mentioned that all the elders were men and he explained that their primary job was to hold him accountable. He also noted that the church's bylaws prohibited having a woman as a lead pastor, something he said might merit revision given the Vineyard's public position on gender equality in leadership. However, it wasn't a priority since he was currently serving as the lead pastor.

Well aware of my propensity to seem like a know-it-all, I brushed aside the small voice in my head that noted the position paper was more than five years old and that accountability is not solely the province of men. Little did I know how prophetic that little voice would turn out to be.

My husband and I were on the liberal end of the diverse spectrum drawn to the Vineyard's "everybody plays" ministry style, and "really good band" worship music. My husband's best friend (and best man at our wedding) was gay and we both had several friends in the LGBTQ community. Although the Vineyard had remained silent on equality at that point, I knew most of those attending viewed homosexuality as a sin. However, I also had years invested in the Vineyard movement and believed we could make a home as well as a difference through our loving influence there. I knew people encountered the Holy Spirit in Vineyard churches. I had met her there myself (although I would have used masculine pronouns for the Spirit then). Also, I knew my husband and I needed as much of the Spirit as we could soak up.

It did not take long for us to plug fully into our new community. We joined small groups. I regularly prayed for our new friends by laying on hands and speaking holy words of encouragement and redemption. I was invited to lead the prayer ministry team, training and coordinating the lay ministers who prayed for congregants at the end of each service. During this time, we had three babies in rapid succession — the first in 2012, the second in 2014, and the third just ten-and-a-half months later in January 2015. Our church community brought us casseroles and baby blankets and welcomed each of our tiny offspring with joy and compassion for our exhaustion.

Our deepening calling to social justice increased our heightened tension with our church as our family grew. Over the next few years, several important things happened: Vineyard USA released a white paper on pastoring LGBT individuals in August of 2014; the U.S. Supreme Court issued a decision on marriage equality in June of 2015; one of my younger brothers came out to me in October 2015; and the North Carolina legislature introduced a bill in 2016 that restricted bathroom usage to the gender assigned on individuals' birth certificates.

Our church had remarkable diversity in age, race, and socioeconomic status, but when it came to equality for our LGBTQ siblings, we were the vocal minority. We tried to be gentle but firm in stating our disagreement with the traditional interpretation of "the" six verses in the Bible. Struck by the dissonance between the approaches to the Bible in the position paper on women in leadership and the paper on LGBT equality, we grappled with how we could share our deep love and respect for the full witness of Scripture and our deeper love and respect for the One we were attempting to follow.

I was called into a number of meetings with our lead pastor and, later, with his successor, explaining that while I loved and respected the leadership in our local church and the association of Vineyard churches more broadly, I would not agree to be silent when I saw injustice or disagreed with the church's approach to loving the world. I would not muzzle or modify my view of truth on social media or in any other venue.

Our church experienced another leadership transition when the lead pastor and his wife left to plant a church in their upper-middle-class white neighborhood. Our economically challenged, diverse congregation promoted our associate pastor who inherited me in my leadership role. I felt a little sorry for him as he sat across from me at lunch. He was attempting to navigate the pressure he was getting some members of the congregation who insisted that I publicly support the association's theological position and my calm insistence they should speak to me directly, rather than speaking through him. I was not going to make it easy on him by resigning and I was not going to compromise my conscience by relenting. He was in a hard place.

By mid-2015, we were down to three elders: the husband of a worship leader, an engineer, and our former pastor. It was a weird time. We tried to support our former pastor's church plant despite our grave misgivings about the wisdom of dividing such a small, diverse community to minister to the upper-middle-class who could easily commute anywhere they chose.

We had deep friendships with our new lead pastor, one of our worship leaders and her husband (who was one of the elders), and a few others. We were all in the same small group. The inclusive views my husband and I occasionally shared no longer shocked people, even if they disagreed with us. We felt like we were growing spiritually and solidifying relationships and community. However, over time, I occasionally picked up on weird vibes between our pastor and one of our friends. There was nothing overt. I could not definitively pointed to anything to prove something was off. I was not an elder and I did not have a clear enough feeling to merit bringing it up with anyone.

We still had no women elders. No women had been considered for the lead pastor role, and no women were in a position to hold the pastor accountable in community with others. So, I was sad and disappointed, but not entirely surprised, when our pastor and a friend confessed to having crossed emotional and physical lines in their relationship.

The church limped along through the summer and fall. The offending pastor was fired. The church discussed the implementation of the "Billy Graham" rule that required male and female members to never be alone together. I pointed out that Graham's rule adds an unnecessary sexual charge to any male/female interaction, and it does nothing at all for those who are attracted to their own gender. Eventually, that conversation got dropped as other practicalities became more pressing.

Throughout the fall, our clothes closet continued to provide for the kids in the neighborhood. Our food pantry continued to provide needed groceries to our neighbors as well as for some of our church friends. Our former pastor continued his role as one of two remaining elders and he began to lay the foundation for shutting down the church. The leadership team included both men and women. However, the elders had decision-making power. Our former pastor seemed to be entirely blind to any conflict of interest inherent in his pastoring a nearby church plant while providing guidance to a congregation with deeper connections and resources.

After announcing to the leadership team that he felt led to close the church, our former pastor finally involved regional leadership (a husband and wife team) from the association. The regional leaders met with the two elders on one evening and the leadership team on the next. Our former pastor did not attend the leadership meeting in which we repeated our view that the church was called to continue its ministry in its current location in this diverse neighborhood. This neighborhood included kids and their moms who walked to church from the nearby apartments. It included those who volunteered in the food pantry and organized the clothes closet, and those who fed and clothed their kids in part from those activities.

Once again, we were in the minority, but it seemed like our voices were being heard. The regional leaders, like us, believed the church wasn't finished yet. However, as the regional leaders departed for a long-planned trip to Europe, it became clear that nothing we had said mattered. We had consistently (but carefully) communicated our perspective only to leadership to avoid causing dissension in the congregation. Sadly, our words had been largely ignored.

After the leadership meeting with the regional leaders, we understood that one of our elders planned to share both perspectives with the congregation to help explain that sometimes seemingly contrary views can be reconciled. The elder felt we would all need to weigh what we heard and determine our own path. Late at night, before our final Sunday service, that elder emailed the leadership team to inform us that they would not be sharing both views.

I sincerely believed that the failure to explain the full range of perspectives was wrong. I texted both elders as soon as I read the email and then spoke to both before the service began. They stated that it was merciful to "protect the flock from whiplash." They felt that as the local elders they had autonomy not bound by regional leadership. I was struck by the injustice of two middle-class white men deciding to dismantle a community by failing to inform them that anyone had advocated for its survival. When I tried to point out that, in this instance, that their "protection" was actually deception, and that we could trust the Lord to shepherd his flock, to speak and care for his own, I was entirely shut down.

One image our regional leadership had shared was that of a clear line going into a hospital patient that filled the patient with lifeblood. Our former pastor denounced their view as "planting a nuclear bomb" in our congregation and insisted that it was more merciful to proceed with shutting down the church.

As I asked him to reconsider his position, I stood almost on tiptoe. I felt my lack of standing and authority in my short height, and my higher voice while carefully modulating my tone. Our conversation was fraught with tension. Despite our friendship, he seemed unable to engage with me in any way except defensiveness. As I explained that sharing only one view was the equivalent of euthanizing a patient who could heal to avoid their theoretical future suffering, and preventing the patient from deciding whether they wanted to work through that suffering to achieve healing and growth. I felt like I was speaking to a statue. Our former pastor stood a full head taller than I did. When he chose to break eye contact, he looked straight over my head, shutting me out entirely. Eventually, he simply walked around me and executed his plan.

When I look back on that day, I realized that this interaction is steeped in the long tradition of ignoring and silencing inconvenient female voices. That foundation is undergirded with a church structure that refused to allow women a seat at the table where decisions were made. Would having women elders have made a difference in accountability before lines were crossed? Would having women elders have made a difference in ensuring the congregation understood the perspectives in favor and against shutting down their church? There is no way to be sure.

In the end, the congregation testified about the work God has done in that congregation and most never learned that anyone was asked to consider whether there might still be life there. They remained in the dark. They were not trusted with the ability to hear and weigh the options for themselves. They were left with the impression that they could only proceed in one direction. They were not allowed to "do the stuff."

Our church building was sold, the profits distributed to several causes, including the new church plant in the suburbs. The congregation scattered. Some went to other churches, some joined the church plant, and some, went nowhere. Currently, the sanctuary is now a grocery store, the Sunday school a hookah bar.

We found a new church home by way of an invitation at the Wild Goose Festival where we were invited to a progressive community of faith where social justice is valued and no one is excluded. My husband and I are not in the minority there. Women are fully equal and nothing bars them from any leadership roles.

When I consider the role my gender has played in my faith, I cannot help but wonder if the relatively new, and not fully accepted idea of women in leadership, along with my loud and annoying advocacy for the rights of the LGBTQ community combined to prevent the privileged male leadership from hearing me. If I had been an elder, would it have been different? If any woman had been an elder, would it have been different? I will never know.

Meet the Author

Bridget A. Blinn-Spears sometimes calls herself a blood cell in the Body of Christ. She is a mom of four, an employment lawyer, an avid reader (now largely through the medium of audiobooks), a Two on the Enneagram, and an oldest child with a dozen younger siblings ranging in age from their late teens to late thirties. She and her husband, Brian, are covenant partners at Umstead Park United Church of Christ in Raleigh. Bridget and her family can often be found exploring the breweries around the Triangle.

EQUALITY

"My faith in the beautiful boundary-breaking, system-toppling, radical-healing message of Jesus is stronger than ever. However, year after year I have begun to lose faith that the systems we currently have will truly change in the ways we desperately need. There are far too many of my sisters with so much fire, beauty, wisdom, and healing to bring who are stuck in systems that treat them as 'less than,' silence their voice, patronize their ideas, and squelch their gifts. They are not 'less than!'"

KATHY

WATERS OF FAITH

Libby Tedder Hugus

"Tell the faith stories to your children, so the next generation knows them, even the children yet to be born, and they in turn will tell their children. So each generation should set its hope anew on God, not forgetting the glorious miracles . . ." (Paraphrase, Psalm 78)

In my childhood home there hung a frame with four different pictures of my mother. She's wearing the same clothes, and it is clearly during the same occasion — but the expressions on her face are wildly different. Four very expressive moments in time captured the same event: my mother while preaching. Behind a pulpit. In a church. With authority and as the photographs revealed, *very* animated. I can still hear the inflections and cadence with which she preaches, although we currently live continents apart.

In the water in which I swam through my childhood, I was heavily buoyed by the experience of women. Women giving voice to the experience of faith, leading others to find nourishment, influencing the spiritual health of others. Spirited, passionate, humorous, story-saturated, zealous, emotional, stubborn, boundaried, and compassionate. All of these characterized the faith experience of my mother and seeped into my bones, flowing through my consciousness to raise me up to float wide-eyed and curious on the current of God's wider story. I was intertwined with the story of God as told by my mother and grandmothers before her. One daughter in a long and complicated flow of history;

each pursuing God's love on earth. I never questioned that women could preach or hold authority in a church because I learned directly from my mother that women preachers were not only possible, but amazing.

To me, she was normal. To others, she was an anomaly. Women as pastors and narrators of God's story was not in question, because I was riding those waves, caught up in those whirlpools. Not until I heard honest stories of my mother's faith experience did I begin to understand how challenging her arrival at Ordained Minister had been. The ridicule, suspicious questioning, dismissal and mansplaining she faced; the way her partnership with my also ordained father somehow legitimized her work.

My mother was not the first woman preacher in our family. My Great-Great Grandmother Taylor was a legendary pioneer church planter in the American South-West. She read through her Bible seventy-two times before she went blind at age ninety-two. Then there was my Grandmother and namesake, Mary Elizabeth "Libby" Perkins, mother of my own mother, who was a much-beloved missionary and preacher. My phenomenal step-grandmother, Rev. Dr. Phyllis Perkins Howard wasn't ordained until her sixties but was a missionary, educator, administrator, preacher, and chaplain until her dying day. Her own mother, Great Grandma Velda Hartley, was a licensed preacher, serving as an evangelist to congregations who couldn't afford big names. Her one-on-one discipleship of Christians left long lasting impact. Each of these women faced obstacles and opposition as they followed the call of God in telling the story of promise, reconciliation, and healing. Each of these women influenced the faith experience of countless others.

My own mother's call came from reading the letter to the Romans chapter ten (verses 14 and 15), *"And how can they hear about [God] unless someone tells them? And how will anyone go and tell them without being sent? That is why the Scriptures say, 'How beautiful are the feet of messengers who bring good news!'"* In my family, women messengers had equal validity and capacity in telling God's story as men, their feet just as much beauty as their counterparts.

I remember distinctly as a little girl having very real, very intense emotional responses to God's story. Crying at the age of two to the film-depiction of Jesus' crucifixion shown on television during Easter, being moved by the televangelism of Rev. Billy Graham at the tender age of four to kneel with my folks at our basement couch to "ask Jesus into my heart." I remember weeping at the altars of summer revivals, children's church, and summer camps. Carrying intense worry about those in our family and friends circles who "didn't know Jesus." I filtered my experience of faith as a child through my embodied emotional experience as female and took strong cues from the females in my family. Gratefully, both of these aspects, being female and being emotional were welcomed in my family. I was not shamed or condemned for either.

Although my mother cried more often and publicly than my father, he easily cried in front of his family and shared his emotions healthily with us. To this day, my Dad is my single biggest cheerleader and encourager. He is far more tender and patient than my mother: characteristics I have sought to bring to bear in life, faith, ministry, and relationships. He easily tears up when speaking of God at work in his life, or of his love for his family (wife, children, and grandchildren particularly).

Intellect was also highly valued in my family. With highly educated parents, grandparents, aunts, and uncles on my maternal side of the family — theological debate and inquiry was a common practice at our family gatherings. Especially around shared meals, my Grandfather could be found holding court as his children and grandchildren brought questions and debate to the fore. My Grandmother, while not a native to the debating culture of the family she married into after my namesake's early death, was imbued with a genteel spirit and could just as easily and firmly express her perspective and be met with equal respect. So I grew up knowing brainy-theological nerds were sexy.

As a junior high student, I led a Bible study that included senior high boys. They interacted fully without ever questioning my age or sex. My voice as an embodied female was appreciated and amplified in all my leadership roles.

At the age of fourteen, right before my fresh(wo)man year in high school, I found myself at a philosophical crossroads: to follow the Jesus-way wholly or give up on it altogether. I chose Jesus, after a great deal of internal wrestling. The choice was difficult because I could sense the high risk of such a commitment, not because I didn't want to choose Jesus. I also made a choice that same summer to own my call to serve God's church as pastor. This to me was a single-hearted choice distinct from simply "surrendering to the family business." This was a choice to live into the generational blessing on my family.

The water I swam in as a girl and youth was stirred significantly when I reached college. In fact, the pond containing my childhood home and culture was blown wide-open into a brand new lake that would lead eventually to an entirely different ocean. And it came from a funny source. From day one, we were notified about the inclusive language policy of the university and the School of Theology and Christian Ministry when it came to written work — both in relation to God and to humanity. "Mankind" was taboo; "humankind" approved. "He/Him/His" pronouns for God were discouraged whenever possible in favor of comprehensive language in reference to Divinity. The immense power of language to shape how we think, believe, and behave is undeniable, and it seeped deep into my experience of faith.

If I swam in the waters of gender equality during my childhood, I was transported to altogether different waters with this revelation: God is not gendered. I knew this theoretically before college, but as my education took shape and I really began to think about who God was, how God loves and why God loves — the great importance of choosing to think about God as un-gendered took root. During childhood, the practice of my faith was peppered with referring to God in male-pronouns. Language can be so limited! I heard sermons and lessons and discussions that referred to God in more feminine ways, but in everyday parlance, God was categorized as male. With the introduction of this writing policy, a whole new water source bubbled up. This was the ocean of the kaleidoscopic, technicolor spectrum of God's full and beautiful image. The waters of my emerging adulthood were diversity: humans were created in the image of God, and God was not limited to male nor female.

Like a cascading waterfall of fresh spring water, practicing the discipline of writing about God without reference to sex or gender brought a new gleaming reflection of who God was and what God was up to in the world. Since the reality of God was no longer limited to "he/him" or "father," it meant that God could also reflect she/her and mother. It meant the presence of God was both feminine and masculine and so much more than the sum total of genders or sexes. It meant relationship to God didn't have to be tied to weird anthropomorphized he/she contexts. It meant that as much as God was strong and mighty God was also tender and sensitive. God was both/and as well as beyond sex or gender.

Writing about God this way challenged me to think of God in new dimensions, which led my practice of faith into far deeper and wider waters. Not only was I freer to live into my embodied life as a female, believing that God's image and character reflected as much of my lived-experience and more — but I was freer to imagine God as more loving than I had once thought. I was also freer to consider the experience of the incredibly diverse human family that was created in God's image. It led me to an inclusive theology of sexuality, gender, and human experience. My experience as a woman mattered, but so did the experience of anyone who identified along the LGBTQIA spectrum of sex and gender. My experience of faith became nuanced. Believe me, this was not an overnight transformation without struggle, deep questioning, and a whole lot of muddied waters. With time, my experience of faith became more expansive. The waters of my faith experience now shimmer and sparkle and ripple with the living, breathing Spirit of God.

As I came to understand God's identity as deep and wide, so too my experience of faith came to make room for the depth and breadth of the experiences of others. I value that the terrain of God's revelation in this world is relationship. God's way of being in this world is in relationship to Godself and in relationship to creation. If God is relational and has held space for each and every human being's experience, so we are gifted the same responsibility to hold space for the particularities of other's lived experience.

Never has holding space for the miraculous particularity of the human experience been realer or more poignant to me than in my journey to becoming a mother. Motherhood has yet again catapulted me to new oceanic depths of relationship to God, self, my spouse, my child, and the created world. I gave birth to my wondrous daughter almost one year prior to writing this reflection. I am forever changed because of and in awe of the utterly intricate miracle that is creation.

My womb was hostess to the conception of human life. I was a necessary co-creator for a new human being. My body nourished, provided for, and grew an extra organ (the wonder-working placenta!) which vitally contributed to the oxygenation and unfolding life of another person. My organs and bones physically expanded to hold literal and precious space for the development of a brand new life. I felt her flutter when she was but a whisper of the human form, I knew her hiccups in their sweet little rhythmic pulse, I heard her heartbeat when she was mere weeks in gestation, I saw and felt the jab of her feet kick at my ribs, and her little body do summersaults through my belly.

Then, in the fullness of time, the beautiful life-giving amniotic waters broke so that that little amphibian-like human could traverse the final canal between heaven and earth to breathe air for the first time. My miraculous body laboriously delivered that person onto the earth from the secret safety of my watered-womb. Now, from its beautiful and ample abundance my body feeds that small person with its own milk. This motherhood thing is nothing short of phenomenal.

God's Eucharistic provision for humanity is realer than it has ever been. This is my literal body, given for you. This is my womb, holding space for and expanding to include you. This is my placenta — grown and birthed and broken-down for you. These are the waters of my womb, broken and spilled out for you. This is my blood poured out for your new and expanding life on earth. This is my milk, continually produced and given for you. Most times, I bring my child to my breast to suckle for her sustenance, well-being, and comfort I marvel at God's wondrous creation.

In ways as transformative as a new language for God, motherhood has introduced a new way of being with God. It is a right here and right now kind of presence. Being a Mama requires me to be present to my child's unfolding life, moment by moment. The inexplicable joy of her existence, the fully-demanding needs of her hunger, sleep, stimulation, exercise, and expulsion of her poop and pee, the utter exhaustion of her lack of sleep encroaching on my own, the heart-squeezing reality of her un-solvable pain and fear. Being her Mama means being with and present to God in waves of pure joy and pure agony; waves of complete hilarity and grave seriousness; waves of preposterous questioning and unshakable knowing.

Without fail, any parent who is further down the path than I comments on how terribly fast it goes. I feel it too, and no doubt will continue to sense it desperately as the years days and weeks and months float by into years and decades. And herein lies another lesson in my current season of experiencing faith: in as much as the obvious whirlwind of my child's life is unfolding at break-neck-tortoise speed during this longest-shortest time of my life, so too is every human life. It is downright obvious in the expansiveness of their growth and development as babies and children. Less so as a youth. But equally as real for every single human — so fleeting, never the same from one minute to the next. We are only ever given the gift of the present moment — right here, right now. As the ethereal poet Mary Oliver once asked, "Tell me, what is it you plan to do with your one wild and precious life?"[50]

---

50. Mary Oliver, *New and Selected Poems, Volume One* (Boston, MA: Beacon Press, 1993), 94.

My faith affirms that the clearest revelation the world has ever known of God's love is in the human, the male, Jesus. I just turned thirty-three years old. Sometimes people joke being thirty-three is a person's 'Jesus year'. It is not lost on me that my Jesus year will be spent deep in the valley of the shadow of diapers even as I live into my vocational call as Pastor to an eclectic bunch of folks who embody God's beautiful diversity. The particularity of when God's love became human in Jesus means that he was a male. And his humanity, his identification with the human experience — warts, farts, sleepless nights, bodily appetites, snort-laughs, aching bones, hair loss and all — means we do not have a God whose love is far off and unreachable. Instead, we have a God who is intimately connected to human lives, human experience.

What if Jesus had been female? It's a lovely thing to imagine. Not because the revelation of God is any less potent or strangely transformative because he was male. But because the idea that God is both/and, beyond sex and gender, is too incredible to miss. Imagine Jesus — stretch marks, kankles, sleepless nights, nausea and hunger, cry-laughs, aching hips, hair loss, leaking boobs, happy-eyes and all. I'll ponder my Jesus year like this as I navigate living into motherhood.

God cannot be limited to one gender or a certain set of chromosomes. God is so much more than that. My current experience of faith as a female is found drowning in the dramatic throes of mothering, pastoring, watching my spouse unfold into a father, and pondering what undercurrent will sweep me into the next waterway of God's deep and wide love.

I sang a song as a little child about the deep and wide flowing fountain. The lyrics are scant and inconclusive, and it is kind of lovely like that — leaving it up to the imagination to wonder after the source of the fountain, the deep and wide and beautifully diverse heart of God spilling love generously and continuously into our lives until we are washed over in fresh mercies for the coming day.

I wonder what my child will say of how she experienced faith through me? I pray it is of the deep and wide and wondrous love of God: sometimes still and quiet and replenishing; sometimes rushing and wild and adventurous.

"So each generation should set its hope anew on God,
not forgetting the glorious miracles."

Psalm 78, paraphrase

"But now, O Jacob, listen to the Lord who created you.
O Israel, the one who formed you says,
"Do not be afraid, for I have ransomed you.
I have called you by name; you are mine.
When you go through deep waters,
I will be with you.
When you go through rivers of difficulty,
you will not drown."
Isaiah 43:1-2a

MEET THE AUTHOR

Libby Tedder Hugus is a Pastor, wife, mama, and caffeine-guzzling podcast consumer. She is married to her darling comedic husband, Jeremy, and together they are raising their wondrous daughter, Harloe. Libby is the daughter of two continents: North America and Africa and maintains dual citizenship between the USA and South Africa. She believes there is always room for one more around the table: both at home and in God's family and that generous hospitality can and will heal the world. She is Pastor to a dinner-church, where doubters + disciples together welcome the hungry into God's Studio of Love. Having moved to Casper in 2011, she has fallen in love with this slice of the windy western frontier, finding breathing room for the soul in Wyoming's wide-open skies.

LESS THAN

Kathy Escobar

I didn't set out to be a pastor. With a master's degree in management and a strong desire to succeed in the corporate world, I was on that fast track for a few years right out of college. However, it wasn't long after we got married 28 years ago that we discovered ourselves in a conservative church where most all the women were stay-at-home moms and the men were the ones being developed professionally. We started our family and with one kid after another, I slipped further away from anything corporate and more deeply into church culture and women's ministry.

While my husband and I were always solid teammates, the culture we lived in was deeply complementarian, with men as the spiritual leaders and women as supporters. An incredible amount of energy was spent on trying to become 'more godly,' which fit with some of my drive to success and mastery. I must say, I was an awesome 'good Christian woman' for a while! I was joyful, helpful, always willing to help. I had cute Christian kids and a husband who provided for me.

This all worked for a short season, but when I began to become more honest in a safe and brave women's group a friend of mine started, things began to fall apart. For the first time in my life, I made myself more vulnerable and shared the truth of how divided I felt inside. On the outside, things were bright, sunny, and prayerful, while on the inside I was filled with insecurity, doubt, and shame. As I began to do more personal work, I realized how easy it was for me to feel 'less than' and how the church system I was in perpetuated that divide. The pastors were better than me, the good Christian mothers were more obedient than me, and the leaders of the different ministries were godlier than me. During that season, I felt like God was constantly disappointed in me and I could never measure up.

I was always 'less than'.

As I processed some of my honest feelings about God, myself, and others in that group, I became more alive and started to tell my real story more openly of hiding a past abortion in high school and the ravages of shame I felt. Each and every time I shared, other women would come up and pour out their story for the first time, too. Soon, some men in different churches we attended also began to a more honest healing journey. I started cultivating a soul care and recovery ministry at a thriving church, and I could feel something begin to bubble inside of me in terms of leadership. I loved nurturing groups, inspiring leaders, and teaching others how to facilitate, too. Soon, I had over 20 men and women leading on my team, yet my role was as a volunteer. It was crystal clear — staff pastoring was for the guys.

Despite all the guts and heart I threw into the ministry, somehow as a female leader I was 'less than'.

If they heard this, I have no doubt the leaders during that time would be shaking their heads, assuring me, "Kathy, that's not how we thought of you. You were never less than." Their intentions were good; yet, they have no idea how hard it was to see all the real power and authority held in the hands of the male leaders while so many of us women were working hard day after day, week after week, year after year, cultivating significant parts of the church's life with little to no support.

I was only there for two years before I was offered a job unexpectedly as a care pastor at a large mega-church. This was a huge step for me, and I was naïve enough to think that maybe with a title, office, and an administrative assistant that I wouldn't be perceived as 'less than'. Sure, they loved my gifts and the juice I brought to ministry, but when it came down to it, I was paid significantly less, and lived and moved as the only female on the senior leadership team, which was lonely and weird. Roles and titles are a start, but until we address issues of hierarchical male power, we will still live in the land of 'less than'.

However, when you're used to 'less than,' anything is better than nothing.

Despite the obstacles to equality, I thrived in that role for a while. During this season of leading, even though it was in a deeply patriarchal system and I was definitely 'less than' my male counterparts, the fire for pastoring was kindled in my belly in a way that can now never be squelched. As I rocked the boat and began to call out some clear and painful dysfunction within the leadership system, I learned that I wasn't just 'less than,' I was also completely expendable. This is what happens to women (and men, too) who buck the system. They are tossed out without a care because the male leadership knows there are hungry ministry leaders who will come up right behind us and toe their line in full obedience. For new ministers, any opportunity feels better than no opportunity.

I remain ever grateful that after being ousted from that mega-church staff that I had a male pastor friend who believed in my leadership and we planted The Refuge, a Christian community and mission center in North Denver, together as co-pastors with a team. It was incredibly painful in those first years because it was hard for me to accept that I was no longer 'less than' in our community. The grooves of inequality were deep, and it took me a while to gain my footing and own that I was indeed called to be a co-lead pastor. It reminds me of the realities of freeing animals from captivity. It sounds good, but we have to remember that opening the cage is only a first step. It takes a long time to feel comfortable enough to move out of the cage, and it always comes tentatively.

Slowly, surely, I began to move out and find my voice in new ways, lead freely, and fan that flame into a greater fire. In The Refuge community, 'less than' began to fade away.

The only problem is that I don't solely live in my sweet and tender egalitarian community. I live in a bigger system and structure of faith where men hold most of the power, and women are often still 'less than'. The head pats, the inappropriate comments about my appearance, the "is your husband the pastor?" comments, the golf games I've never been invited to, and the patronizing over the years are countless. Oh, the stories I have after 15 years of full-time ministry as a female pastor. No matter how you slice it, white male power and privilege dominates, and there's a cluelessness about what it means for those underneath it, that permeates almost everything.

For a long time, I bought into the theology that somehow as a woman I was 'less than'. Eve started it, and misinterpretations of Paul's letters perpetuated it. After my free-fall out of mega-church staff, I began to question whether I could stay in the Christian faith after what I had experienced for so many years.

I couldn't shake how far away the church had strayed from the message of Jesus, who releases the prisoners and frees the oppressed. Is this kind of inequality and bondage what he had in mind? I didn't think so. But I had so few examples of leadership where women weren't somehow 'less than'. I poured over the solid theological work of Christians for Biblical Equality, I nurtured friendships with strong and powerful female leaders, and I began to listen to Jesus instead of the male-dominated systems who proclaimed his name. What remained after unraveling so many deeply conservative-based beliefs was only a remnant, but it's been enough to sustain me.

My faith in the beautiful boundary-breaking, system-toppling, radical-healing message of Jesus is stronger than ever. However, year after year I have begun to lose faith that the systems we currently have will truly change in the ways we desperately need. There are far too many of my sisters with so much fire, beauty, wisdom, and healing to bring who are stuck in systems that treat them as 'less than,' silence their voice, patronize their ideas, and squelch their gifts.

They are not 'less than'!

And here's the reality — if the church doesn't wake up and start doing something different, there is going to be a brain-and-heart drain that will cause it to crumble even further. These strong, wise, amazing women will find somewhere else to lead, somewhere else to teach, somewhere else to serve and live out who they were made to be where they are not treated as 'less than'.

So many of us are done with 'less than'.

I love that in the past 15 years there are more women at the table than ever before, more women in pastoral roles, more women teaching, preaching, and leading more freely. It makes my heart sing. Yet, despite the movement we've made, let us never forget we have a long way to go to true equality where no one is 'less than' another, where submission is mutual, where power is shared.

We need to be done with 'less than'.

I know I am.

MEET THE AUTHOR

Kathy Escobar co-pastors The Refuge, a Christian community and mission center in North Denver. A speaker, writer, advocate, and spiritual director, she is the author of several books including Faith Shift: Finding Your Way Forward When Everything You Believe is Coming Apart. *She has a Master of Arts in Management and a Certificate in Spiritual Direction from Denver Seminary. Her passion is creating safe and brave spaces for transformation and healing in a variety of contexts, and you can read her blog and more about her work at www.kathyescobar.com.*

Working Toward Change

Pastor Meggan Manlove

"Oh! A woman pastor." Uh oh, I thought to myself. Our church office administrator had just connected me to a woman on the phone who was inquiring about Trinity Lutheran Church. It turns out this caller was delighted to be talking to a woman pastor; it simply had not been what she had expected. This was a welcome encounter, but her initial declaration was one more reminder that I am not normal in the city of Nampa, Idaho.

The first spring I was serving as Trinity's pastor, Trinity took part in a midweek Lent supper and worship series. Each Thursday the whole ecumenical group went to a different church. Clergy took turns preaching, never preaching when his or her congregation was hosting. As I walked out of a building after worship one Thursday evening another clergy person shouted, "Goodbye, Reverend Hunter." Karen Hunter is the Episcopal priest in Nampa and, as far as I know, after seven years here, we are the only two women who are solo or senior clergy in town who are not part of a clergy couple. There are two of us, and people cannot remember who is who?

Since moving to Idaho, I have seen lots of surprised faces and heard many "wows" when I have told people I am a pastor. I now know that behind my back there are people who have looked down on me, as well as Trinity Lutheran Church for calling me.

A few summers ago, a new signal light was built on the church's corner — Midland Blvd and Lone Star Road. Our parking lot was used to park regular sized vehicles, and occasionally people working on the light came in to use our restrooms. One day a flagger came in just as our office administrator and I were about to leave. "Can I use your bathroom?" he asked. To which one of us replied, "Yes. Down the hall on the right." He came back, tablet in hand, and asked if I knew scripture. "Yes," I answered with curiosity in my voice." He proceeded to quote a passage from scripture in which it's made quite clear that women should not be in leadership. Whenever I tell this story, I'm asked what my response was, and I honestly don't remember.

This kind of attack has been happening to women clergy for years. It simply had never happened to me, and I am not good on my feet. I could not recall anything from my studies, sermons, or conversations, and I knew he was not interested in a dialogue. I was also annoyed that he used the restroom as a ruse to get into the church. I wanted to point out that his zipper was down, which it was. I think what I said was something like, "Yes. That is in the Bible, but the author did not have one of his best moments there." Meanwhile, our office administrator realized that this was happening. He began to instruct the man to leave. The intruder went on to quote something from Revelation and tell me that I should know better than to be in the pulpit. That was when I found my voice and said, "You need to leave now." I got the shivers every time I saw him at the intersection until the project finished.

I could tell many other stories about how, since moving to Nampa, I have been reminded how far we have to go when it comes to women's equality. Fortunately, none of those stories have to do with my parishioners, who have always treated me as their pastor, (with my strengths and my areas needing growth,) not as a "woman" pastor. In my interview, I think someone mentioned that I would be their first woman pastor, but that was it. Perhaps their lack of discrimination inside the church has made the discrimination I have witnessed outside the congregation even more glaring. But how to combat it?

One of the less talked about, at least in the entertainment news, but important films in 2015 was *Suffragette*, set in the early 20th century in the United Kingdom, starring a perfectly cast Carey Mulligan, along with Helena Bonham Carter and Romola Garai. There is also an explosive five-minute performance by Meryl Streep, in which she channels the fire and passion of the Emmeline Pankhurst, the movement's leader. *Suffragette* is:

A drama that tracks the story of the foot soldiers of the early feminist movement, women who were forced underground to pursue a dangerous game of cat and mouse with an increasingly brutal State. These women were not primarily from the genteel educated classes, they were working women who had seen peaceful protest achieve nothing. Radicalized and turning to violence as the only route to change, they were willing to lose everything in their fight for equality — their jobs, their homes, their children, and their lives. Maud was one such foot soldier. The story of her fight for dignity is as gripping and visceral as any thriller, it is also heart-breaking and inspirational."[51]

I am thankful for the work of the Suffragettes, and for giants in the Women's Rights movements in the United States, from Elizabeth Cady Stanton to Betty Friedan. Professionally, I am grateful for the first Lutheran women clergy in the United States. I do not know if I would condone the militant actions portrayed in *Suffragette*, and I recognize that the film tells one small piece of the suffragette story, but I understand why they were used. I am also not sure what role I would have taken or how brave and determined I would have been if I had been born in an earlier decade. However, there is still much to be done, and I am part of the movement.

Several encounters made clear what my role is today in Nampa, Idaho. Several young women who are working towards ordination, always in traditions not as friendly towards women pastors as the Evangelical Lutheran Church in America (ELCA), have asked to speak with me about ministry. Sometimes it is a referral and other times the women find me on their own. The conversation is never about women's ordination. Still, they seem to be joyful to have sought out and found a woman pastor with whom to talk. I am honored to be part of their journeys.

About a year after the stoplight incident I became aware in a new way of what laywomen and other women professionals were facing in Nampa, and I began asking systemic questions like, "Why do churches not allow women in lay leadership positions?" "Why, if I want to have to hear from other women professionals (bankers, real estate agents, and small business owners) do I have to attend the Chamber women's luncheon?" "Why are they not represented equally on panels with men?"

---

51. *Suffragette* promotional materials, directed by Sarah Gavron (Focus Features, 2015) https://www.imdb.com/videoplayer/vi3207115545

In early July 2017, I met with Donna Shines, Executive Director of the Mentoring Network, who has lived in Canyon County for decades and in Nampa for the last seven years.[52] A few years ago, she served on a panel of non-profit representatives hosted by the Chamber of Commerce. When I presented my issue to Donna, she agreed that patriarchy is a problem in our community. (An interesting side-note, Donna herself grew up Roman Catholic but considers herself Spiritual but Not Religious now.)

The Mentoring Network has been in the community since 2005 and Donna is now tracking the high school graduates who have come through the Network. It is true that the population she works with is overwhelmingly at-risk, but she is still saddened by the trajectory of many of the youth — one year of college or vocational school, and then they drop out, (for a variety of reasons). She shared an anecdote of a young Hispanic woman who dropped out to take care of her parents, a reminder to both Donna and myself of the complexities of being a Hispanic woman in Canyon County in the 21st Century.

Donna gave me the names of other professional women in the community whom she is looking to for leadership and inspiration; both within their organizations and within the larger Nampa community. She asked me what I thought of the relationship between the church and the patriarchy we witness — *does the church foster patriarchy or does it adopt the existing patriarchy of the society?* That is a hard question. Certainly, I have seen and heard enough to believe that if anyone is looking for justification of patriarchy, there is a plethora of clergy in Nampa who seem happy to help. I recalled that a few years ago, Northwest Nazarene University held a panel on similarities and differences between the Nazarene and LDS (Mormon) traditions. A defining moment came when the NNU religion professor made the LDS woman on the panel explain, after she told us the many leadership positions she had held in her ward, why she could not be a bishop (the highest position in a local ward). "Because women are more naturally caretakers." was her response. She did not even quote scripture.

One suggestion given to me by my Doctor of Ministry classmates at San Francisco Theological Seminary was to look at what is happening in other parts of the country and other industries. The cover for the April 2017 issue of *The Atlantic* made me very hopeful until I read the article and become downright

---

52. Donna Shines, interview by Meggan Manlove, Nampa, ID, 13 July 2017.

depressed.[53] Lisa Mundy writes about how Silicon Valley recognizes its diversity problem. "Women today hold only about a quarter of U.S. computing and mathematical jobs — a fraction that has actually fallen slightly over the past 15 years . . . Women not only are hired in lower numbers than men are; they also leave tech at more than twice the rate men do."[54] Mundy records how many companies have embraced unconscious-bias training over the past few years, ". . . as a ubiquitous fix for Silicon Valley's diversity deficit"[55] but it has helped very little.[56]

That made me wonder about what might work better. Intel started linking bonuses to diversity hiring. This seems to be working. Also, Mundy adds, we can place our hope in the "venture-capital firms formed specifically to invest in start-ups run by women, and certain colleges . . . have dramatically increased the number of female students in their computer-science programs."[57] From this, I feel that dialogue and training are important. Locally, in my context, it might be more productive to simply have a roster of women willing to speak in public (Donna's idea), and insist in whatever way I can that every panel and speaking engagement is made up of 50% women.

In order to do this, I want to create a roster of professional women willing to speak in public at various events and about various topics. My congregation and I are well respected in the community, and I think people will be receptive to sitting down and talking with me. If they are not interested in setting this up, and if there is resistance to this idea, then I will have to take other action. I cannot predict the outcome, but there might be some seeds to sow.

53. Liza Mundy, "Why is Silicon Valley So Awful to Women? An industry tries to reform itself — and the American workplace," *The Atlantic* (April 2017): 61-73.
54. Ibid., 65.
55. Ibid., 69.
56. Ibid., 70-71.
57. Mundy, 73.

MEET THE AUTHOR

Meggan grew up in the Black Hills of South Dakota and spent many summers paddling canoes in the Northwoods of Wisconsin and Minnesota. She graduated from Concordia College, Moorhead and spent a year in the Jesuit Volunteer Corps. Meggan then attended and graduated from the Univ. of Chicago Divinity School and was ordained a pastor in the ELCA in 2004. She served a congregation in rural Iowa for six years and moved to Nampa, Idaho in 2010 to serve as pastor of Trinity Lutheran Church. She blogs about faith, community, and film at megganmanlove.com.

PASS THE MIC

Alexis James Waggoner

Irecently participated in a conference of ministers and inter-faith leaders — largely attended by conservative, white, male, Protestants. When we
had a Q and A session with the leadership of the event, I asked the obvious
(obvious-to-me) question: "How can we get perspectives from a more diverse
representation of faith leaders? More women, more people of color, more
people from different faith traditions, and more people from the LGBTQI+
community?"

Out of the eight or so people on the leadership team, one was a person of
color, two were women, and the rest were white men. All of the white men
spoke up in response to my question. One of the women spoke. I never heard
from the other woman (who was a Rabbi), or the person of color. I wish I could
have heard their perspectives. But no one passed the mic to them.

Of course, any of them could have raised their hand or I could have specifically asked to hear their opinion. But my story illustrates a blind spot I experience more frequently the longer I'm in ministry. On my good days, I realize it's
born not from malice, but from ignorance. However, ignorance is no longer an
excuse I'm willing to tolerate.

PASS THE MIC

The act of using our voices to lift up and — literally — pass the mic to those
who have been kept voiceless is a need that infiltrates all areas of our culture.

We should bring about opportunities to hear from diverse perspectives in our government, in our workplaces, in our schools, in our families, and — most definitely — in our churches.

It's not only men who should demand this action. Any individual with a scrap of power or privilege should endeavor to use their position to raise up another individual. (I experience this most in the context of working with white men in positions of power.) In this context, I believe that if men in leadership positions in the church fail to use their power to lift up women, they continue to wound the mission, witness, and call of the church.

It's not enough for someone who cares about the church to say, "That's not my thing" or "I'm not called to this area of ministry." It should be your thing and it is your calling. Anyone that feels compelled to serve the church, in any capacity, accepts the responsibility to empower the powerless. Empowering others is the message of the Hebrew scriptures. They pulse with the drumbeat of concern for the quartet of the vulnerable: the widow, the orphan, the poor, and the stranger. This is also the message of Jesus. He insisted that the systems of the world were so far inverted that, ultimately, he was murdered for his beliefs and actions.

Individual to Collective

The problems we encounter and the resistance we feel towards actually *doing* the work of Jesus in this area are multi-dimensional. But I believe they fall into two main categories: hyper-individualization and collective denial.

For many people, it is simply easier to maintain egalitarian, even empowering, one-on-one relationships with people without ever addressing more significant problems of injustice. For example, I was once on staff at a church that had mission and outreach down to a science. We sponsored dozens of community programs, opened our doors to the needy, took in the homeless during the winter, built houses, performed service projects, sponsored kids, and performed a myriad of other tasks both at home and abroad.

We had a tough time when we learned that issues we put Band-Aids on continued to get worse. We were comfortable and, to be honest, sometimes complacent, and even complicit in their continuation. We didn't want to be reminded that, because of our socio-economic status, race, or gender, there were things we could be *doing* to turn the tables for the people in our community.

For the most part, we didn't want to address the systems that were causing the issues that required our outreach programs in the first place.

This mindset can easily translate to supporting — or not supporting — women in leadership in the church. There are plenty of people in my life who know me, see the work I'm doing, and wildly support my calling as a minister. Yet, they cannot acknowledge the *concept* of women in ministerial leadership. They belong to denominations that don't ordain women, they attend churches that keep women out of the pulpit, or they participate in patriarchal and hierarchical relationships.

In each of these examples above, action and belief are hyper-individualized. Awareness develops from personal relationships but the problem comes in turning awareness into action. When people are unwilling to engage in reflection about the incongruity, and are unaware for the need of deeper reflection, the ability to root out injustice fails. When there is an unwillingness to let those awarenesses of inequality, which awaken when watching a friend or coworker suffer or succeed in ways we don't expect, develop more fully through reflection and education, we lose the ability to turn awareness into action, and fight the roots of injustice.

Of course, the converse is true as well. For each example of hyper-individualization, I can think of just as many issues that run the other way. For example, people who have a "not in my backyard" approach to women in church leadership. They may belong to denominations that affirm women's ordination, but they would have a hard time voting to call a women minister. Perhaps there's an unspoken quota: it's ok to have a woman or two on the staff, but not as the senior minister, and not comprising the entire leadership team.

Then there are the roles women get relegated to in church ministry, even in churches that claim to support women in ministry fully. Women still find themselves as the children's pastor (or director), the youth minister, or the women's ministry coordinator. Being part of a community that, on paper, affirms women's leadership roles is a far cry from actually living out that affirmation.

And that's the trouble with both of these viewpoints. In subscribing to either of these mentalities, we let ourselves off the hook. If we're *focused on the individual*, we may think we're supportive because we have that one friend or that one experience with a woman in ministry. But what are we doing to address the broader issues of gender injustice perpetrated by our churches? If we're *focused on the communal*, we lead ourselves to believe we are doing better because we have a larger worldview that allows for women in such positions of leadership, but fail to see that it hasn't trickled down to actually affect our lives or the lives of the women in our church pews.

Of course, these are not the only two options. There are other ways to deny women full inclusion in the life of the church. And there are plenty of faith communities that are doing their best to get it right. But if we *think* we're getting it right, perhaps we should examine our own experience, beliefs, and motives — as well as the experiences and stories of those around us — to make sure we're not just trying to let ourselves off the hook.

OUTNUMBERED IN A MILITARY CONTEXT

My role as a chaplain in the Air Force Reserves gives me an additional perspective from which to analyze these responses to women in ministerial leadership. As a female chaplain in the Air Force, I am part of a vastly outnumbered group. There are about 30 female chaplains in the Air Force Reserves out of roughly 300 total chaplains. I have experienced both individual and communal responses from my peers as translated into a military setting.

Yes, I can tell personal stories of harassment and bias; instances that resulted in other chaplains being discharged and instances that resulted in absolutely nothing happening. My women colleagues tell frustrating and upsetting stories about their service as chaplains, but they also have stories of support and empowerment. No environment is perfect.

And yet, even in the military environment, my experience overall has been positive. My male colleagues value my presence and perspective. They often go out of their way to "pass the mic" and specifically ask me to speak up or contribute in a meeting, during a presentation, or at an event. My supervisors continually encourage me to live out my calling and my ministry. I have even received affirmation from chaplains who belong to denominations that very often do not support women's full inclusion in ministry.

Some of my interactions with these chaplains may fall into the hyper-individualization category — they support and interact with me on a personal level but still would not advocate for women in leadership in a broader sense. However, I also know multiple male chaplains, from conservative denominations, who join in the fight for equality on a systemic level.

When I ponder why that is, and why I've had a largely positive experience as a woman in ministry in a context where I am so outnumbered, I conclude that it is because the military has a mandate for egalitarianism. That mandate is not carried out perfectly, and the military-industrial complex surely has its own set of skeletons in the closet. I can only speak from my experience, which has predominantly been a reflection of a commitment to equal treatment and equal opportunity. The military has a direct order to do so.

This makes me realize, however, that as people who follow Jesus, we also have a mandate — from a higher authority than the US military — for inclusion and equality. I wonder why so many of us neglect to take this seriously.

WHERE CAN WE SACRIFICE?

Though I frame this essay and this question about people who may be keeping women from full inclusion, it's a question for all of us. It's not just a question about whether or not we're comfortable in a church led by a woman senior minister (although as a minister I am concerned with answering this question in a church context). It's a question for all of us no matter where we spend the majority of our time. It's a reminder that most of us have some position of power and influence somewhere in our lives. How are we using that to lift up the voices of those who are too often pushed to the side or ignored altogether?

I want to see significant results. I want to see more women leading churches, more women as military chaplains, and more women feeling that anything they want to do to serve God is possible. As we move forward on this journey, we need to be aware of the hundreds of little decisions we make about how to affirm — or not — the calling of the women in our lives. Sometimes, for me, it's as simple as noticing when, for example, in a church staff meeting, other women are struggling to get a word in edgewise and then taking the initiative to ask explicitly to hear their opinion.

Sometimes it's as simple — and profound — as passing the mic.

Meet the Author

Rev. Alexis James Waggoner is a theologian and educator working as the Marketing and Digital Education Director for the Westar Institute (www.westarinstitute.org) an interfaith organization dedicated to bridging the gap between religious scholarship and culture. She's ordained with the Christian Church (Disciples of Christ) and serves as a Minister of Religious Education in addition to her role as a Chaplain in the Air Force Reserves. Alexis has a M.Div. from Union Theological Seminary in the City of New York and lives in New York City with her husband, Ryan, and their toddler, Junia.

Engaging Racism

Wendie Brockhaus

"You're part of the problem! You're a gentrifier," an older black woman declared, pointing at my younger white co-pastor in the middle of our evening worship gathering. He looked stunned for a moment, and I could tell his wheels were turning. Was she just here to pick a fight? Should he continue to engage? What would people think? Our community fell silent, waiting to see what would happen. A second or two went by after she made her statement, and then, to his credit, my co-pastor received her feedback without being defensive and kept the worship service going. After it was over, he made a beeline for our new guest to see if she'd be willing to have some further dialogue regarding her comments. Initially she declined, but reluctantly changed her mind and invited him to contact her later.

We were just beginning a series on race at The Open Table, the dinner church I'd been serving for the past two years as Assistant Curator. A nontraditional church plant, we had an informal worship service which included dinner around tables in the social hall, a bit of indie rock music, and conversations facilitated by guest teachers who were experienced in whatever topic we were engaging at the time. So instead of having the same preacher every week, we used a dialogical format which enabled us to hear God's story from a variety of voices. It occasionally meant receiving unpredictable comments of this nature from people attending the service, but it was worth the risk. I'm not sure what white folks fear more — death, or being called out by a black woman in public — but I was glad we had created a worship space where these kinds of conversations could happen. It's hard to love your neighbors if you never talk to them, after all.

It takes some listening, too. As the 2016 election cycle ended, the leaders of The Open Table discerned a need for some kind of response to the concerns about racism we were hearing from our community. There had been an uptick in hate crimes, not just nationally, but in our own city. The Muslim owner of a nearby restaurant came in one day to find his windows shattered. A clergy colleague of ours shared that he had been walking down the street in a busy shopping district when he heard someone hurl a racial slur at a black person as they walked by, and this pastor confessed that he froze and didn't know what to do. If a pastor doesn't know how to respond to racism, what about the rest of the church? This question drove us to scrap our previously scheduled programming and host a bystander intervention training we titled, "Disrupting Racism". We quickly got in touch with our contacts from a local racial justice organization and invited them to partner with some of our leaders to host practical, skill-building workshops as part of several breakout sessions.

Normally we would expect around 60 people to attend one of our worship gatherings, but for this event over 150 people said they were coming on Facebook, and about 800 people said they were "Interested". Clearly, this topic had struck a nerve. Since we are a dinner church, we were a little worried about having enough food for that many people. I remember looking at our leaders that night, speechless, when over 150 people began trickling through our doors and sitting down at the tables together. They represented different racial and ethnic backgrounds, religious traditions, sexual orientations, abilities, political leanings, and age groups, and it felt to me like I was seeing the Gospel happen before my eyes. It truly became a loaves and fishes moment, as people showed up for the potluck with armloads of casseroles, desserts, and vegetables. We had to keep setting up additional buffet tables to hold the weight of all the food being shared. In the breakout sessions, we practiced nonviolent communication, "third ways" such as distraction and disruption, and how to respond to and support others who were the target of racism. We were only scratching the surface of the work that needed to be done, but that night helped our church solidify racial justice as part of our core mission, to be a community of peace and reconciliation in a city divided.

It's taken me a while to get there. When I was growing up and went to gatherings with extended family, it wasn't uncommon to hear a grandparent, an uncle, or a cousin utter a racist slur. We never talked about race at home, in church, or at school, except for a rare mention of Lincoln emancipating slaves as part of my history lessons, so I didn't understand the gravity of my family's actions until I went to college. I gave myself a pass. "My parents and I never use those words," I would think to myself, ". . . so I'm ok. I'm not racist." Until my mid-twenties, the only image of Jesus I knew was an unassuming white man, usually blond and blue-eyed. He showed up in children's books, the church's stained glass, artwork, and in my picture Bible. He was safe and respectful, never kneeling during the National Anthem or wearing a Black Lives Matter shirt.

Imagine my surprise on meeting Middle Eastern Jewish Jesus when I went to seminary! It was a different experience entirely to read the Bible through his eyes, and to compare that with the message of womanist or liberation theology which gave preference to the marginalized. This knowledge gave me a new perspective on the experience of my neighbors of color, but one cannot educate racism away. It would take a more sustained effort and the difficult work of self-transformation before I could admit the truth to myself. And the truth would be hard to swallow:

I can ignore the concept of race because my privilege gives me the option to do so, while for others it is a daily awareness and potentially life-threatening reality. I no longer believe it is possible for me not to be racist as a white person living in the United States because our systems are set up to benefit me. No laws have been passed which excluded my family from particular neighborhoods, jobs, or schools. I do not have to worry about my child being pulled over by the police. I can go into a drugstore and find makeup or Band-Aids which match my skin color. I can see any number of movies with a cast whose skin matches mine. When I go into a school, church, or government building, I can usually be assured that the dominant culture will reflect my own whiteness. I can talk about colorblindness because I do not have to think about race.

Last year The Open Table received a $50,000 grant from Leadership Education at Duke Divinity to do a one-year project in which we would train a multiracial team of 20 leaders (10 people of color and 10 white people) to host anti-racism trainings for religious and nonreligious organizations in our city. Thanks to the generous grant funding, we were able to hire a nationally recognized community organizer to facilitate our team training, and have been able to explore the idea of making this an ongoing offering of our church to the community. As I write this, we are beginning our pilot runs of the trainings in different churches and businesses around Kansas City. The timing of this seems providential, after the recent event in the news regarding the two black men who were arrested unjustly at a Philadelphia Starbucks. Since that story came out, local coffee shops and restaurants have been contacting us requesting the anti-racism training for their staff members. We received similar requests from the public library, an atheist group, a nonprofit organization, and multiple churches, including our parent congregation, Second Presbyterian Church. By making this work a central part of our mission, we have been able to respond to the needs of our city in meaningful and practical ways.

Remember the woman at the beginning of my story? After that night, she began meeting with my co-pastor and me for further conversation. She invited us over to the nonprofit she directs and made us breakfast before giving a tour and explaining her passion for their mission. She deeply cares about building a community for black families in an area of town which has traditionally been a racial dividing line. We ended up inviting her to be a guest teacher for a panel conversation later on in our series on race, where she shared her story of living in her neighborhood for decades and watching as it became gentrified. When I shared with her about my spouse's health concern, she offered a ritual for healing. And when we put out the invitation for leaders to apply for our anti-racism project, she joined our team.

The table continues to be a central image and metaphor for our community, and we keep coming back to it in our conversations about racial reconciliation. Talking about race has never been easy, but I'm beginning to understand that silence is not an option. It's not enough to be anti-racist or anti- any other evil; I must also act. I want to use whatever voice and power I have to make the world a better and more loving place for future generations of neighbors, which means organizing with others to move towards that goal together.

That is why I do this work, and why I have faith in our power to make change. Sometimes we may end up partnering with someone we did not expect, perhaps even someone who first appeared as an antagonist. We may feel unsure as to whether or not we can trust each other. We may feel the problem is too large and that we are too small. We may worry there is not enough food to go around. We may feel frightened that we are not in control. But we are all invited to God's table together, and while it can sometimes be a place of discomfort, it is also a place of wild abundance and surprises.

MEET THE AUTHOR

As the only child of two entrepreneurs, I learned that creativity (somewhat more than cleanliness) was next to godliness. I became passionate about the integration of spirituality, theology, and the arts at a young age, and could often be found engaged in teaching and learning with my local church. My work has taken me into Title I classrooms as a music teacher, into the chapel as the Director of Spiritual Formation for a seminary, into the library as a writer, into an urban trauma center as a chaplain resident, and most recently, around the table as Assistant Curator of a dinner church called The Open Table. I love to find connections between people and ideas, provoking thought that propels us forward as a community which follows the law of love. With the understanding that faithful engagement with Jesus will look and feel different for my generation, I also value the hands, hearts, and minds which helped build the church into which I was born, as well as the contributions of other faith traditions to the wells of the world's wisdom. A big part of my life's work is to ensure the next generations of spiritual leaders have the support and empowerment they need to endure.

A Place at the Table

Piper Ramsey-Sumner

At twelve years old, during the annual family camp meeting for all of the Nazarene churches in West Texas, I wrote a sermon on I Corinthians 13 and preached it from the top bunk in our cabin to my patient family below. That summer, I determined that I would be a pastor. Growing up, I hoped that God would be able to use me *despite* my gender. Even though my church affirmed women in leadership, I understood that there was a barrier I would have to cross to be taken seriously in the Church. As a woman in ministry, you are invited to the Table, but you are faced with the challenge to push your way past two thousand years of exclusion, marginalization, and violence to find your seat.

That history has shaped the narrative of Christianity: from the Bible and theology to the sacraments and leadership. This narrative is comprised of the stories that we tell in order to sculpt our identity as Christians, yet many communities have been excluded from those stories. The experiences of women have rarely been recorded in the archives of history. Not only are they not remembered but women are intentionally silenced and disenfranchised by men. I believe the Table, at which we, the people of God, are meant to join, has been corrupted since nearly the beginning because of our exclusion of marginalized identities. Let us remember that there has always been enough room for us all at the Table of Divine Love! But, we have made the mistake of building boundaries that oppress and control and are difficult to break down. I believe that we, as women, play a significant role in the transformation of the Christian narrative. We will ensure that our humanity is recognized and our participation with the Divine is made valuable and essential at the Table of Divine Love. In the following pages, I will explore women in the Christian narrative through my experience as a woman, a Christian, and a theologian.

My gender is something I have been aware of since early in my life. I knew what it meant to be a girl: girls were smarter, nicer, and cleaner than boys. But girls were also less strong, less brave, and more emotional than boys. Gender operates as a social structure that is built upon hierarchy, dualism, and domination. Western ideology promotes a gender dualism, in which there are two genders, determined by biology. Men are thought to be superior in strength, intelligence, agility, wisdom, and leadership skills. Women are seen as maternal, domestic, delicate, and submissive. The oppression of women is directly related to these concepts of gender, which quickly lead to sexist stereotypes that cultivate a culture in which women experience a lack of social mobility, damaging religious ideologies, oversexualization, and ultimately, violence against not only women but also those who challenge gender normativity. Sexism is commonplace in our culture and can be witnessed in all areas of a woman's life, professional, educational, personal, etc.

I recall a time when a man asked my father how many kids he had, and he replied, "Three girls." The man responded with pity towards my father for living in a house with all those women and no sons. I wondered; are daughters really so bad? Did dad wish he had sons instead of my sisters and me? How different am I as a woman from a man? What does it mean to be a woman? Is it about my body? My chromosomes? The way I dress or act? Sociologists and gender theorists have argued this question, and come to a multitude of differing conclusions. Gender is not easy to define. For some, it is understood as biological, and by others as performative. Still other theories imagine gender as a spectrum or as ordained by God. For me, the essence of who I am is wrapped up in my self-understanding as a woman. My reality is shaped by the lens of my gender identity, which enriches my sense of self, as well as my relationships, sexuality, spirituality, and every day the realities that I experience as a cisgender woman in America. For me, being a woman is not about my body or my gender expression, being a woman means being strong, clever, soft, and resilient because those are the traits I seek exemplify. Being a woman also makes me a human: imperfect, mortal, and worthy of love along with the rest of humankind.

Biblical womanhood and gender complementarianism are ideas that are used as a tool of fundamentalist Christianity to advocate for a complementary gender dualism in which men and women fulfill their roles, women submitting to and honoring the man, who leads, protects, and provides for the home. Of course, these ideas can be observed outside of the marriage in the public spaces like religious organizations, schools, businesses, and politics. Being exposed to life-limiting gender expectations for my entire life, I have rebelled against Christian concepts of Biblical womanhood and complementarianism. There are too many remarkable examples of womanhood in my life for me to be held back; these strong, intelligent, unyielding, and creative women instilled in me a sense of pride in sharing a piece of my identity with them. Growing up, I was surrounded by intelligent, witty, empathetic, fierce, and innovative women. My grandmothers inspired me to embrace my femininity and to find strength and dignity in who I choose to be. So why were Bible teachers and Sunday school leaders of my adolescence teaching me that my gender prevents me from leading the church and requires me to be submissive to my husband? It is argued that complementarianism does not oppress women; but when a woman is not given the freedom to exist outside of the expectations and limitations of her "complementary" gender role, she is oppressed.

I believe that all of humankind reflects the image of God along with the rest of creation. In the creation myth of the Book of Genesis, humans are made in the image of God, "male and female he created them" (Gen. 1:27 NRSV). God's love and holiness are revealed in our humanity, our relationships, and our communities. The *imago Dei* is not about gender; rather our shared humanity is a reflection of the beauty and love of God. Yet, women are historically excluded from theological anthropology, and when we are included, women are seen as image-bearers *despite* our gender. Although academics attempt to address gender through theological and sociological exploration, the story of Christianity remains a narrative that is centralized upon the experience and works of men. We witness this in the early Church fathers denying the image of God in women, in the dismissive and demonizing definitions of the feminine from Reformation leaders, and in the domestication of women by most evangelical Christian denominations. We must remember that the Bible is an ancient collection of sacred texts that is imperfect, contradicts itself, and tells the story of God's people through myth and poetry. The text does not often treat women well. Women are mistreated, abused, and often absent within the narrative. The New Testament contains theological instruction that disallows women in leadership and claims their subordination under the authority of men. The Bible reflects much of the male-dominated cultural frameworks of the ancient world, and it is used today as a tool for heteronormative, patriarchal ideologies.

Surrounded by interpretations of these writings that encourage the marginalization of women and the domination of men, I still cling to Jesus. When I read the Gospels, I am met with the story of a man who challenged the injustices and inequalities of his society by bringing about a new way of being in the kingdom of God. He treated people with dignity and compassion, touching lepers, socializing with tax collectors, feeding the hungry, and protecting women. And this same man was executed for his teachings and his disruption of the *status quo*. Jesus preached a gospel of Divine Love, in which all people are adopted as God's children and called to participate in a kingdom built upon radical love. The kingdom of God brings about redemption and reconciliation, it seeks justice and abundant life, and above all else it, brings about the salvation of the world. In the kingdom of God, the Table is never full; there is always room.

When I was twenty-one and wondering what my future would hold, I picked up the Bible. This book had been my anchor in the storm. When difficulties with school or relationships came, I knew I could come to the Bible to find comfort and guidance. Flipping through the pages, I found myself reading I Corinthians 14:34 (NRSV), "Women should be silent in the churches. For they are not permitted to speak, but should be subordinate, as the law also says." I cried in my dorm room, reading the words over and over again. I knew that I could not believe in a God who reduced my gender to a silent, passive presence in the Church. I cried as I remembered pastors, friends, and peers dismissing my passions and abilities. I recalled all of the times I have been literally silenced in the presence of men because my contributions were considered unwanted and unneeded in Christian leadership. I wondered, maybe they were right, maybe I was never meant to pursue a vocation in Christian leadership, and maybe I was going against God's will in my theological education.

But, then I remembered the story of Jesus at Jacob's well. Jesus was in Samaria, the land of a people rejected and despised by the Jewish people. In the middle of the day, a lone woman went to fetch water at the well, and Jesus provoked a conversation. Not only was she a woman alone, but this Samaritan was also a social outcast among her people, living with a scarlet letter on her chest. He listened to her, engaged with her questions and challenges. In their conversation, Jesus revealed to her that he is the *I AM*, the Messiah, the deliverance of the people of Israel. He taught her about living water that fulfills and sustains those who drink it. Jesus chose this woman to reveal himself as the divine source of life and truth, not only proclaim his Gospel, but also to bring the news to the Samaritan people through her testimony and experience. To Jesus, the Samaritan woman mattered. Jesus did not see her gender as a reason to devalue her experiences or to distrust her; instead, Jesus left her with a gift that breaks social and religious boundaries and gives life everlasting for all who seek it. Jesus asked her to pull up a chair at the Table.

I was reminded that day that despite the brokenness and chaos of this world, there is a God who sits down with the rejects, the sick, the forgotten, and the ignored and sees them for who they are: beloved and known by God. That is the true story of Christianity; it is the narrative that I want to hold on to. Christianity is incomplete without the stories of all of those who are touched by Holy Love. The table of God's people is ever growing and always open. Let us make room for one another.

MEET THE AUTHOR

∞

Piper is a M.Div. student at Iliff School of Theology and a novice barista. She is a passionate vegan and social activist who loves to make music, cook, and do yoga. She is married to her grad school sweetheart, Kyle, and has a beautiful cat named Rosie. Although she's from the great state of Texas, Piper currently lives in North Florida, enjoying her quiet house in the woods and the beach just an hour away. She visits Denver every few months to get her fix of mountains, low humidity, and her favorite Coloradan friends. You can follow her on Instagram at @cbfplr.

OUTRO

Never Enough

Janel Apps Ramsey

(Please take a moment to listen to "Never Enough"
from *The Greatest Showman*)

I'm trying to hold my breath
Let it stay this way
Can't let this moment end[58]

The mountaintop experience is a phrase I've heard in the church my entire life. The mountaintop experience is not just a mountain view, but it represents those moments when you feel closest to God. They are the moments you feel inspired, full of hope and joy, and ready to take on the world. You also know that life can't be this way all the time and that these moments will end. Life is about living in the valleys. God blesses us with a mountain top experience every once in a while, to remind us of His greatness, of the possibilities, and of the reward that awaits us when we are faithful to him. Our purpose, our

---

58. Justin Paul and Benj Pasek, "Never Enough" from *The Greatest Showman* (NYC, NY: Sony/ATV Music Publishing LLC, Kobalt Music Publishing Ltd.) Sung by Loren Allred. December 20, 2017.

direction, and our call all become clearer on the mountaintop. That is where God moves mountains and changes the world.

One hot summer day in the middle of Michigan, sitting in an old wooden tabernacle, I had one of those moments. I had just completed camp with InterVarsity, where I was blatantly told women couldn't lead. It was that afternoon that I first saw her preach. And she was glorious. Glorious! She was a preacher, and a very important leader in our denomination. And I was going to meet her before the day was over.

As my jaw was resting on the old wooden bench I was sitting on, the man next to me, an old veteran preacher (who never showed emotion) leaned over, with a smile on his face and said, "Maybe women can preach." It's a moment I can still picture in my head today. I was shocked when he said it. In hindsight, maybe he was trying to encourage me in a backhanded way.

In that moment and in the days that followed, the memory of seeing her set off a dream inside of me. A few months later, after a vibrant and unmistakable vision, I knew that I was called to preach. I knew that the moment I witnessed that summer day, was something I could live out in my own life as an ordained woman preacher. I was going to preach to the world and make a difference.

I never wanted that moment to end. Clearly, God wanted me in ministry. He wanted me. And The Church verified that they wanted me too. I could be a trailblazing woman preacher. Like many of the women before me. (I aimed at being the exception, when exceptions were, and are, few and far between.)

You set off a dream with me
Getting louder now
Can you hear it echoing?

The Church set off a dream in me long before God did. A dream to do the thing that very few people are called to do. God had spoken to me. And now I was going to work toward living that dream out. Answering the call. Giving it my all. No matter the cost.

The call on my life grew, and changed, and pulled me forward. It changed my major in college and continued to draw me into the most important life a person could have. The life of a preacher of the Gospel. This is no mere career choice; this is the call from God.

And so I pursued it. I shared it. I longed to be affirmed as a pastor. I did all things. Filled out all the paper. Led people into Sanctification. Went to camps, assemblies, and every service. I learned theology and church history. Passed my annual interviews. I served, gave, taught, and dreamed of the future.

I dreamed of the day when my husband and I would have a church of our own to lead. To create or serve a community that upheld the perfect doctrine of Holiness. That we would help people live moral lives, free from sin, and reach the people in the community we lived in. A dream fulfilling all the things a pastor should do when faithfully answering the call.

And maybe someday, if God allowed it, lead more people. Maybe God would make space for me to help on the district. Or even serve as a leader of many churches, helping them perpetuate the dream of a world full of Nazarenes.

Take my hand
Will you share this with me?
'Cause darling without you

And so I did what you're supposed to do and got licensed right away in my local congregation. Soon after, I was licensed by the District. I built my life around doing all the things that the leadership told me do. I worked on myself and worked on being a better evangelist. I made the church my top priority, at the expense of everything else. I held my hand out to The Church hoping that all my hard work would prove how worthy I was to be part of the team.

I longed to be mentored. I longed to be an example so that others might follow along. I pursued all the benchmarks, gave all the money I had, and wore myself out doing it. But I never complained or felt taken advantage of, because I thought I was on a team. I thought I was in it, hand and hand with The Church; that we were all moving the same direction.

But I was never paid. I was never given a title. I was never found worthy of more than being a glorified volunteer. Which now, looking back, makes me feel like my hand wasn't clasped in theirs; it was just sitting on a high school music stand.

Do you remember high school music stands? Those black ones that as they age, start to slip. Over time, with wear and tear, the stand stops staying where you put it. It gently slides down while you're playing music. And the rack that holds your music, or more specifically the joint that holds the rack, gets looser and looser. Your music either tips forward and dumps, or gravity pulls it backwards and it you can't see it anymore.

As the years go by, you lean on this object at your own risk. It wobbles widely from side to side. It might hold you up, or it might not. You might slide off onto the floor. You might get hit in the head as it falls over on top of you.

And soon, it's that music stand in the back of the instrument room that everyone knows doesn't work, but doesn't want to throw out. (Sometimes it's fun to give it to a freshman to watch and laugh as they try to fix it.)

But it's no longer capable of being a dependable partner. There is no solution. It needs to be discarded and replaced. The problem is, sometimes a weird little thing like a music stand can be your favorite. Maybe you've used it every day of middle school. It was your companion. Maybe you even brought in some grease and a wrench from your dad's shop to try and keep it working. It's yours. It did all the things. And now it doesn't work.

All the shine of a thousand spotlights
All the stars we steal from the night sky
Will never be enough
Never be enough

Metaphors always fall short. Whether it's a big thing or a small thing, when you've built a picture of what something should be, or it has told you for years what it is, and then it's gone, there isn't much left you can do. But grieve.

Grief is hard. It doesn't make sense. It's random. And grief often can't explain why something failed. For some of us, we just want a clear, coherent answer. Why did this happen?! But more often than not, there isn't one.

I know: move on, get over it, and let God make beautiful things out of the dust. I know. And for some people that's easy. And for some of us, it's not easy at all. There are lots of people that can move past this kind of disappointment without blinking an eye. But I'm not one of them. I was promised something that never happened, and maybe could never happen. I was given a dream, one that was so clearly articulated and delineated by The Church. And it was a lie; maybe not because it was a falsehood on its face, but because the systemic biases and discrimination were so deeply rooted, that only a few survived.

For me, that vision and that path are gone. Like a thousand spotlights, my path was made clear to me from the time I was 18. I knew where I was going. Everything was clear. At least, that's how I understood it.

But, the thing about spotlights is that while you are in them you can't see anything else. You are blind to the world and all it contains. You can only see the thing you are looking at. You can't see the warning signs, or bumps coming along the road, because everything is light. Everything is the way you dreamed it would be (because you can't see anything else.) The Church creates a blind spot around you to the very world you're supposed to reach, so that you don't question what you're doing or how the system works.

That's also how you expect life to work out as a pastor. You reach up and steal the stars from their places, because you are doing God's work. The work you are doing aligns with all of creation. You are doing the work of fulfilling the redemption of humanity. You matter and what you do matters.

When in reality, you are simply a glorified fundraiser working to get butts in seats, and to keep the offering plates full. Making space for new staff members, buying the latest gear, and bringing in those lapsed Baptists and Catholics.

With this vision, this call to the church, life is prebuilt. All you have to do is walk the path. Do what the church says, read the books, run the campaigns, and host VBS. Don't get creative, unless you learned it at a conference, because you could find yourself out of a job if you fail.

Be careful, because *when* you fail, as so many pastors do each year, you will be left with Plan B, guilt and shame, and condemnation. You will lose your identity, your title, your church, and your community. You may even lose your family.

Towers of gold are still too little
These hands could hold the world but it'll
Never be enough
Never be enough
For me

When you finally are able to stand up again — after having failed to miraculously restore a remnant of a church in a tiny, dried up town, with a rag-tag group of broken, closed-minded people who refuse to face reality (that the church needs to close) and call you to be their pastor instead — you soon realize that you will NEVER, ever have the dream that was promised to you.

The allure of the call. The promise of pastoral success. The dream of preaching in a suit to an audience that's listening is dead. And with it, your hope. And probably your faith. And the realization sets in that you will never fulfill God's Plan A for your life. You are a failed pastor.

No career you find will ever fill the hole in your life. You were indoctrinated with that message from very young. There is no call, unless you get to be a missionary, which is greater than being a Pastor. Even if you can find a fulfilling career, then it is crystal clear that you were mistaken and God did not call you to ministry. (Nice little paradox The Church has built to make sure you never feel successful or whole.)

If a career that pays well, provides for your family, comes with insurance, and gives you a little extra spending money, does feel good — you're greedy and sold out. If you end up in life that is actually happy, fulfilling, and good, then you need to give more away. If you enjoy having Sundays free to go to the mountains, you were never committed. If you think you can be Christian and drink a beer . . . it's never enough.

It's never enough for The Church. And it's never enough for you.

NEVER ENOUGH

This volume of essays is full of different kinds of stories. They cover a wide range of experiences and emotions that reflect a diversity of voices. Sadly, in these stories, The Church often fails — especially for women.

I shared this part of my journey because things ARE moving forward for me, in spite of where I have been. They are looking better. I have so many opportunities I could never have dreamed of on my own. I am beyond blessed to minister with my friend, Ryan. I am humbled to walk with others through their own faith transitions. I have Brew Theology, and a podcast, and this book + podcast project. I am part of a team of out-of-the-box pastors dreaming up new futures. I have a husband who works super hard for our family and is my number one advocate. I'm feeling physically better after an acute bout of chronic illness, I have a new niece and nephew, and my parents are healthy. I live in a truly amazing city surrounded by God's creation.

Then why isn't it enough?

Because some days, it's still not enough. And if it were just me, I'd gladly own that. I do try to own my baggage and work on it. I do own that my personality is a little more pessimistic than optimistic. I do own that my desire to see things whole, means broken things really bug me. But, the reality is that it's not just me who lives in a state of never enough. It's not just me by a long shot.

So many people are coming out of fundamentalist evangelical traditions like mine. Whether formally pursuing ministry or not, we are all stuck feeling like it's Never Enough. SO MANY WOMEN — powerful, talented, courageous, confident, amazing women — are told they are *never enough*. So many women leaders are constantly told, in big and small ways, that they are *never enough*. So many LGBTQIA folks, people of color, divorcees, persons with disabilities, people with chronic health conditions, and every other human that doesn't conform to the list of the hour, feels like they are *never enough*.

The old narratives are so strong. The old biases run so deep. The unconscious messages are so prevalent. It becomes clear that our personal faith will *never be enough*, if it can survive. Our lives will *never be enough* if we're not giving God every last tidbit of ourselves. Our careers can *never be enough* because they are a meaningless Plan B. It will never, ever be enough again. Never.

And that's what The Church wants us to believe, so that we will come back — broken and bleeding — and fill the pews, and pay our tithe, and stop thinking so much. Because if we can settle for what was and stop dreaming, then that should surely be enough . . .

If we give in, stop speaking, and give up on the world and church, nothing will change. If we keep doing church the way it's been done, nothing will change. But as much as possible, each in our own way, place, and space, we must continue to bring about newness in our faith practices and in the world. The call carried in the minds, hearts, and souls of women will not be silent. We will never stop dreaming of world in which redemption and re-creation blooms in the lives of humanity and the world.

That is why, after I left my tradition and saw the same behavior in the independent church, I was fortunate to find Brew Theology. I help nurture a space where people can talk about faith and find solidarity amidst the changing religious landscape. Brew Theology is a safe place for people experiencing faith shifts, where 'dones' are welcome, and where people from other traditions can all gather around the table and find a home.

We are in the midst of what the Rt. Rev. Mark Dyer called "The Giant Rummage Sale" (as referenced by Phyllis Tickle). Where elements of faith will be kept and discarded, where the church will be forced to change, and most of us will never see the result of that transition. It's frustrating to live in the midst of change, without knowing what will make it to the next iteration of Church.

But we can do our best to make the world, and the world of faith, a better place. The Church will have to change and be made new. And I sincerely hope that the Church will choose to throw out patriarchy, oppression, misogyny, and white supremacy as we move into the future. In the meantime, let us continue to cultivate a beautiful, powerful, egalitarian church wherever we are. May that spill over into a world that can start to reflect the beauty of creation where all people can stand side-by-side, equal and free.

MEET THE AUTHOR

Janel Apps Ramsey is the Co-Editor of Women Experiencing Faith. *She is the Co-Director of Brew Theology, an organization that helps people have healthy, meaningful, and eclectic conversations in their communities. You can learn more at brewtheology.org and you can listen to the Brew Theology Podcast wherever podcasts are found. Janel is also the founder of womenandchurch.com, a website that provides information about women in the church. She lives in Denver, CO with her husband, Baird. They have several cats: Yao, Aurora, and Onyx. She enjoys mountains, creating things (and embellishing her bullet journal) with washi tape, and journeying with people through faith transitions.*

Acknowledgements

WE APPRECIATE . . .

- all the contributors for bearing their hearts, souls, and minds on paper and trusting us to share their stories well.

- our spouses and families for giving us space to work on this project.

- everyone who has encouraged us along the way. We couldn't have done it without you.

JANEL WOULD LIKE TO THANK . . .

- Tom for this amazing opportunity. I could never have dreamed of doing this on my own. Your collaboration and trust mean so much. It is a privilege to work with you.

- Baird Ramsey for making space in our lives for me to bring this project to completion and for supporting me in my various branches of ministry.

- Ryan Miller for making room for me to work on this in the midst of our summer season, and for giving me the chance to share this with our Brew Theology community. You're the best ministry partner a person could ask for.

- For the encouragement and patience all of my friends have offered. If I try to name you, I will forget some of you, so this is for ALL of you!

- Jen Fulmer for giving words to a vague idea and helping me formulate the thesis for this project. Cheers, my friend! I am forever grateful.

TOM WOULD LIKE TO THANK . . .

- Janel for having the vision for this project and devoting so much of her time and energy to making it a reality.

- His family for modeling positive examples of what it means to be girls and women.

- The many friends who agreed to write *amazing* essays for this book. You inspire me!

SacraSage Press publishes high quality books with high quality content that explore themes of spiritual importance in the service of wisdom.

Find other books in the **SacraSage Press** line at www.sacrasagepress.com.

The Women Experiencing Faith Project continues online. At **womenxfaith.com** you can find the podcast, online reflections, and future dreams for the project. You can also find graphics to go along with the project, a discussion guide, and other information.

If you would like to contribute your story to a future volume or online, you can make your submission at womenxfaith.com.

Made in the USA
San Bernardino, CA
25 November 2018